European Yearbook of International Economic Law

Special Issue

The European Yearbook of International Economic Law (EYIEL) is an annual publication in International Economic Law, a field increasingly emancipating itself from Public International Law scholarship and evolving into a fully-fledged academic discipline in its own right. With the yearbook, the editors and publisher intend to make a significant contribution to the development of this "new" discipline and provide an international reference source of the highest possible quality. The EYIEL covers all areas of IEL, in particular WTO Law, External Trade Law for major trading countries, important Regional Economic Integration agreements, International Competition Law, International Investment Regulation, International Monetary Law, International Intellectual Property Protection and International Tax Law. In addition to the regular annual volumes, EYIEL Special Issues routinely address specific current topics in International Economic Law.

More information about this subseries at http://www.springer.com/series/8848

Anastasios Gourgourinis
Editor

Transnational Actors in International Investment Law

Springer

Editor
Anastasios Gourgourinis
School of Law
National and Kapodistrian
University of Athens
Athens, Greece

ISSN 2364-8392 ISSN 2364-8406 (electronic)
European Yearbook of International Economic Law
ISSN 2510-6880 ISSN 2510-6899 (electronic)
Special Issue
ISBN 978-3-030-60678-7 ISBN 978-3-030-60679-4 (eBook)
https://doi.org/10.1007/978-3-030-60679-4

This Springer imprint is published by the registered company Springer Nature Switzerland AG.
The registered company address is: Gewerbestrasse 11, 6330 Cham, Switzerland

Preface

This edited volume mainly draws from papers that were presented and discussed during the International Colloquium on "Actors in International Investment Law: Beyond Claimants, Respondents and Arbitrators". The colloquium, which took place at the University Paris 2 Panthéon-Assas on the 26th and 27th of September 2019, was jointly organized by the CERSA, research centre of the French National Centre for Scientific Research (CNRS) and of the University Paris 2 Panthéon-Assas, the University of Zaragoza and its Faculty of Law, and the Athens Public International Law Center (Athens PIL) of the National and Kapodistrian University of Athens School of Law and was hosted by Catharine Titi. The call for papers of this colloquium noted the fact that traditional studies of actors in international investment law have tended to focus principally on arbitrators, claimant investors, and respondent states, leaving a number of other seminal actors outside the main scope of this field of law, a view that was duly reaffirmed as the event unfolded.

There is, hence, a direct connection of this book with two other volumes simultaneously published by Springer: *Public Actors in International Investment Law* (edited by Catharine Titi) and *Private Actors in International Investment Law* (edited by Katia Fach Gómez). These three books not only aim to make a relevant academic contribution to the aforementioned fields but also to promote a scholarly discussion that lays the foundations for future legal debates on international investment law. The present book is dedicated to the actors of international investment law who are engaged in "transnational" activity. The use of the term "transnational" herein, instead of "international", is largely influenced by Philip Jessup's definition of "transnational law", taken from his seminal work (*Transnational Law*, New Haven: Yale University Press, 1956). The approach taken in this book is to focus on actors of international investment law, such as UNCITRAL, the EU, and the World Bank, international standardizing bodies, as well courts and tribunal, international or domestic, who engage in "transnational situations", i.e. situations which "involve individuals, corporations, states, organizations of states, or other groups". Hence, and irrespectively of whether these actors may/could otherwise qualify as public and/or private, emphasis is placed on their activities which in fact transcend national frontiers by influencing the evolution of international investment law.

The first chapter by Bruno Sousa Rodrigues zooms into the role of UNCITRAL a *par excellence* transnational actor in international investment law. The focal point is the evolution of UNCITRAL's mission from the mere harmonization and unification of municipal commercial law, to its quite incidental interference with the administration of international investment disputes and finally to its consolidation in the ISDS sphere through the development of the transparency rules and the current mandate of its Working Group III.

Rosario Ojinaga Ruiz and Maria Lina Leiva co-authored the chapter on the topic "EU as a Driver in the Judicialization Process of International Investment Disputes: ISDS Reform and EU Judicial System". The current tension between EU law and the ISDS lies in the centre of this chapter's discussion. The purported autonomy of EU law is examined as the driving force behind the judicialization of the ISDS and the reiteration of the EU's role in the international investment system. Exploring EU's modern investment treaty-making practice, the claims regarding the legal standing of the EU as a respondent, and the possibility of dialogue between investment tribunals and EU authorities, the authors highlight the contemporary and strengthened role of the EU as a key transnational actor in investment arbitration.

In the chapter entitled "Compulsory Optionality: International Standardizing Bodies as Transnational Actors in International Investment Law", Eleni–Amalia Giannakopoulou and Marios Tokas discuss the contemporary role of international standardizing bodies, a largely neglected transnational actor in international investment law. Inspired from the role of international standard-setting in World Trade Organization law, the authors seek to determine how international standards influence the interpretation and application of rights and obligations under international investment agreements.

Krystle Baptista's chapter entitled "New Actors in Investment Arbitration: The Legitimate Government" provides an account regarding the legitimate government of the respondent state and the relevant role of institutions such as the World Bank. In view of the coexistence of two governments in Venezuela, the author tackles the question whether ICSID tribunals and ad hoc annulment committees have jurisdiction to determine the proper representation of the respondent state, concluding that the question is more political than legal.

Ioannis Prezas authors a chapter which explores the impact of international non-investment courts in the normal unravelling of an investment dispute. The scope of analysis ranges from case-law cross-referencing, to the adjudication of investment disputes in the European Court of Human Rights, the limited jurisdiction of the International Court of Justice for the interpretation and application of the ICSID Convention, and finally the impact of sovereignty disputes on the territorial application of the BIT and the legality of the investment. The author advocates that an international non-investment adjudicative body may become a real transnational actor in investment law and arbitration, if its case law, proceedings, and decisions are likely to influence or impact the shaping of investment law and/or the functioning of investment arbitration.

The chapter by Fulvio Maria Palombino and Gustavo Minervini delves into the details of external precedent in international investment law. After a thorough examination of specific investment cases where arbitral tribunals have used external precedent in order to corroborate their own findings, the authors deconstruct and restructure the potential value of cross-referencing in de-fragmenting public international law and, finally, re-take stock of the role of non-investment courts as actors in international investment law.

Ksenia Polonskaya's chapter offers a Canadian perspective on domestic courts as transnational actors in international investment law. Focussing on the judicial process and practices of setting aside arbitral awards in Canada, the author investigates how Canadian courts themselves perceive their role, their interactions with arbitral tribunals, and their potential as active participants in international investment law. She posits that the way relationships between arbitral tribunals and domestic courts evolve may contribute to the legitimation or delegitimation of the international regime for foreign investment protection.

The last chapter is authored by Aikaterini Florou and is entitled "A Middle Path of ISDS Reform: The Principle of Comity as a Means of Strengthening the Role of National Courts in the Enforcement of Investment Arbitral Awards". The author explores the dynamics of domestic courts and international investment arbitration at the stage of the enforcement of arbitral awards. She places emphasis on the increasing tension between EU law and international investment law in the context of intra-EU ISDS and puts forward the principle of comity as a method for solving the Gordian knot; this, it is argued, may subsequently strengthen the role of national courts in international investment law.

Athens, Greece Anastasios Gourgourinis

Contents

UNCITRAL and the Governance of International Investments 1
Bruno Sousa Rodrigues

EU as a Driver in the Judicialization Process of International Investment Disputes: ISDS Reform and EU Judicial System 19
Rosario Ojinaga Ruiz and Maria Lina Leiva

Compulsory Optionality: International Standardizing Bodies as Transnational Actors in International Investment Law 45
Eleni-Amalia Giannakopoulou and Marios Tokas

New Actors in Investment Arbitration: The Legitimate Government . . . 73
Krystle Baptista

International Non-investment Courts and Tribunals as Transnational Actors in International Investment Law and Arbitration? 105
Ioannis Prezas

Apropos of the External Precedent: Judicial Cross-Pollination Between Investment Tribunals and International Courts 133
Fulvio Maria Palombino and Gustavo Minervini

Domestic Courts as Transnational Actors in International Investment Law: A Canadian Perspective 151
Ksenia Polonskaya

A Middle Path of ISDS Reform: The Principle of Comity as a Means of Strengthening the Role of National Courts in the Enforcement of Investment Arbitral Awards 171
Aikaterini Florou

UNCITRAL and the Governance of International Investments

Bruno Sousa Rodrigues

Contents

1 Introduction 2
2 "An International Clearing House for Unification Activities" 3
3 Business as Usual: The Legal Implications of the NIEO 7
4 Tectonic Shifts Under UNCITRAL? ISDS Reform and Institutional Imagination 11
5 Conclusion 15
References 17

Abstract Has the performance of UNCITRAL's mandate evolved over time in relation to the governance of international investments? The chapter argues that UNCITRAL's activities concerning investment law may be divided in two discrete instants. A first period is marked by an attentive performance of UNCITRAL's mandate to promote "the progressive harmonization and unification of the law of international trade", focused only on the private dimensions of international investment transactions. A second period begins recently with UNCITRAL's involvement in the governance of investment arbitration. In particular, the project of ISDS reform has been undertaken at UNCITRAL under a presumably expanded understanding of its mandate and mission. It is, however, unclear whether this reconstruction of UNCITRAL's mandate merely reflects a stronger engagement with public international law or an attempt to pursue activities of institutional imagination seemingly geared towards the transnational constitutionalization of the international investment regime. In any event, the new set of tasks conducted by UNCITRAL will require changes to the methods and practices historically developed for the transnational harmonization of municipal commercial law. This chapter aims at contributing to a reflection on the obstacles that UNCITRAL may face in the years to come regarding its evolving role as one of the centres for the transnational governance of international investments.

B. S. Rodrigues (✉)
Sciences Po Law School, Paris, France
e-mail: bruno.sousarodrigues@sciencespo.fr

A. Gourgourinis (ed.), *Transnational Actors in International Investment Law*,
European Yearbook of International Economic Law,
https://doi.org/10.1007/978-3-030-60679-4_1

1 Introduction

The term transnational law is usually attributed to Philip Jessup, who in 1956 published a seminal book precisely entitled "Transnational Law".[1] The opening of his book frames a discussion on the insufficiency of the existing legal vocabulary to grasp awkward phenomena that would hardly fit in the dichotomy national/international law. Transnational law, thus, was a concept developed to look into "law which regulates actions or events that transcend national frontiers", encompassing public and private law and "other rules which do not wholly fit into such standard categories".[2]

It now seems clear that lawyers have formed transnational alliances and have created normative practices that can no longer be confined to the geopolitical configuration of the world. In some cases, these transnational legal practices have been recognized by the community of States and were conducive to investing certain actors with formal prerogatives concerning transnational norm production.

Transnational law, within this framework, is marked by polycentric norm-making, and by a correlative explosion of normative voices materialized in the most diverse types of documents such as guidelines, standard contracts and model laws. This chapter is part of an edited book that pays tribute to Jessup's insight, exploring actors of international investment law "who are engaged in 'transnational situations'".

The United Nations Commission on International Trade Law (UNCITRAL or Commission henceforth) is certainly one of these actors—and one of paramount importance. The transnational normative instruments produced by the Commission are numerous and comprise both hard law and soft law. In order to contemplate UNCITRAL's role as one of the normative centres of transnational economic governance, it may suffice to refer to the Model Law on International Commercial Arbitration, Rules on Transparency in Treaty-based Investor-State Arbitration (Rules on Transparency) and the United Nations Convention on Transparency in Treaty-based Investor-State Arbitration (Mauritius Convention).

The Commission also provides an interesting vantage point for the study of the ambiguous relations entertained by private and public international lawyers. This body has traditionally been associated with private international law and its seats had been primarily occupied by private international lawyers. However, the interest of public international lawyers towards a forum discussing private international law has recently peaked with the emergence of a project of Investor State Dispute Settlement ("ISDS") reform sponsored by UNCITRAL.

The current discussions on ISDS reform—and the Commission's previous work on ISDS, notably the drafting of the Rules on Transparency and the adoption of the Mauritius Convention—are certainly an important part of the portrait depicting its involvement in the transnational governance of international investments. Still, these

[1]See Jessup (1956).

[2]See Jessup (1956), p. 1.

elements do not give a full account of the story, and one should be careful not to see the forest for the trees.

The objective of this chapter is to explore UNCITRAL's evolving influence over the governance of international investments, moving beyond an exegetic research that merely dissects its normative instruments. The question that will be addressed in this chapter is the following: has the performance of UNCITRAL's mandate evolved over time in relation to the governance of international investments? It seems that this matter has not yet attracted sufficient attention in investment law scholarship.

The argument put forth in this chapter claims that the Commission's role in the governance of international investments may be divided into two discrete instants. In a first moment, UNCITRAL closely followed its original mandate to promote "the progressive harmonization and unification of the law of international trade", which was done through its work on the transnational uniformization of legislation governing the private dimensions of investment transactions. In a second, more recent moment, UNCITRAL adopted an expanded understanding of its mandate, which could be reflective either of a stronger engagement with public international law or of an attempt to pursue activities of institutional imagination seemingly geared towards the transnational constitutionalization of the international investment regime.

This chapter is divided into three sections. The first section reviews the creation of UNCITRAL, highlighting the process through which its mandate to foster the unification and harmonization of domestic commercial law was created. The second section analyses UNCITRAL's work on the legal implications of the New International Economic Order ("NIEO"), trying to demonstrate how UNCITRAL did not stray far from its original mandate in its first direct incursion in the field of international investments. Finally, the third section explores UNCITRAL's works on ISDS reform and the constitutional ambitions voiced within this process by some member States that advocate for a complete and systemic overhaul of the international investment regime. This chapter concludes with some considerations on UNCITRAL's work methods in relation to the new set of tasks with which it is now entrusted.

2 "An International Clearing House for Unification Activities"

UNCITRAL was established by the resolution 2205 (XXI) of 17 December 1966 adopted by the United Nations General Assembly (General Assembly henceforth).[3] The process leading to the creation of UNCITRAL took place a few months after the Convention on the Settlement of Investment Disputes Between States and Nationals

[3] See General Assembly Resolution 2005 (XXI), The establishment of UNCITRAL (17 December 1966), reproduced at UNCITRAL Yearbook, Volume I: 1968–1970, (last accessed 29 June 2020),

of Other States ("ICSID Convention") was opened to signature on the 18 March 1965. Yet, investment or the settlement of investment disputes did not appear on the radar of those involved in the creation of UNCITRAL. Rather, this body was envisioned as an organ in charge of promoting the "progressive development of the law of international trade", as stated in the aforementioned resolution.

A series of factors informed the decision to create the Commission, such as the perceived modest results obtained up until that point by other institutions, the lack of coordination amongst the various formulating agencies and the limited representation and participation of developing countries in the processes of unification and harmonization of the law of international trade.[4] Furthermore, the creation of a new body to deal exclusively with the harmonization and unification of the law of international trade was based upon the inexistence of an organ within the United Nations (UN) that was both technically competent on the matter and able to devote the resources necessary for the success of that endeavour.

The Commission was set, therefore, as a central formulating agency for international trade law. It was thought that this new body would be in the best position to coordinate the efforts of the diverse agencies operating in the field, while commanding higher authority due to UN's broad constituency. In other terms, UNCITRAL was to act as "a kind of international clearing house for unification activities",[5] i.e., a transnational legislative forum in which experts ought to play a central role. Indeed, the performance of a quasi-legislative function has been at the core of most of UNCITRAL's activities ever since, and the Commission has developed a number of normative documents aiming at the unification of domestic commercial law.

At the root of UNCITRAL's creation lies a document entitled "Steps to be taken for the progressive development of private international law with a view of promoting international trade",[6] which was submitted by the delegation of Hungary to the

p. 65. For accounts on the creation and functioning of UNCITRAL, see Ustor (1967), David (1970), Honnold (1979).

[4]See Report of the Secretary-General, Progressive development of the law of international trade, A/6396, reproduced at UNCITRAL Yearbook, Volume I: 1968–1970, https://www.uncitral.org/pdf/english/yearbooks/yb-1968-70-e/yb_1968_1970_e.pdf (last accessed 29 June 2020), p. 41, para. 210.

[5]On this matter, the Secretary-General's report read as follows: "It would be essential to assure the most active and broadly-based support of Governments, and at the same time to provide for the participation of recognized authorities in this field of law. It would therefore appear advisable to provide that the membership of such a commission should be composed of an appropriate number of States, elected by the General Assembly, and to provide further, that the representatives of these States, appointed by them to serve on the commission, should be persons of eminence in the field." Report of the Secretary-General, Progressive development of the law of international trade, A/6396, reproduced at UNCITRAL Yearbook, Volume I: 1968–1970, https://www.uncitral.org/pdf/english/yearbooks/yb-1968-70-e/yb_1968_1970_e.pdf (last accessed 29 June 2020), p. 44, para. 226.

[6]Background paper by the delegation of Hungary, Steps to be taken for the progressive development of private international law with a view to promoting international trade, A/C.6/L.571, reproduced at UNCITRAL Yearbook, Volume I: 1968–1970, https://www.uncitral.org/pdf/english/yearbooks/yb-1968-70-e/yb_1968_1970_e.pdf (last accessed 29 June 2020), pp. 5–12.

General Assembly.[7] That document argued that it was time for the UN to adopt a new agenda concerning the progressive development of international law and that the legal work within the UN system had been unduly focused on public international law.

A narrow approach to international law, claimed the Hungarian proposal, would not find support in Article 13, 1(a) of the Charter, which referred to the progressive development of international law without the qualification of its public or private dimensions.[8] Therefore, the proposal ventured beyond a strict public-private divide, engaging with economic governance as a transversal issue of major interest to international law and with the law on international trade as a topic of central importance for economic development.[9]

The proposal was also well aware of the obstacles that could be posed by the division of labour between public and private international lawyers. It suggested that previous discussions at the Sixth Committee of the General Assembly on expanding the agenda of the International Law Commission to cover issues of private international law did not produce any concrete results precisely as consequence of this divide.[10]

The Hungarian proposal gained momentum at the General Assembly and prompted further works, leading the UN Secretariat to produce a note entitled

[7]The Hungarian proposal was an initiative of Endre Ustor, a Hungarian diplomat and jurist who is usually attributed the paternity of UNCITRAL. Ustor was a member of the International Law Commission and of the Institut de Droit International.

[8]Among other issues, the Hungarian submission discusses the previous work of the League of Nations for the development of international law, as well as explores the scope of the idea of progressive development of international law within the UN system. In particular, it notes that the expression "progressive development of international law" was crafted in the United Nations Conference on International Organizations, held in 1945 in San Francisco, as a way of striking a balance between stability and change in international law. The term came to be incorporated in Article 13 of the Charter, paragraph 1(a). In particular, the document asked "whether the United Nations General Assembly's activities aimed at the progressive development of international law under Article 13, paragraph 1 a, of the Charter can be extended beyond the traditional area of public international law." Background paper by the delegation of Hungary, Steps to be taken for the progressive development of private international law with a view to promoting international trade, A/C.6/L.571, reproduced at UNCITRAL Yearbook, Volume I: 1968–1970, https://www.uncitral.org/pdf/english/yearbooks/yb-1968-70-e/yb_1968_1970_e.pdf (last accessed 29 June 2020), p. 8, para. 32.

[9]In relation to the centrality of the law on international trade for economic development, see Background paper by the delegation of Hungary, Steps to be taken for the progressive development of private international law with a view to promoting international trade, A/C.6/L.571, reproduced at UNCITRAL Yearbook, Volume I: 1968–1970, https://www.uncitral.org/pdf/english/yearbooks/yb-1968-70-e/yb_1968_1970_e.pdf (last accessed 29 June 2020), p. 11, para. 56.

[10]See Background paper by the delegation of Hungary, Steps to be taken for the progressive development of private international law with a view to promoting international trade, A/C.6/L.571, reproduced at UNCITRAL Yearbook, Volume I: 1968–1970, (United Nations Publication, New York, 1971), pp. 9–10.

"Unification of the law of international trade".[11] This preliminary study, which was submitted to the Sixth Committee of the General Assembly, stated that "[t]he impetus for the unification of the law of international trade stems from difficulties typically faced by those who engage in international commercial transactions as a result of the multiplicity of, and divergencies in national laws".[12] In particular, the Secretary-General endorsed the idea advanced by the Hungarian delegation, pursuant to which it was necessary for the UN to be involved in the unification of municipal commercial law.

In light of this preliminary study, the General Assembly requested the UN Secretariat to submit a comprehensive report on the unification and harmonization of the law of international trade and included in the provisional agenda for its twenty-first session an item on the topic. The report produced, which was entitled "Progressive development of the law of international trade",[13] laid the foundational contours for the creation of UNCITRAL. The report was based on a preliminary study commissioned to Professor Clive M. Schmitthoff,[14] which was later revised by Professor Margarita Argúas,[15] Dr. Taslim O. Elias,[16] Professor Gyula Eörsi,[17] Professor Willis L. Reese,[18] and Professor Mustafa Kamil Yasseen.[19]

A central pillar of the Secretariat's report is the definition of international trade law as the "the body of rules governing commercial relationships of a private law nature involving different countries".[20] In this regard, the report produced a list of topics that would illustrate the scope of the law of international trade, which included the international sale of goods, negotiable instruments, the conduct of business

[11] See Note by the Secretariat, Unification of the law of international trade, A/C.6/L.572, reproduced at UNCITRAL Yearbook, Volume I: 1968–1970, https://www.uncitral.org/pdf/english/yearbooks/yb-1968-70-e/yb_1968_1970_e.pdf (last accessed 29 June 2020), pp. 13–17.

[12] Note by the Secretariat, Unification of the law of international trade, A/C.6/L.572, reproduced at UNCITRAL Yearbook, Volume I: 1968–1970, https://www.uncitral.org/pdf/english/yearbooks/yb-1968-70-e/yb_1968_1970_e.pdf (last accessed 29 June 2020), p. 14, para. 6.

[13] Report of the Secretary-General, Progressive development of the law of international trade, A/6396, reproduced at UNCITRAL Yearbook, Volume I: 1968–1970, https://www.uncitral.org/pdf/english/yearbooks/yb-1968-70-e/yb_1968_1970_e.pdf (last accessed 29 June 2020), pp. 18–66.

[14] Professor Schmitthoff, an Anglo-German scholar specialized in the law of international trade and serving at the City of London College, was considered a leading authority in the field of international trade law.

[15] Professor Argúas was an Argentinean judge and scholar specialized in private international law.

[16] Dr. Taslim O. Elias was the Nigerian minister of justice at the time and would become a president of the International Court of Justice.

[17] Professor Eörsi was a Hungarian scholar specialized in comparative private law.

[18] Professor Reese was an American scholar specialized in private international law.

[19] Professor Yasseen was an Iraqi scholar specialized in public international law.

[20] Report of the Secretary-General, Progressive development of the law of international trade, A/6396, reproduced at UNCITRAL Yearbook, Volume I: 1968–1970, https://www.uncitral.org/pdf/english/yearbooks/yb-1968-70-e/yb_1968_1970_e.pdf (last accessed 29 June 2020), p. 20, para. 10.

activities, insurance, transportation, commercial arbitration, and copyrights and industrial property. Undeniably, this report echoed a well-established division of labour between private and public international lawyers.

In addition, the report further endorsed the divide between private and public international law by implicitly subscribing to the dichotomy of acta jure imperii and acta jure gestionis. Notably, it excludes from the scope of the law of international trade the "international commercial relations on the level of public law, such as those relating to the attitude and behaviour of States when regulating, in the exercise of their sovereign power, the conduct of trade affecting their territories", while including within the scope of the law of international trade the "international commercial relations on the level of private law entered into by governmental and other public bodies or, particularly in countries of centrally planned economy, by foreign trade corporations".[21]

In sum, UNCITRAL was not envisioned as a forum for the governance of the economic relations of States in their capacity as sovereigns, or even for the governance of international investments in their public law dimension. Under the idea of harmonization and unification of the law of international trade, UNCITRAL should focus on the production of normative instruments to govern cross-border economic relations of a private nature.

The next section examines how this mandate was strictly performed when UNCITRAL was asked to deal with the legal implications of the NIEO—its first direct engagement with the governance of international investments.

3 Business as Usual: The Legal Implications of the NIEO

The movement for the establishment of a new international economic order was launched by the Group of 77 at the third session of the United Nations Conference on Trade and Development (UNCTAD), held in 1972.[22] The initiative, emerging in the context of decolonization, advocated for an extensive and deep reform of the legal order governing economic relationships amongst developed and developing states. At the centre of the demands of the "Third World" was the notion of permanent sovereignty over natural resources, and the immediate consequence of such a notion was the revision of the law on expropriation of foreign assets.[23] In the following years, the movement would gain traction within the General Assembly, leading to the adoption in 1974 of three foundational documents, i.e. the "Declaration on the

[21]Report of the Secretary-General, Progressive development of the law of international trade, A/6396, reproduced at UNCITRAL Yearbook, Volume I: 1968–1970, https://www.uncitral.org/pdf/english/yearbooks/yb-1968-70-e/yb_1968_1970_e.pdf (last accessed 29 June 2020), p. 21, paras 11–12.

[22]See UNCTAD's resolution 45 (III) of 18 May 1972, Vol. I: Report and Annexes, TD/180, (United Nations Publication, New York, 1973).

[23]For more on the NIEO, see García-Amador (1980) and Ferguson (1980).

Establishment of a New International Economic Order",[24] the "Program of Action on the Establishment of a New Economic Order"[25] and the "Charter of Economic Rights and Duties of States".[26]

The NIEO's agenda reached UNCITRAL in 1978, when member states decided that the Commission would work on "[t]he legal implications of the new international economic order". In particular, a working group dedicated to the NIEO was created that same year, holding seventeen sessions in total between the years of 1979 and 1994. The Commission's work on the topic can be divided into two phases, with the first phase extending from 1979 to 1987 and the second phase extending from 1988 to 1994.

The first phase of UNCITRAL's work on the legal implications of the NIEO gravitated around "the harmonization, unification and review of contractual provisions commonly occurring in international contracts in the field of industrial development".[27] This was to be done through the drafting of a legal guideline concerning international contracts in the field of industrial development.[28] This programme of work occupied UNCITRAL for the next six years, running its course only in 1987 at the Commission's twentieth session when it adopted the "UNCITRAL Legal Guide on Drawing up International Contracts for the Construction of Industrial Works".[29]

---

[24]See General Assembly resolution, Declaration on the establishment of a New International Economic Order, A/RES/S-6/3201 (1 May 1974), https://digitallibrary.un.org/record/218450?ln=en (last accessed 29 June 2020).

[25]General Assembly resolution, Programme of action on the establishment of a New International Economic Order, A/RES/S-6/3202 (1 May 1974), https://digitallibrary.un.org/record/218451?ln=en (last accessed 29 June 2020).

[26]General Assembly resolution, Charter of Economic Rights and Duties of States, A/RES/29/3281 (12 December 1974), https://digitallibrary.un.org/record/190150?ln=en (last accessed 29 June 2020).

[27]For the Working Group's propositions, see Report of the Working Group on the New International Economic Order, A/CN.9/176 (14–25 January 1980), https://undocs.org/en/A/CN.9/171 (last accessed 29 June 2020), para. 39 (d). Despite the decision taken at the twelfth session on the membership of the Working Group, the Commission revisited its previous position and decided that all of its member-states should be part of the Working Group on the NIEO.

[28]The drafting of the guideline was largely entrusted to the Commission's Secretariat, and it was "generally agreed that the Secretariat in carrying out the preparatory work should have a certain measure of discretion". See Report of the United Nations Commission on International Trade Law on the Work of its Thirteenth Session, A/35/17, para. 141, https://undocs.org/en/A/35/17(SUPP) (last accessed 29 June 2020). For the decision on entrusting the Secretariat with the task of drafting the legal guide, see records of the Commission's fourteenth session, see Report of the United Nations Commission on International Trade Law on the Work of its Fourteenth Session, A/36/17, https://undocs.org/en/A/36/17(SUPP) (last accessed 29 June 2020), para. 84, 2(b).

[29]For the text of the guide, see UNCITRAL Legal Guide on Drawing up International Contracts for the Construction of Industrial Works, A/CN.9/SER.B/2 (7 December 1987), https://uncitral.un.org/sites/uncitral.un.org/files/media-documents/uncitral/en/legal_guide_e.pdf (last accessed 29 June 2020). For the full record of the Commission's twentieth session, see Report of the United Nations Commission on International Trade Law on the Work of its Twentieth Session, A/42/17, https://undocs.org/en/A/42/17 (last accessed 29 June 2020), paras 306–316.

The second phase of UNCITRAL's work on the NIEO focused on preparing a model law for public procurement and a legal guide on countertrade. The suggestion to pursue such a programme was advanced at the Commission's nineteenth session, held in 1986. In that occasion, and upon the suggestion of the Secretariat to explore the topics of joint ventures, countertrade and public procurement, the Commission decided that priority should be given to work on procurement.[30] The reasoning behind that decision was that the working group on the NIEO could not explore more than one topic at a time. Still, at its twenty-first session, held in 1988, the Commission decided to open another frontline, asking the Secretariat to prepare a draft outline of the contents and structure of a legal guide on countertrade contracts.[31]

The second phase of UNCITRAL's work programme on the NIEO was concluded in instalments. Notably, the Commission's activities on countertrade were finished earlier than those on public procurement, with the adoption of the "Legal Guide on International Countertrade Transactions" at the Commission's twenty-fifth session, held in 1992. UNCITRAL's decision to adopt the legal guide on countertrade paid tribute to the NIEO by highlighting "its mandate [...] to further progressive harmonization and unification of the law of international trade, [bearing] in mind the interests of all peoples, and in particular of developing countries".[32]

Moreover, UNCITRAL's work on public procurement gave rise to two different model laws—which were, in reality, variations of the same main text. The first was the "Model Law on Procurement of Goods and Construction", adopted by the Commission in its twenty-sixth session in 1993.[33] A year later, this document was considered ill-adapted to the regulation of the procurement of services, leading to the adoption of a second document that was a consolidated version of the first text including provisions for the procurement of services. Thus, in 1994, the "Model Law on Procurement of Goods, Construction and Services" was established.[34] Both

[30]Report of the United Nations Commission on International Trade Law on the Work of its Nineteenth Session, A/41/17, https://undocs.org/en/A/41/17 (last accessed 29 June 2020), para. 243.

[31]See Report of the United Nations Commission on International Trade Law on the Work of its Twenty-First Session, A/43/17, https://undocs.org/en/A/43/17 (last accessed 29 June 2020), para. 35. Later on, the working group on international payments was designated to deal with this unfolding of the NIEO's agenda. See Report of the United Nations Commission on International Trade Law on the Work of its Twenty-Third Session, A/45/17, https://undocs.org/en/A/45/17 (SUPP) (last accessed 29 June 2020), para. 17.

[32]See Report of the United Nations Commission on International Trade Law on the Work of its Twenty-Fifth Session, A/47/17, https://undocs.org/en/A/47/17(SUPP) (last accessed 29 June 2020), para. 137.

[33]See Report of the United Nations Commission on International Trade Law on the Work of its Twenty-Sixth Session, A/48/17, https://undocs.org/en/A/48/17(SUPP) (last accessed 29 June 2020), para. 258.

[34]This decision was taken at the Commission's twenty-seventh session, held in 1994. For the records of the session, see Report of the United Nations Commission on International Trade Law on the Work of its Twenty-Seventh Session, A/49/17, https://undocs.org/en/A/49/17(SUPP) (last accessed 29 June 2020), para. 97.

documents were adopted with references to UNCITRAL's mandate and to NIEO's commitment to the advancement of developing countries' interests. The adoption of these documents marked the end of the working group on the NIEO. With the winds of neoliberalism blowing stronger, UNCITRAL was already envisioning potential work to be done on the legal implications of privatization.[35]

The Commission's efforts to explore the legal implications of the NIEO are a good illustration of its own understanding of the mandate adopted in 1966 by the General Assembly. In particular, UNCITRAL's competence was predominantly construed within a strong public-private divide. This precluded incursions on clear legal implications of the NIEO, such as the law on expropriation or on state responsibility. Indeed, the Commission interpreted its mandate as concerned with the private dimensions of the NIEO only.

In its thirteenth session, some delegates observed that "the dividing line between private and public law was not always easily discernible" and that "participation of governmental agencies in international trade was considerable and public law relationships could therefore not be ignored". Still, a number of other delegates also pointed out that the Commission was "primarily concerned, if not solely, with matters of private law".[36] Given the consensual approach traditionally adopted at UNCITRAL, such a view prevailed within the Commission.

The aforementioned understanding of UNCITRAL's mandate is not merely an endogenous interpretation espoused by the delegates to the Commission. There seemed to be, at that moment in time, a well-established division of labour within the UN system for the governance of economic relations. In this regard, while UNCITRAL would be entrusted with the mission of unifying municipal commercial law, UNCTAD and the General Assembly would be the preferential fora for the governance of the international economy.

This division of labour is certainly suggestive of the then prevalent public-private divide, but also representative of a strict separation between national and international law. Indeed, the NIEO did not put into question the underlying foundations of international law, relying heavily on the ideas of national sovereignty and self-determination. To some extent, one could say that the NIEO attempted to carve out the law of development from the international law domain, attributing a larger margin of domestic action to States in relation to foreign capital.

For all these reasons, it is possible to state that the Commission's involvement with the NIEO did not deviate from its business as usual mode. Indeed, all normative

[35]See Report of the United Nations Commission on International Trade Law on the Work of its Twenty-Seventh Session, A/49/17, https://undocs.org/en/A/49/17(SUPP) (last accessed 29 June 2020), paras 307–310.

[36]Report of the United Nations Commission on International Trade Law on the Work of its Thirteenth Session, A/35/17, https://undocs.org/en/A/35/17(SUPP) (last accessed 29 June 2020), para. 136.

instruments produced on the legal implications of the NIEO consisted of widely accepted tools for the unification of domestic private law.[37]

4 Tectonic Shifts Under UNCITRAL? ISDS Reform and Institutional Imagination

It has been argued above that UNCITRAL's involvement in the governance of international investments was, at first, marked by a deference to the public-private divide in international law and by a focus on the transnational harmonization of municipal law concerning international economic relations. Yet, recent events suggest that there are considerable changes taking place within the Commission when it comes to the governance of international investments. UNCITRAL has taken the lead in the discussions on ISDS reform, gaining the status of a central formulating agency for the law on investment dispute resolution.

The Commission's work on the procedural dimension of investment law is the result of a double life undertaken by the UNCITRAL Arbitration Rules (Arbitration Rules henceforth). Intended to govern commercial arbitration between private parties, the Arbitration Rules were adopted as an alternative to the ICSID system, especially in a series of cases against States that had denounced the ICSID Convention (Bolivia, Ecuador and Venezuela).

This somewhat accidental involvement with ISDS was consolidated with the adoption of the Rules on Transparency and the Mauritius Convention. Both instruments were also somewhat accidental themselves, as they were side products of the revision process of the Arbitration Rules.

Faced with an ever-growing backlash against the opacity of ISDS,[38] the Commission had to decide the extent to which the Arbitration Rules should contain detailed provisions on ISDS. The resulting agreement was that work on ISDS should not delay the revision process, but that "the topic of transparency in treaty-based investor-state arbitration was worthy of future consideration and should be dealt with as a matter of priority immediately after the completion of the current revision of the UNCITRAL Arbitration Rules".[39]

---

[37]The Secretary-General's report substantiating the creation of UNCITRAL surveys the different methods of unification of domestic private law. See Report of the Secretary-General, Progressive development of the law of international trade, A/6396, reproduced at UNCITRAL Yearbook, Volume I: 1968–1970, https://www.uncitral.org/pdf/english/yearbooks/yb-1968-70-e/yb_1968_1970_e.pdf (last accessed 29 June 2020), pp. 40–41. For a scholarly work on the topic, see David (1968).

[38]There exists a vast literature exploring the shortcomings of ISDS. See, for instance, Waibel et al. (2010) and Choudhury (2009).

[39]See Report of the United Nations Commission on International Trade Law on the work of its forty-first session, A/63/17, https://undocs.org/en/A/63/17(SUPP) (last accessed 29 June 2020), para. 314.

The success of the Mauritius Convention as a method of extending the application of the Rules on Transparency for treaties in force prior to the adoption of that set of rules raised UNCITRAL's status as a centre for the production of procedural investment law. The Commission suddenly became an obvious choice of forum when talks on ISDS reform gained momentum.[40]

In 2017, the Commission felt empowered to entrust its working group III with a broad mandate and a wide discretion to explore potential reforms for ISDS. In addition, the process was to be government-led, marking an express deviation from the traditional expert-led production process adopted at UNCITRAL. The mandate of working group III was laid out in the following terms:[41]

> The Commission entrusted Working Group III with a broad mandate to work on the possible reform of investor-State dispute settlement. In line with the UNCITRAL process, Working Group III would, in discharging that mandate, ensure that the deliberations, while benefiting from the widest possible breadth of available expertise from all stakeholders, would be Government-led, with high-level input from all Governments, consensus-based and fully transparent. The Working Group would proceed to: (a) first, identify and consider concerns regarding investor-State dispute settlement; (b) second, consider whether reform was desirable in the light of any identified concerns; and (c) third, if the Working Group were to conclude that reform was desirable, develop any relevant solutions to be recommended to the Commission. The Commission agreed that broad discretion should be left to the Working Group in discharging its mandate, and that any solutions devised would be designed taking into account the ongoing work of relevant international organizations and with a view to allowing each State the choice of whether and to what extent it wished to adopt the relevant solution(s).

This new status as a privileged locus for the governance of international investments reflects a change of paradigm concerning the Commission's construction of its mandate. The concept of "law of international trade"[42] and the mission of promoting its progressive harmonization is now construed in a more flexible way. Its direct engagement with matters that were traditionally framed as public law issues indicates that UNCITRAL no longer feels bound to exclusively promote the transnational uniformization of municipal commercial law. Yet, the extent of this paradigm shift is unclear and the outcome of the process of ISDS reform can be decisive in shaping the future role the Commission may play in the transnational governance of international investments.

---

[40] See Kaufmann-Köhler and Potestà (2016), Can the Mauritius Convention serve as a model for the reform of investor-State arbitration in connection with the introduction of a permanent investment tribunal or an appeal mechanism? Analysis and Roadmap, https://www.uncitral.org/pdf/english/CIDS_Research_Paper_Mauritius.pdf (last accessed 1 June 2020), pp. 27–31.

[41] See Report of the United Nations Commission on International Trade Law on the work of its fiftieth session, A/72/17, https://undocs.org/en/A/72/17 (last accessed 29 June 2020), para. 264.

[42] See General Assembly resolution 2005 (XXI), The establishment of UNCITRAL (17 December 1966), reproduced at UNCITRAL Yearbook, Volume I: 1968–1970, https://www.uncitral.org/pdf/english/yearbooks/yb-1968-70-e/yb_1968_1970_e.pdf (last accessed 29 June 2020), p. 65, section I.

At least two scenarios could be reasonable projections of the Commission's role in the years to come. In a first scenario, UNCITRAL is in the process of focusing its attention on public international law issues, performing a sort of "public law turn". Thus, issues that were once felt to be outside the scope of its mandate are now being interpreted as falling under the purview of UNCITRAL. In other words, the term "law of international trade" that was once construed as a private international law category is being transformed into a public international law concept. This could lead UNCITRAL to become a body of interstate economic governance like any other. Within this framework, the Commission may consolidate its position as a specialized agency for the production of procedural international investment law, for it already commands great authority on transnational dispute resolution.

The wording used to entrust working group III with the mission of reforming ISDS could support the thesis that UNCITRAL is taking a "public law turn". Indeed, ISDS reform was mandated as a "government-led" process, expressly affirming that states' interest will carry more weight than those of arbitration experts. This proactive attitude of states has been further translated into a demographic change at UNCITRAL meetings. What was once a forum predominantly composed of private lawyers has become an institution with an ever-growing presence of state officials and public international lawyers.[43] This scenario may likely reinforce the perception that UNCITRAL is like any other international organization—created by states to cater for states.

A second scenario, however, could relate to a more profound change in UNCITRAL's role in the governance of international investment. Globalization, it has been argued, is marked by an "accelerated differentiation of society into autonomous social systems, each of which springs territorial confines and constitutes itself globally".[44] Accordingly, the codes legal/illegal, having/not having, power/no power are acquiring new contours at the transnational and global sphere. This

[43]Compare, for instance, the facts surrounding the election of the chairperson for the working group on the reform of Arbitration Rules (working group II) and for the working group on ISDS Reform (working group III). On the one hand, working group II chose its chairperson without any controversy and through the normal UNCITRAL consensus-based process. Michael E. Schneider, who was part of the Swiss delegation, was appointed chair. Schneider was not a government official, but rather a partner and founding member of Lalive—a leading law firm in arbitration. On the other hand, the election of the chairperson for working group III was surrounded by controversy and had to be done through secret ballot—something unusual in the context of UNCITRAL. Finally, the chairperson elected was Shane Spelliscy, a state official acting as the Director and General Counsel for the Trade Law Bureau of the Government of Canada. For information on the election of the chairperson of Working Group II, see Report of the Working Group on Arbitration and Conciliation on the work of its forty-fifth session (Vienna, 11–15 September 2006), A/CN.9.614, https://undocs.org/en/A/CN.9/614 (last accessed 29 June 2020), para. 11. For the records on the election of the chairperson of Working Group III, see Report of Working Group III (Investor-State Dispute Settlement Reform) on the work of its thirty-fourth session (Vienna, 27 November – 1 December 2017), https://www.uncitral.org/pdf/english/workinggroups/wg_3/WGIII-34th-session/930_for_the_website.pdf (last accessed 29 June 2020), paras 11–15.

[44]Fischer-Lescano and Teubner (2004), p. 1006.

functional differentiation of society is also accompanied by further "specialization" within each of its social systems.

Investment law represents one example of this transversal legality, as it operates the binary code legal/illegal within a discrete epistemic community that is not bound by territorial borders. The constituency of this transnational normative regime cannot be reduced to a circle of private or public international lawyers—and, in fact, the stakeholders of investment governance cannot be limited to any group of lawyers or state officials. As a result, this hybrid world becomes one of tension and conflict, as "the various rationalities confront other rationalities in this manner, each with a claim to universality".[45] Within this framework, a number of stakeholders of the investment regime may perceive constitutionalization as a tool to curb some of these tensions, engaging with UNCITRAL as the place to promote such endeavour.

In this scenario, ISDS reform may be transformed into a transnational constitutional moment, aiming at the demise of the public-private and national-international divides. Beyond theoretical formulations discussing transnational or global law,[46] the work on ISDS at the Commission could mean that the hybridity of investment law[47] is now taken seriously as an empirical phenomenon. In that case, the UNCITRAL's mandate to promote "the progressive harmonization and unification of the law of international trade"[48] could be taken to mean a duty to reformulate the whole system of investment governance under a constitutional-like framework.

The activities of working group III on ISDS are still ongoing, but there is a strong rhetoric for systemic change. Evidently, this carries different meanings depending on who is voicing this agenda. There seems to be, however, an effervescent activity of institutional imagination, especially when it comes to the very controversial issue of creating a multilateral investment court.[49] The debates around this topic suggest that UNCITRAL may be performing a different role than merely promoting the

---

[45]Neves (2013), p. 19.

[46]For an early analysis of transnational law, see Jessup (1956). For accounts on global law, see Fischer-Lescano and Teubner (2004); Kingsbury et al. (2005).

[47]An early elaboration on the hybridity of the investment regime can be found in Douglas (2004). For a recent analysis on the investment regime's contribution to the blurring of lines between public and private international law, see Fernández Arroyo and Mbengue (2018), and Roberts (2014).

[48]See General Assembly resolution 2005 (XXI), The establishment of UNCITRAL (17 December 1966), reproduced at UNCITRAL Yearbook, Volume I: 1968–1970, https://www.uncitral.org/pdf/english/yearbooks/yb-1968-70-e/yb_1968_1970_e.pdf (last accessed 29 June 2020), p. 65, section I.

[49]In particular, the European Union and its member states have been main advocates for the systemic nature of changes needed in ISDS, proposing as a solution to these systemic concerns the creation of a two-tier standing court. See the Submission from the European Union, Possible reform of investor-State dispute settlement (ISDS), A/CN.9/WG.III/WP145 (12 December 2017), https://undocs.org/en/A/CN.9/WG.III/WP.145 (last accessed 29 June 2020); and Submission from the European Union and its Member States, Possible reform of investor-State dispute settlement (ISDS), A/CN.9/WG.III/WP159/Add.1 (24 January 2019), https://undocs.org/en/A/CN.9/WG.III/WP.159/Add.1 (last accessed 29 June 2020).

harmonization of procedural international investment law, pointing to the direction of the transnational constitutionalization of the investment regime.[50]

The final outcome of projects on ISDS reform could very well be the production of a new institutional setting for the governance of international investments. Accordingly, the second scenario emerging out of ISDS reform may be one in which UNCITRAL is in the process of becoming a type of constituent assembly, where a multifarious constituency is brought together to imagine an overarching institutional framework in charge of controlling the validity of investment agreements between states and between investors and states.

One should guard against a conservative reflex to claim that UNCITRAL must deal exclusively with private international law. Although conservatism could provide an easy way out of future dilemmas, legal institutions tend to evolve over time and extend their arms to embrace areas not envisioned by their founders. If the lines between public and private international law were blurred in the 1970s, when the Commission was dealing with the NIEO, they are now barely definable. The appropriate attitude towards UNICITRAL's eventual new mission may indeed be one of understanding the challenges and limitations that would arise from the performance of an extended mandate.

5 Conclusion

The public-private divide is embedded in UNCITRAL's genetic code, as one may easily realize from the preparatory works leading to its creation. Public international lawyers have never paid much attention to the Commission's activities, preferring other UN venues for their intervention, including UNCTAD, the International Law Commission and the Sixth Committee of the General Assembly.

As a consequence, all of UNCITRAL's concerns and work methods catered, at first, for the needs of private international law. In blunt terms, UNCITRAL was created by private international lawyers for private international lawyers. In this respect, even if the progressive harmonisation of the law of international trade has generated transnational legal norms, this transnationalization has been limited to what was perceived as the private dimension of economic governance.

The consolidation of the division of labour between public and private international law made no exception to the governance of international investments. Prior to the existence of investment-treaty arbitration, international investment transactions were under the purview of arbitrators as a type of contractual dispute. Notably, international investments were underpinned by different types of contractual

[50] Some have written on the constitutionalization of the investment regime, but with a slightly different focus from the one followed by this chapter. See, for instance, Petersmann (2009), Stone and Grisel (2009) and Behrens (2007).

arrangements (concessions contracts, public-private partnerships, production sharing agreements) referring disputes to commercial arbitration.

Within this framework, much of investment law was but a branch of contract law—and international investment law, a special case related to certain international contracts. Contracts produced by economic agents were largely meant to be self-regulatory, while the occasional disputes arising therefrom would be adjudicated by commercial arbitration. State courts would exercise the role of ultima ratio, having the last say on the administration of violence whenever enforcement of arbitral awards was required.

In the pre-investment arbitration world, UNCITRAL was an institution producing the normative infrastructure for the governance of international investments. This was reflected in a variety of documents, such as the Rules of Arbitration and the model laws on public procurement.[51] This normative production paid tribute to UNCITRAL's mandate of unifying and harmonizing domestic commercial law. Still, the emergence of investment arbitration seems to have moved the Commission towards unchartered waters, and its current work on ISDS could affect its status in the broader system of economic governance.

UNCITRAL's increasing influence on procedural investment law may suggest a consolidation of its normative authority and its transformation into a constitutional assembly for the transnational constitutionalization of the investment regime. The potential creation of a constitutional framework for the governance of international investments at UNCITRAL, which could be materialized in a standalone appellate body or in a two-tiered permanent investment court, would represent a considerable change in the range of tasks and missions undertaken by the Commission.

It may be necessary, therefore, to adapt the methods and practices historically developed for the harmonization of municipal commercial law to the needs of constitutional imagination. Some of these changes are already being implemented, such as the growing participation of state officials and public international lawyers, and the overall enlargement of the constituency of working group III.[52]

Even though working groups are meant to have a smaller number of participants than the Commission's plenary session, the opposite is true for working group III. As this chapter is being written, the last session of working group III, held from 14 to 18 October 2019, was attended by representatives of the 60 UNCITRAL member

---

[51]Many of the normative instruments which structure transnational investments can fall under the normative framework produced by UNCITRAL, such as concessions contracts, public-private partnerships, production sharing agreements. Similarly, the default jurisdiction that governs these contracts are also particularly influenced by UNCITRAL's work. It is clear, then, that UNCITRAL, beyond its work on ISDS, has already left a lasting imprint on the governance of the micro-dimensions of international investments.

[52]In relation to the diverse constituency of the Commission's working group III, it is important to draw attention to the Academic Forum and to the Practitioner Group. Both groups of stakeholders, one of academics active in the field of ISDS and the other of lawyers and arbitrators practicing ISDS, are acting as observers and aim at influencing the outcome of the ISDS reform process. See Report of the United Nations Commission on International Trade Law on the work of its fifty-first session, A/73/17, https://undocs.org/en/A/73/17 (last accessed 29 June 2020), para. 144.

states plus 31 representatives of observer states. In addition to these state officials, there were over 30 representatives of intergovernmental organizations and international institutions.[53]

Certainly, this enlarged constituency raises the legitimacy of the reform process, but it also creates challenges in drafting a text that is acceptable to all stakeholders. Therefore, beyond engaging in constitutional imagination, the successful discharge of the mission entrusted to working group III will require considerable methodological creativity.

The times ahead may be of anxiety or excitement, but they will certainly not be dull ones. Investment arbitration brought an exotic animal, quite distinct, to the international law's vivarium. Some would refer to the investment normative regime as a sort of platypus,[54] a normative system that blurs the boundaries between public and private international law in an unsurmountable way due to its polycentricism and fragmentation.

Amongst the multitude of bilateral and multilateral investment treaties in force and the variety of institutional arrangements in place to adjudicate them, UNCITRAL could be but one of various loci for the governance of international investments. Yet, the Commission could also become the main source of authority of a future constitutional framework for the governance of international investments. Time will tell.

References

Behrens P (2007) Towards the constitutionalization of international investment protection. Archiv des Völkerrechts 45(2):153–179

Choudhury B (2009) Democratic implications arising from the intersection of investment arbitration and human rights. Alberta Law Rev 46(4):983–1008

David R (1968) The methods of unification. Am J Comp Law 16(1):13–27

David R (1970) La commission des nations unies pour le droit commercial International. Annuaire Français de Droit International 16:453–474

Douglas Z (2004) The hybrid foundations of investment treaty arbitration. Br Yearb Int Law 74 (1):151–289

Ferguson CC (1980) The new international economic order. Univ Ill Law Forum 3:693–706

Fernández Arroyo DP, Mbengue MM (2018) Public and private international law in international courts and tribunals: evidence of an inescapable interaction. Columbia J Transnl Law 56:797–854

Fischer-Lescano A, Teubner G (2004) Regime-collisions: the vain search for legal unity in the fragmentation of global law. Mich J Int Law 25:999–1046

García-Amador FV (1980) The proposed new international economic order: a new approach to the law governing nationalization and compensation. Univ Miami Inter-Am Law Rev 12:1–59

[53]See Report of Working Group III (Investor-State Dispute Settlement Reform) on the work of its thirty-sixth session, A/CN.9/964, paras 6–9, https://undocs.org/en/A/CN.9/964 (last accessed 29 June 2020).

[54]The image is attributed to Anthea Roberts. See Roberts (2013), p. 45.

Honnold J (1979) The United Nations Commission on International Trade Law: mission and methods. Am J Comp Law 27:201–211
Jessup P (1956) Transnational law. Yale University Press, New Heaven
Kaufmann-Kohler G, Potestà M (2016) Can the Mauritius Convention serve as a model for the reform of investor-State arbitration in connection with the introduction of a permament investment tribunal or an appeal mechanism? Analysis and roadmap. Geneva Center for International Dispute Settlement, available at https://www.uncitral.org/pdf/english/commissionsessions/unc/unc-49/CIDS_Research_Paper_-_Can_the_Mauritius_Convention_serve_as_a_model.pdf
Kingsbury B, Krisch N, Stewart RB (2005) The emergence of global administrative law. Law Contemp Probl 68:15–61
Neves M (2013) Transconstitutionalism. Hart, Oxford
Petersmann EU (2009) Constitutional theories of international economic law. In: Dupuy PM, Petersmann EU, Francioni F (eds) Human rights and international investment law and arbitration. Oxford University Press, Oxford, pp 137–194
Roberts A (2013) Clash of paradigms: actors and analogies shaping the investment-treaty system. Am J Int Law 107(1):45–94
Roberts A (2014) State-to-State investment treaty arbitration: a hybrid theory of interdependent rights and shared interpretive authority. Harv Int Law J 55:1):1–1)70
Stone S, Grisel F (2009) Transnational investment arbitration: from delegation to constitutionalization? In: Dupuy PM, Petersmann EU, Francioni F (eds) Human rights and international investment law and arbitration. Oxford University Press, Oxford, pp 118–136
Ustor E (1967) Le développement progressif du droit commercial international. Un nouveau programme juridique de l'ONU. Annuaire Français de Droit International 13:289–206
Waibel M, Kaushal A, Chung KH, Balchin C (2010) The backlash against investment arbitration: perceptions and reality. Wolters Kluwer, Alphen aan den Rijn

Bruno Sousa Rodrigues is a doctoral researcher and lecturer at Sciences Po Law School, where he has taught classes on "Public International Law", "Law and Society" and "Comparative Constitutional Law and Political Institutions". His research interests gravitate around the globalization of law, the theory of arbitration and economic governance. Bruno has been admitted to practice law by the Brazilian Bar Association (OAB/BA) and he has experience with dispute resolution of public and private law cases in both arbitral and judicial proceedings.

EU as a Driver in the Judicialization Process of International Investment Disputes: ISDS Reform and EU Judicial System

Rosario Ojinaga Ruiz and Maria Lina Leiva

Contents

1 Introduction 20
2 UNCITRAL and ISDS Reform Alternatives 23
2.1 The EU Proposal for a Multilateral Investment Court 26
2.2 An Important Feature: The Open Architecture 28
3 Judicialization of ISDS and EU Judicial System 31
3.1 Jurisdictional Clauses 33
3.2 Determination of the Respondent 35
3.3 Jurisdiction and Applicable Law 38
3.4 Disconnection or Judicial Dialogue? 40
4 Conclusions 42
References 42

Abstract With judicialization of ISDS as a hallmark of the EU investment policy and its proposal for the multilateralization of the investment court system, ISDS reform is increasingly associated with challenges arising from the multiplication of international tribunals and judicial dialogue. This includes challenges concerning the relation between the investment court system and the EU judicial system. In particular, the main feature regarding the compatibility of the CETA ICS with the autonomy of the EU legal order is the ISDS disconnection from EU Law and its judicial system. As a result, in Opinion 1/17 the CJEU has considered that the safeguards embodied in CETA rules and procedures are sufficient guarantee to the autonomy of the EU legal order, but the need of judicial dialogue with CETA Tribunals has been dismissed. Nevertheless, taking into account the possible

The authors are grateful for the valuable input and comments from Catharine Titi.
The research for this chapter was conducted as part of the project "European Union in the World: International Law and Politics", Erasmus + Programme-Jean Monnet Activities, Ref. 587791-EPP-1-2017-1-ES-EPPJMO-MODULE.

R. O. Ruiz · M. L. Leiva (✉)
University of Cantabria, Santander, Spain
e-mail: ojinagar@unican.es; maria-lina.leiva@alumnos.unican.es

A. Gourgourinis (ed.), *Transnational Actors in International Investment Law*,
European Yearbook of International Economic Law,
https://doi.org/10.1007/978-3-030-60679-4_2

outcome of the ongoing process of ISDS reform at the UNCITRAL and the current trend towards judicialization of international adjudication, new legal approaches may become necessary for the promotion of judicial dialogue and cooperation between the CJEU and other international jurisdictional structures.

1 Introduction

After the Lisbon Treaty, in the context of current reform of international investment governance,[1] the European Union ("EU") international investment policy (or the emerging unwritten EU Bilateral Investment Treaty model)[2] has been geared towards a comprehensive reform of investment protection rules and of the investor-state dispute settlement mechanism ("ISDS"). In the current global reform matrix, the EU has opted to carried a systemic procedural reform by promoting a shift from investment arbitration to an institutionalized and court-like ISDS system,[3] through its initiatives for the establishment of an investment court system ("ICS") and the creation of a multilateral investment court ("MIC").[4]

This approach is the result of the Brussels Investment Consensus[5] and it was embodied in recent practice, since almost all of the EU new generation free trade agreements ("FTAs")[6] with investment chapters, provide an investment court system, including the EU – Canada Comprehensive Economic and Trade Agreement

[1]UNCTAD, World Investment Report 2015. Reforming international investment governance (2015), http://unctad.org/en/PublicationsLibrary/wir2015_en.pdf (last accessed 1 June 2020).

[2]Hoffmeister and Alexandru (2014), p. 380.

[3]Lenk (2015) p. 14.

[4]Roberts (2018b), p. 194. This author makes a classification to disaggregate the level of ISDS reform, giving examples with different states. The states are classified in incremental, systemic and paradigmatic reformers considering the scale of proposed changes, not their merits. In this particular classification, the EU has been considered an incremental reformer actor in its form and substance, and a systemic reformer in procedure.

In its role as a driver of the judicialization process of ISDS, the EU has become one of the key supporters of a horizontal recalibration of ISDS, from private to public authority without altering (or even reasserting) its international character. At the multilateral stage, however, reform options are polarised between those actors that pursue a very modest horizontal recalibration and those who aspire to a significant dismantling of international authority. Herranz-Surrallés (2020), p. 344. For a more comprehensive approach to the process of judicialization of private transnational power and authority, Cutler (2018).

[5]OJ 2012 C 296E, European Parliament Resolution 2010/2203 of 6 April 2011. OJ 2017 C 265/05, European Parliament Resolution 2014/2228 of 8 July 2015. OJ 2018 C 101/30, European Parliament Resolution 2015/2105 of 5 July 2016.

[6]Titi (2015), p. 640.

("CETA"),[7] EU – Mexico Trade Agreement,[8] and the Investment Protection Agreements ("IPAs"): EU – Singapore,[9] EU – Vietnam,[10] with other ongoing negotiations.[11] The ICS would provide consistency and experience for a multilateral investment court. Even CETA, Singapore and Vietnam agreements (as was the case with the proposed Transatlantic Trade and Investment Partnership text), contain express provisions or "bridging" procedures anticipating the transition from a bilateral investment court system to a permanent MIC.[12]

Seeking support for its approach, the EU engaged with partners to build consensus for a permanent MIC, which has gathered specific interest in Canada.[13] In fact, several instances were used to promote the creation of a MIC.[14] The European Commission stated from the beginning that "the objective would be to multilateralise the court either as a self-standing international body or by embedding it into an existing multilateral organization".[15]

---

[7]OJ 2017 L 11, p. 23. Comprehensive Economic and Trade Agreement (CETA) between Canada, of the one part, and the European Union and its Member States, of the other part. OJ 2017 L 11, p. 1. Council Decision (EU) 2017/37 of 28 October 2016 on the signing on behalf of the European Union of the Comprehensive Economic and Trade Agreement (CETA) between Canada, of the one part, and the European Union and its Member States, of the other part. OJ 2017 L 11, p. 1080. Council Decision (EU) 2017/38 of 28 October 2016 on the signing the provisional application of the Comprehensive Economic and Trade Agreement (CETA) between Canada, of the one part, and the European Union and its Member States, of the other part.

[8]Current state of EU – Mexico negotiations, https://trade.ec.europa.eu/doclib/press/index.cfm?id=1833 (last accessed 1 June 2020).

[9]Curent state of EU – Singapore negotiations, https://trade.ec.europa.eu/doclib/press/index.cfm?id=961 (last accessed 1 June 2020).

[10]Current state of EU – Vietnam negotiations, https://trade.ec.europa.eu/doclib/press/index.cfm?id=1437 (last accessed 12 June 2020).

[11]There are ongoing negotiations with Chile, Australia and New Zealand, among others. No investment protection chapter was included in the EU-Japan Economic Partnership Agreement. Overview of TFA and Other Trade Negotiations, update February 2020, https://trade.ec.europa.eu/doclib/docs/2006/december/tradoc_118238.pdf (last accessed 1 June 2020).

[12]The "bridging clause" from a bilateral ICS to a MIC it is considered in article 8.29 of CETA, article 3.12 of the EU – Singapore IPA, article 3.41 of the EU – Vietnam IPA and article 12 of the proposed TTIP text. On challenges facing by the EU in relation to the gradual transition from the bilateral (ICS) to the multilateral (MIC) phase in terms of efficiency, costs, predictability and coherence, see Titi C, The European Union's proposal for an international investment court: Significance, innovations and challenges ahead. Transnational Dispute Management TDM 1, 2017, https://www.transnational-dispute-management.com (last accessed 1 June 2020).

[13]Article 6 (i) of the Joint Interpretative Instrument on the CETA between Canada and the European Union and its Member States, OJ 2017 L11.

[14]Some of the meetings used to introduce the MIC idea were: United Nations Commission on Trade and Development ("UNCTAD")'s World Investment Forum held in Nairobi, Kenia (2016); Organization for Economic Co-operation and Development ("OECD") Investment Treaty Dialogue, Paris (2016); Intergovernmental expert meeting, Geneva (2016) and Informal meeting at World Economic Forum, Davos (2017).

[15]European Commission, Concept Paper, 5 May 2015, Investment in TTIP and beyond – the path for reform. Enhancing the right to regulate and moving from current ad hoc arbitration towards an

Currently, the EU is also pursuing the creation of a MIC in the ongoing multilateral ISDS reform negotiations in Working Group III ("WGIII") of the United Nations Commission on International Trade Law ("UNCITRAL").[16] In November 2018, WGIII agreed by consensus that reforming the current system of investor-state arbitration was "desirable" in order to address concerns relating to: (1) consistency, coherence, predictability, and correctness of arbitral decisions; (2) independence, impartiality, and diversity of decision-makers; and (3) costs and duration of proceedings. On 18th January 2019, the EU made a submission to establish a standing mechanism for the settlement of international investment disputes,[17] including a possible work plan for achieving this aim.[18]

The current EU role as a driver in the judicialization process of ISDS has developed in parallel with extensive debates on the legitimacy of ISDS and recourse to the Court of Justice of the European Union ("CJEU") regarding the scope of the EU competence in foreign direct investment ("FDI")[19] and the compatibility of ISDS in intra-EU Bilateral Investment Treaties ("BITs") with the EU legal order.[20]

Nonetheless, the EU's leading role in the ongoing negotiations at UNCITRAL will be facilitated by the recent Opinion 1/17 of the CJEU on the compatibility of the Investment Court System in Chapter 8 (F) of CETA with the autonomy of the EU legal order.[21] In Opinion 1/17, the CJEU distinguished the external dimension of the

---

Investment Court, https://trade.ec.europa.eu/doclib/docs/2015/may/tradoc_153408.PDF (last accessed 12 June 2020), p. 12.

[16]Following a public consultation and impact assessment, the Commission made a recommendation to start negotiations on a MIC and the Council adopted negotiating directives. European Commission, Commission Staff Working Document Impact Assessment, SWD(2017) 302 Final. https://eur-lex.europa.eu/legal-content/EN/TXT/PDF/?uri=CELEX:52017SC0302&from=EN (last accessed 15 June 2020). European Commission, Recommendation for a Council Decision authorising the opening of negotiations for a Convention establishing a multilateral court for the settlement of investment disputes, COM(2017) 493 Final 7. https://ec.europa.eu/transparency/regdoc/rep/1/2017/EN/COM-2017-493-F1-EN-MAIN-PART-1.PDF (last accessed 15 June 2020). Negotiating directives for a Convention establishing a multilateral court for the settlement of investment disputes. Council Document of 20 March 2018, No 12981/17. http://data.consilium.europa.eu/doc/document/ST-12981-2017-ADD-1-DCL-1/en/pdf (last accessed 15 June 2020).

[17]UNCITRAL, Possible reform of Investor-State dispute settlement (ISDS): Submission from the European Union and its Members States, 24 January 2019, A/CN.9/WG.III/WP.159/Add.1, https://undocs.org/en/A/CN.9/WG.III/WP.159/Add.1 (last accessed 1 June 2020).

[18]UNCITRAL, Possible reform of Investor-State dispute settlement (ISDS): Submission from the European Union and its Members States, 24 January 2019, A/CN.9/WG.III/WP.159/Add.1, https://undocs.org/en/A/CN.9/WG.III/WP.159/Add.1 (last accessed 1 June 2020).

[19]In this case, the CJEU stated that ISDS clauses are susceptible to remove investment disputes from the jurisdiction of the courts of the EU Member States in favour of an international arbitral body and cannot therefore be established without the Member State's consent. CJEU, Opinion 2/15, 16 May 2017, ECLI:EU:C:2017:376, paras 291–292.

[20]CJEU, case C-284/16, *Slovak Republic v. Achmea BV*, ECLI:EU:C:2018:158.

[21]CJEU, Opinion 1/17, 30 April 2019, ECLI:EU:C:2019:341. The CJEU was also asked to assess the compatibility of the ISDS mechanism in CETA with the general principle of equal treatment,

ICS in CETA from the intra-EU dimension in *Achmea*[22] and, by adopting a very formalist approach, it concluded that ISDS in CETA is compatible with the EU legal order, among others because it is wholly separate from the legal (not the factual) universe of EU law.[23]

Against this fluid and changing background, this chapter examines both the opportunities and challenges that the EU is facing regarding the systemic reform of ISDS, mainly in the light of the current process of judicialization of international investment law. The main two arguments of this chapter are: the flexibilization of the EU MIC proposal to be able to negotiate with a wide spectrum of states within the same multilateral forum, and the disconnection as the main feature for the compatibility of CETA ICS with the autonomy of the EU legal order and its judicial system. Consequently, this chapter starts by examining the EU proposal within the ISDS reform alternatives. Next, it addresses how this proposal has been deconstructed to make it flexible in response to the multilateral forum requirements. Finally, the chapter concludes with the analysis of the judicialization of ISDS and the articulation with the EU law and judicial system, from the perspective of a broader need of a more systemic approach to international dispute settlement in a multijurisdictional world.

2 UNCITRAL and ISDS Reform Alternatives

With the establishment of UNCITRAL WGIII in December 2017, the engagement on ISDS reform gained prominence, and the first goal of the EU to move this discussion into a multilateral level was finally achieved. WG III began its work on its 34th session (2017) and has continued through several sessions taking place in Vienna and New York. Although reform of ISDS has been a matter of discussions for some years at the national, regional, as well as multilateral levels, the multilateral debate on reform of ISDS is now expected to be largely concentrated at UNCITRAL.[24]

The General Assembly of UNCITRAL entrusted the Working Group III with a narrow but clear three stage mandate, requiring it to: I. identify and consider concerns regarding ISDS; II. consider whether reform is desirable in the light of any identified concerns; III. if the WG concludes that reform is desirable, develop

with the requirement of effectiveness and with the right of access to an independent tribunal. These specific issues will not be analysed in this chapter.

[22]CJEU, case C-284/16, *Slovak Republic v. Achmea BV*, ECLI:EU:C:2018:158.

[23]Schepel H, A Parallel Universe: Advocate General Bot in Opinion 1/17, European Law Blog, https://europeanlawblog.eu/2019/02/07/ (last accessed on 7 February 2019).

[24]Mohamadieh (2019), p. 1.

any relevant solutions to be recommended to the Commission.[25] From a European strategic point of view, it was crucial that the latter mandate "to develop any relevant solution to be recommended" was indicated by the General Assembly of UNCITRAL, and *not* by the EU.

Even when EU had already made the decision to shift ISDS into a more court-like system, this engagement within the multilateral level, rather than bilaterally, would have unified the judicialization process and would have allowed the EU to lead this improvement more effectively. If a MIC is created through the UNCITRAL process, it could potentially depart from the EU proposed model and the system pursued by the EU would have the potential to extend beyond its initial design, consolidating its leadership position in the global investment governance.[26]

As the legitimacy crisis of ISDS is not actually new,[27] within the last years many states have been taking actions and implementing many ISDS reforms in their international investment agreements ("IIAs"). However, there are significant divergences in countries' approaches to reforming ISDS as the traditional international flows of FDI—from developed to developing countries—has completely moved to a more interchanged scenario, with new actors and needs, resulting in new requirements of a more inclusive and flexible approach.[28]

Among the broader approaches, three categories of reform proposals could be identified: incremental, paradigmatic and systemic reform. The first one would institute modest reform to redress specific concerns on the actual ISDS system. The second would require important changes, more significant and structural reforms such as replacing investor-state arbitration with a multilateral investment court and appellate body. The third one would entail a paradigm change, dismissing the existing system as irrevocably flawed and in need for wholesale replacement.[29] In general, these changes could be seen as oriented to *reform* or to *replace* traditional ISDS.

Regarding the WGIII's concern pertaining to consistency, coherence, predictability and correctness of arbitral decisions by ISDS tribunals, states have revealed a clear trend to reform the existing ISDS by improving its features or replacing it, through the reinforcement of other existing mechanisms or through the creation of something new.

---

[25] General Assembly Report of the United Nations Commission on International Trade Law, Fiftieth session (3–21 July 2017), A/72/17, https://undocs.org/en/A/72/17 (last accessed 1 June 2020), para. 264.

[26] Puig and Shaffer (2018), p. 398.

[27] Schill SW (2014), The sixth path: reforming investment law from within, https://papers.ssrn.com/sol3/papers.cfm?abstract_id=2446918 (last accessed 15 June 2020), p. 2; Sornarajah M (2012), Starting anew in international investment law http://ccsi.columbia.edu/files/2014/01/FDI_74.pdf (last accessed 1 June 2020), p. 2.

[28] Roberts (2018a).

[29] Roberts A and Tylor J, UNCITRAL and ISDS Reforms: Agenda-Widening and Paradigm-Shifting, https://www.ejiltalk.org/uncitral-and-isds-reforms-agenda-widening-and-paradigm-shifting/ (last accessed 30 April 2020).

On the one side, some states believe that to allow effective progress on ISDS reform, they should prioritize the concerns identified in WGIII and try to solve one by one,[30] this means to improve ISDS features progressively. For example, inconsistencies in the arbitral awards could be addressed in various ways, such as increasing the role of states by providing the possibility of joint interpretations from the treaty parties binding for arbitral tribunals, as well as other similar mechanisms to revise, amend or update investment treaties.[31] Another way to reform ISDS could be limiting the access to it by introducing local litigation requirements as a precondition to ISDS.[32] The application of the rule of exhaustion of local remedies has been a major concern from the beginning of the WGIII sessions.[33]

In this same vein, treaties could limit the time periods to submit claims, or they could even limit the investor's access to ISDS by reducing the subject-matter scope, or circumscribing the range of arbitrable claims, or excluding policy areas from ISDS coverage.[34] This selective judicialization[35] would address a concern related to the preservation of the states' "right to regulate" that has been debated in the last years within the ISDS system.[36] This selective judicialization could narrow access to ISDS and so shield some policy areas from dispute settlement.[37]

On the other side, some states have decided to take measures more focalized in order to replace the ISDS system or at least to prevent the escalation of conflict. For example, by promoting the use of mediation and negotiation as institutionalized

---

[30]UNCITRAL, Possible reform of Investor-State dispute settlement (ISDS): Submission from the Government of Chile, Israel and Japan, A/CN.9/WG.III/WP163, 15 March 2019, https://undocs.org/en/A/CN.9/WG.III/WP.163 (last accessed 1 June 2020), p. 4.

[31]UNCTAD, *World Investment Report* 2018 (UNCTAD/WIR/2018), https://unctad.org/en/PublicationsLibrary/wir2018_en.pdf (last accessed 15 June 2020).

[32]A Treaty may include a requirement to exhaust local judicial remedies (or to litigate in local courts fro a prolonged period) before turning to arbitration. UNCTAD, World Investment Report 2019, UNCTAD/WIR/2019, https://unctad.org/en/pages/PublicationWebflyer.aspx?publicationid=2460 (last accessed 15 June 2020). Also see UNCITRAL, Possible reform of investor-State dispute settlement (ISDS): Submission from the Government of South Africa, 17 July 2019, A/CN.9/WG.III/WP176, https://undocs.org/en/A/CN.9/WG.III/WP.176 (last accessed 15 June 2020), p. 8.

[33]UNCITRAL, Report of Working Group III (Investor-State Dispute Settlement Reform), 14 May 2018, A/CN.9/935, https://undocs.org/en/A/CN.9/935 (last accessed 1 June 2020). Roberts (2018b), p. 195. Returning to domestic courts has been a strong perspective in the India's 2015 BIT Model. India has been considered as a paradigmatic reformer in this view.

[34]Many states have been taking this option through including "carve outs" in their treaties. Some examples could be found in Australia adding a "tobacco carve out" in recent treaties, such as CPTPP/TPP.

[35]Schill SW and Vidigal G (2019), Cutting the gordian knot: investment dispute settlemet à la carte, https://uncitral.un.org/sites/uncitral.un.org/files/rta_exchange_-_investment_dispute_settlement_-_schill_and_vidigal.pdf (last accessed 1 June 2020), p. 4.

[36]Titi (2014), p. 10.

[37]As an example, chapter twenty eight of CETA gives the EU and Canada the right to exclude certain areas, either from specific chapters of CETA, or from the whole agreement. They can do so for a variety of reasons, such as to ensure public safety, prevent tax evasion, or to preserve and promote cultural identity.

alternatives to ISDS. These mechanisms already exist in many of the BITs, so the aim of replacing ISDS could be achieved just by giving them a more leading role.[38]

Other states have decided to replace ISDS entirely by accepting only state-to-state arbitration in their BITs. The innovation in this regard is the tendency of rethinking this kind of mechanism as a way of cooperation rather than confrontation. The Brazilian Model Cooperation and Facilitation Investment Agreement ("CFIA") highlights the benefits of this system when complemented with a dispute prevention mechanism.[39] Ombudsmen offices as a first contact point have been proposed as a way to assess problems with a foreign investor and prevent disputes from escalating to arbitration proceedings.[40]

Within all the alternatives on ISDS reform, the most innovative idea is that of replacing the existing ISDS system with a new international jurisdictional structure; in particular, the EU proposal for the establishment of a new permanent multilateral investment court.

2.1 The EU Proposal for a Multilateral Investment Court

The proposal of the EU and its Member States submitted to UNCITRAL WGIII in January 2019, is in accordance with the Negotiation Directive ("ND") 12981/17 (from March 2018).[41] This ND contains the authorization to open negotiations, allowing the European Commission to negotiate a potentially legally binding agreement. This Directive authorized the European Commission to work on step three of the UNCITRAL mandate of reforming ISDS, when the WGIII was in phase one. First, a description of this proposal will be exposed. Then, an analysis of how this

[38]For example, the states parties of MERCOSUR (Argentina, Brazil, Paraguay and Uruguay) signed in April 2017 the Protocol on Investment Cooperation and Facilitation ("MERCOSUR Protocol"), https://www.mercosur.int/documento/protocolo-de-cooperacion-y-facilitacion-de-inversiones-intra-mercosur/ (last accessed 1 June 2020).

[39]UNCITRAL, Possible reform of investor-State dispute settlement (ISDS): Submission from the Government of Brazil, 11 July 2019, A/CN.9/WG.III/WP171, https://undocs.org/en/A/CN.9/WG.III/WP.171 (last accessed 1 June 2020), p. 4. Another recent example could be the Southern African Development Community ("SADC").

[40]UNCITRAL, Possible reform of investor-State dispute settlement (ISDS): Submission from the Government of Korea, 31 July 2019, A/CN.9/WG.III/WP179, https://uncitral.un.org/sites/uncitral.un.org/files/wp179_new.pdf (last accessed 1 June 2020), p. 5. UN General Assembly, Possible reform of investor-State dispute settlement (ISDS): Submission from the Government of Brazil, 11 July 2019, A/CN.9/WG.III/WP171, https://undocs.org/en/A/CN.9/WG.III/WP.171 (last accessed 1 June 2020), p. 4. UNCITRAL, Possible reform of investor-State dispute settlement (ISDS): Submission from the Government of South Africa, 17 July 2019, A/CN.9/WG.III/WP176, https://undocs.org/en/A/CN.9/WG.III/WP.176 (last accessed 1 June 2020), p. 8.

[41]Negotiating directives for a Convention establishing a multilateral court for the settlement of investment disputes. Council Document of 20 March 2018, No 12981/17. http://data.consilium.europa.eu/doc/document/ST-12981-2017-ADD-1-DCL-1/en/pdf (last accessed 15 June 2020).

proposal has been relaxed to include other important actors with different position about the creation of a MIC, will be included.

The EU proposal identified systemic concerns about ISDS, considering that an accurate response would be a standing mechanism, with full-time adjudicators and combining a first instance tribunal and an appellate tribunal.[42] The first instance would hear disputes, and conduct fact finding as arbitral tribunals do nowadays, and then apply the applicable law to the facts. It would also deal with cases remanded back from the appellate tribunal when the latter could not dispose on the case. The appellate tribunal would hear appeals from the first instance tribunal, and it cannot engage in a de novo review of the facts. The grounds of appeal should be error of law or manifest errors in the appreciation of the facts. Moreover, and following new trends, a structured dialogue between the court and the treaty parties has also been included.[43]

Regarding arbitrators, deep concerns have been shown about the requirements of independence and impartiality of decision makers in actual ISDS,[44] as well as other characteristics related to selection and appointment of arbitral tribunals.[45] Addressing some of these concerns, the EU proposes full time salaried adjudicators appointed by the treaty parties for fixed non-renewable terms, with high qualifications and ethical requirements, including geographical and gender diversity.[46]

A MIC would be able to rule on disputes under the large stock of existing and future agreements by making use of the "opt-in" mechanism envisaged in the Mauritius Convention on Transparency in ISDS and in the Multilateral Convention to Implement Tax Treaty Related Measures to Prevent Base Erosion and Profit Shifting (BEPS Convention).[47] This mechanisms allow to rule not only on disputes

---

[42]UNCITRAL, Possible reform of Investor-State dispute settlement (ISDS): Submission from the European Union and its Members States, 24 January 2019, A/CN.9/WG.III/WP.159/Add.1, https://undocs.org/en/A/CN.9/WG.III/WP.159/Add.1 (last accessed 1 June 2020).

[43]UNCITRAL, Possible reform of Investor-State dispute settlement (ISDS): Submission from the European Union and its Members States, 24 January 2019, A/CN.9/WG.III/WP.159/Add.1, https://undocs.org/en/A/CN.9/WG.III/WP.159/Add.1 (last accessed 1 June 2020), p. 6.

[44]UNCITRAL, Report of Working Group III (Investor-State Dispute Settlement Reform), 6 November 2018, A/CN.9/964, https://undocs.org/A/CN.9/964 (last accessed 1 June 2020), para. 66 ss.

[45]UNCITRAL, Possible reform of investor-State dispute settlement (ISDS): Selection and appointment of ISDS tribunal members, 31 July 2019, A/CN.9/WG.III/WP.169, https://undocs.org/en/A/CN.9/WG.III/WP.169 (last accessed 1 June 2020).

[46]UNCITRAL, Possible reform of Investor-State dispute settlement (ISDS): Submission from the European Union and its Members States, 24 January 2019, A/CN.9/WG.III/WP.159/Add.1, https://undocs.org/en/A/CN.9/WG.III/WP.159/Add.1 (last accessed 1 June 2020), p. 4.

[47]UNCITRAL, Possible reform of Investor-State dispute settlement (ISDS): Submission from the European Union and its Members States, 24 January 2019, A/CN.9/WG.III/WP.159/Add.1, https://undocs.org/en/A/CN.9/WG.III/WP.159 (last accessed 1 June 2020), p. 8. Kaufmann-Köhler G and Potestà M (2016), Can the Mauritius Convention serve as a model for the reform of investor-State arbitration in connection with the introduction of a permanent investment tribunal or an appeal mechanism? Analysis and Roadmap, https://www.uncitral.org/pdf/english/CIDS_Research_Paper_Mauritius.pdf (last accessed 1 June 2020), p. 75. Titi (2018), p. 150.

of future agreements but also in existing agreements through a combination of two methods, (1) accession to the instrument establishing the standing mechanism and (2) a specific notification ("opt-in") that a particular existing or future agreement would be subject to the jurisdiction of the standing mechanism.[48]

The effective enforcement of awards would be another vital feature for a standing mechanism. Thus, the EU suggests creating an enforcement regime within the same instrument establishing the MIC. Another option would be to include the enforcement mechanism of the New York Convention on Recognition and Enforcement of Foreign Arbitral Awards, on the basis that MIC awards could be considered as a "permanent arbitral body" within Article 1 (2) of this Convention.[49]

Despite the fact that the European Commission has initially elaborated a full and concise proposal for the creation of a MIC, the debates developments in WGIII and state's submissions, obliged to design a special feature to allow the potential inclusion of all the relevant actors in the international investment scene, even to those states whose position was not fully in favour of the creation of a MIC.

2.2 *An Important Feature: The Open Architecture*

The "Open architecture" is a special feature in the EU proposal which allow for the adhesion of countries that might want to use the standing mechanism for state-to-state dispute settlement but do not use ISDS in their agreements, or even for countries that may like to retain the flexibility to utilize only an appeal mechanism.[50]

This special feature was rather forced by the wide support that many states have shown on another replacing ISDS reform option, called the Stand-Alone review or Appellate Body ("AB").[51] An AB could provide a quality control procedure to an

---

[48]UNCITRAL, Possible reform of Investor-State dispute settlement (ISDS): Submission from the European Union and its Members States, 24 January 2019, A/CN.9/WG.III/WP.159/Add.1, https://undocs.org/en/A/CN.9/WG.III/WP.159 (last accessed 1 June 2020), p. 8. "Once the contracting parties to an agreement that are also parties to the instrument establishing the standing mechanism have made a notification concerning a particular agreement, then the standing mechanism would decide disputes arising under that agreement. For agreements concluded after the establishment of the standing mechanism, a reference could be made in the agreement conferring jurisdiction on the standing mechanism, or it could be added later."

[49]UNCITRAL, Possible reform of Investor-State dispute settlement (ISDS): Submission from the European Union and its Members States, 24 January 2019, A/CN.9/WG.III/WP.159/Add.1, https://undocs.org/en/A/CN.9/WG.III/WP.159 (last accessed 1 June 2020), p. 7.

[50]UNCITRAL, Possible reform of Investor-State dispute settlement (ISDS): Submission from the European Union and its Members States, 24 January 2019, A/CN.9/WG.III/WP.159/Add.1, https://undocs.org/en/A/CN.9/WG.III/WP.159/Add.1 (last accessed 1 June 2020), p. 9.

[51]Roberts A and John T, UNCITRAL and ISDS Reforms: China's Proposal, https://www.ejiltalk.org/uncitral-and-isds-reform-chinas-proposal/ (last accessed 30 April 2020); Roberts A and John T, "UNCITRAL and ISDS Reforms: Moving to Reform Options. . .the Politics, https://www.ejiltalk.org/uncitral-and-isds-reforms-moving-to-reform-options-the-politics/ (last accessed 30 April 2020).

award before it becomes final, without creating a new first instance. There is a suggestion that this task could be carried out by an independent body under one of the existing arbitration organizations.[52] The AB could review awards and decisions made by arbitral tribunals, a standing investment court, regional investment courts, international commercial courts and domestic courts in case of denial of justice.[53]

The AB appears as a possible option in many states' submissions to UNCITRAL WGIII,[54] including China submission.[55] China has recently emerged as one of the top FDI home countries and FDI host countries as well. It has been assuming a key role in international investment system, making innovations over the last few years, shifting from a cautious to a proactive attitude towards ISDS.[56] Even more, some developing states believe that China could assume the position that the West countries are losing so rapidly in this field.[57]

At the multilateral level, however, China is not able to exert an influence equivalent to its economic power, and at the same time China has not been involved in many ISDS cases.[58] But the complexity and uniqueness of the relationship between China and the EU,[59] obliged the latter to further approximate positions on ISDS reform in a multilateral framework negotiation rather than bilaterally.

There is a gap between the core principles of the EU's proposal and China's key concerns towards ISDS system. One of China concerns about ISDS is related to the fairness and correctness of each award, rather than the consistency of different awards. From China's perspective, correctness could be merely achieved through an AB without the need of a MIC. Even more, an appeal mechanism that could

[52]UNCITRAL, Possible reform of investor-State dispute settlement (ISDS): Submission from the Government of Morocco, 4 March 2019, https://undocs.org/en/A/CN.9/WG.III/WP.161 (last accessed 1 June 2020), A/CN.9/WG.III/WP.161, p. 5.

[53]UNCITRAL, Note by the Secretariat: Possible reform of investor-State dispute settlement (ISDS), 30 July 2019, A/CN.9/WG.III/WP.166, https://undocs.org/en/A/CN.9/WG.III/WP.166 (last accessed 1 June 2020), p. 6.

[54]UNCITRAL, Note by the Secretariat: Possible reform of investor-State dispute settlement (ISDS), 30 July 2019, A/CN.9/WG.III/WP.166, https://undocs.org/en/A/CN.9/WG.III/WP.166 (last accessed 1 June 2020), p. 6.

[55]UNCITRAL, Possible reform of investor-State dispute settlement (ISDS): Submission from the Government of China, 19 July 2019, A/CN.9/WG.III/WP.177, https://undocs.org/en/A/CN.9/WG.III/WP.177 (last accessed 1 June 2020), p. 4.

[56]Ning and Qi (2018) pp. 156, 159; Liu (2019), p. 267.

[57]Sornarajah (2018), p. 224; Cai (2018), p. 188.

[58]Ning and Qi (2018), p. 161. There has been three cases against China and eight cases involving Chinese investors. "Concerns of Chinese scholars are not related to the inconsistency of awards based on similar treaty provisions, but rather related to the correctness of interpretations given by arbitral tribunals."

[59]China has concluded BITs with 26 EU member states. China and the EU launched their negotiation rounds for BIT in 2013, and has concluded their 27th round of negotiation in March 2020. See, European Commission, Report of the 27th round of negotiations on the EU-China Comprehensive Agreement on Investment, 9 March 2020, TRADE.B2/Ares(2020)1434741, https://trade.ec.europa.eu/doclib/docs/2020/march/tradoc_158663.pdf (last accessed 1 June 2020). The aim is to finalize negotiations for an ambitious investment agreement on 2020.

ensure a more accurate interpretation of the international investment treaties, need in depth analysis and assessment.[60] Consequently, the EU MIC proposal raises new questions and concerns from China position.

In the bilateral negotiations between China and the EU, this existing gap in their interests must be tackled, as both countries are strategic markets for each other.[61] However, the overall challenge would be to lump *together* the different perspectives on investment dispute settlement and articulate an inclusive system that allows these different views to co-exist.

The flexibilization of the EU original MIC model could be considered as a recognition that, even when there are significant divergences in the reform approaches, there is a slight trend in seeking a combination of different dispute settlement options under a common institutional structure, which would be able to offer and administer different modes of settling investment disputes. Inspiration for this idea can be drawn from dispute settlement system under United Nations Convention on the Law of the Sea of 10 December 1982 ("UNCLOS").[62] The dispute settlement system within UNCLOS has a common framework in which different modes of dispute settlement are included. The "Choice of procedure" in article 287 of UNCLOS establish a system that preserves the flexibility for states in the choice of their preferred means of adjudication.[63]

Considering the core elements of dispute settlement in investment, there is a key possibility to construct a common framework—an umbrella agreement—which would include the creation of a MIC (whose jurisdiction can be voluntary for states and organizations) coexisting with the option of investor-state arbitration and even inter-state arbitration.[64]

Finally, it is worth to notice that even when the investment dispute reform process has been open up to a wider range of possibilities—from the initial debates of the WGIII up to nowadays-, the pioneering idea of judicialization of ISDS still retains its major features and EU is performing a leadership role in this field.

[60]Ning and Qi (2018), pp. 165–166.

[61]EU and China are actually negotiating a Comprehensive Agreement on Investment (CAI) from 2014. They agree that an agreement would go beyond a traditional investment protection agreement and it would contain, among others, a dispute resolution. Current state of negotiations: https://trade.ec.europa.eu/doclib/press/index.cfm?id=2115 (last accessed 1 June 2020).

[62]Schill SW and Vidigal G (2019), Cutting the gordian knot: investment dispute settlemet à la carte, https://uncitral.un.org/sites/uncitral.un.org/files/rta_exchange_-_investment_dispute_settlement_-_schill_and_vidigal.pdf (last accessed 1 June 2020), p. 4.

[63]The free choice of forum system embodied in Article 287 of United Nations Convention on the Law Of the Sea also includes special rules regarding the participation of EU. See Ojinaga (2016), p. 980.

[64]Schill and Vidigal (2020), p. 315.

3 Judicialization of ISDS and EU Judicial System

With the judicialization of ISDS as a hallmark of the EU investment policy and its proposal for the multilateralization of the ICS at UNCITRAL, the ISDS reform has become increasingly associated with challenges arising from the proliferation of international tribunals and judicial dialogue. Even if the ICS and MIC represent an improvement on the traditional ISDS model, it could give rise to a number of new challenges. Among particular challenges facing the EU are those concerning the relationship between ICS, or MIC, and the EU judicial system.

The EU participates in international multilateral regimes and dispute settlement systems, such as in World Trade Organization ("WTO") and UNCLOS, but not yet in the more specific European Convention on Human Rights ("ECHR") system. As noted by the CJEU, the competence of the EU in the field of international relations and its capacity to conclude international agreements necessarily entails the power to submit to decisions of International Dispute Settlement ("IDS") bodies on the interpretation and application of those agreements.[65] In its opinion on the European Economic Area ("EEA"), the CJEU stated that "an international agreement providing for system of courts, including a court with jurisdiction to interpret its provisions, is not in principle incompatible with Community Law".[66] Hence, the EU could be considered as entitled to negotiate compromissory clauses, eventually including judicialized ISDS procedures, in international agreements.

However, those agreements must respect the indispensable conditions for safeguarding the essential character of the powers of EU institutions and the autonomy of the EU legal order.[67] In particular:

> That autonomy accordingly resides in the fact that the Union possesses a constitutional framework that is unique to it. That framework encompasses the founding values set out in Article 2 TEU, which states that the Union 'is founded on the values of respect for human dignity, freedom, democracy, equality, the rule of law, and respect for human rights', the general principles of EU law, the provisions of the Charter, and the provisions of the EU and FEU Treaties, which include, inter alia, rules on the conferral and division of powers, rules governing how the EU institutions and its judicial system are to operate, and fundamental rules in specific areas, structured in such a way as to contribute to the implementation of the process of integration described in the second paragraph of Article 1 TEU[68]

---

[65]CJEU, Opinion 1/17, 30 April 2019, ECLI:EU:C:2019:341, para. 106; CJEU, Opinion 2/13, 18 December 2014, ECLI:EU:C:2014:2454, para. 182; CJEU, Opinion 1/09 8 March 2011, ECLI:EU:C:2011:123, para. 74; Opinion 1/91, 14 December 1991, ECLI:EU:C:1991:490, paras 40 and 70; Rosas (2018), pp. 4–6; Wessel (2013), pp. 23–30.

[66]CJEU, Opinion 1/91, 14 December 1991, ECLI:EU:C:1991:490, para. 40.

[67]CJEU, Opinion 1/17, 30 April 2019, ECLI:EU:C:2019:341, para. 107; Opinion 2/13, 18 December 2014, ECLI:EU:C:2014:2454, para. 183; Opinion 1/00,18 April 2002, ECLI:EU:C:2002:231, paras. 20 and 21.

[68]Opinion 1/17, 30 April 2019, ECLI:EU:C:2019:341, para. 110. Opinion 2/13,18 December 2014, ECLI:EU:C:2014:2454, para. 158.

Then, the compatibility of the judicialized ISDS procedures with the EU legal order and its judicial system should be considered in the light of the CJEU case-law regarding the external dimension of the principle of autonomy,[69] including the guarantee of jurisdictional autonomy vis-à-vis international courts and tribunals and IDS bodies.[70] The notion of jurisdictional autonomy, emphasised by the CJEU in its previous Opinion 2/13, refers to the safeguarding of the jurisdictional order laid down in the EU Treaties[71] and, more particularly, to the CJEU exclusive jurisdiction to give the definitive interpretation of EU law, mainly in the framework of the preliminary ruling procedure provided for in Article 267 of the Treaty on the Functioning of the European Union ("TFEU"), in accordance with Article 19 of the Treaty of the European Union ("TEU").[72] Then, the external dimension of autonomy of EU law is engaged in situations where an international dispute resolution mechanism might apply or interpret EU law.[73]

Certainly, CETA offers a number of safeguards, both substantive and procedural, in order to preserve the autonomy of EU Law. The main element regarding the compatibility of the ICS in CETA with the autonomy of the EU legal is the ISDS disconnection from EU Law and its judicial system. In Opinion 1/17, the CJEU has considered that the safeguards embodied in CETA rules and procedures are sufficient guarantee to the autonomy of the EU legal order, because the CETA Tribunals stands outside the EU judicial system[74] and lacks jurisdiction to interpret or apply EU law other than that relating to the provisions of that agreement.[75] However, the CJEU is silence on how the role of domestic courts in the Union may be affected by new judicialized ISDS mechanisms and international investment tribunals.[76]

In addition, in Opinion 1/17 the CJEU highlights the constitutional relevance of the "right to regulate" for the autonomy of the EU legal order. Nevertheless, it considers that, by virtue of the express restriction of the scope of Sections C and D of Chapter Eight of CETA, the CETA Tribunal has no jurisdiction to declare incompatible with the CETA the level of protection of a public interest established by the EU Law and, on that basis, to order the Union to pay damage. So, a major sensitive issue will be that of the risk of divergent interpretation by the CJEU and the CETA Tribunals of certain restrictive clauses as, for example, article 28.3.2 of the CETA.

---

[69] CJEU, Opinion 2/13, 18 December 2014, ECLI:EU:C:2014:2454, para. 170. See Rosas (2007).

[70] Eckes (2019), pp. 185–223; Odermatt (2018), p. 304.

[71] CJEU, case C-459/03, *Commission v Ireland*, ECLI:EU:C:2006:345, para. 154.

[72] CJEU, Opinion 1/17, 30 April 2019, ECLI:EU:C:2019:341, para. 111; Opinion 2/13, 18 December 2014, ECLI:EU:C:2014:2454, paras 174–176 and 246. Vajda C (2019), Achmea and the autonomy of the EU legal order, https://www.lawttip.eu/uploads/files/UNIBO%20Vajda_WP.pdf (last accessed 1 June 2020), pp. 10–11.

[73] Vajda C (2019), Achmea and the autonomy of the EU legal order, https://www.lawttip.eu/uploads/files/UNIBO%20Vajda_WP.pdf (last accessed 1 June 2020), p. 18.

[74] Opinion 1/17, 30 April 2019, ECLI:EU:C:2019:341, paras 113–114.

[75] Opinion 1/17, 30 April 2019, ECLI:EU:C:2019:341, para. 136.

[76] On the view taken by the AG Bot, opinion delivered on 29 January 2019, ECLI:EU:C:2019:72, paras 171–172.

In Opinion 1/17 the notion of autonomy has become more flexible, as the result of the more prominent role recognised by the CJEU to the need of finding a balance between ensuring the EU constitutional framework and enabling the EU to develop its external action, its involvement in international dispute settlement and the development of a rule-based international legal order.[77] To a great extend however, the approach adopted by the CJEU to the notion of jurisdictional autonomy in Opinion 1/17 seems widely consistent with its relevant case-law in previous Opinion 2/13 and the MOX Plant case, since "the focus is almost entirely on what might be called the negative dimension of autonomy"[78] or in protecting EU Law from external threats. As a result, the need of judicial dialogue with other jurisdictional structures has been dismissed by the CJEU. However, taking into consideration the ongoing negotiations at UNCITRAL and their possible outcome, the CJUE reasoning on the compatibility of the ICS in CETA with the EU legal order might be in need of further development and adjustment. In particular, as a brief look at the autonomy safeguards embodied in CETA suggests, some potentially problematic concerns could arise regarding the application of mutual exclusiveness clause, the determination of the respondent by an investor and the examination of domestic and EU Law as matter of fact by the CETA tribunals. So, the need of new procedural rules and tools for judicial dialogue and cooperation between the CJEU and other international courts and tribunals should be further considered in the future;[79] in particular, in order to guide the ICS Tribunals, or other international jurisdictional structures, with binding rulings in its usage of EU Law.

3.1 *Jurisdictional Clauses*

The procedural rules for the settlement of disputes under CETA and other EU FTAs include jurisdictional clauses aimed to prevent the recourse by the investor to other national or international judicial action in parallel with, or in addition to, a claim

[77] CJEU, Opinion of AG Bot, delivered on 29 January 2019, ECLI:EU:C:2019:72, paras 173–178 and 72 to 90.

[78] Odermatt (2018), p. 2.

[79] Both the growing need of procedural mechanisms to mitigate the risks of overlapping jurisdiction and parallel proceedings and the role that the international economic law is playing as a laboratory for the development of these mechanisms and procedural cross-fertilization have been emphasised by authors. Boisson de Chazournes (2017). Ruiz Fabri and Paine (2019), The procedural cross-fertilization pull, https://poseidon01.ssrn.com/delivery.php?ID=989065009005112086027088120116119122028021001019074056118072080086029111121002109123020121038120049012114064124089028020108019025042021040033079103126091068065085089059002063007026026088101110107078068097083118119107125088006098084005117123006095026026&EXT=pdf (last accessed 29 June 2020); Burgorgue-Larsen L (2003), Le fait régional dans la juridictionnalisation du droit international, https://hal.archives-ouvertes.fr/hal-01743274/document (last accessed 1 June 2020), p. 38.

submitted to ICS Tribunals.[80] There are two sets of procedural rules in CETA to order coexisting jurisdiction with different significance for the relationship between the ICS and the EU judicial system: the "mutual exclusiveness" clause and other rules on "related actions".

The mutual exclusiveness clause[81] obliges the investor to choose between make use of ISDS mechanism filing their claim for compensation before the CETA Tribunals with respect to a measure alleged to constitute a breach of CETA or to submit a claim before a domestic (or international) court or tribunal.[82] The last option includes the recourse to the domestic courts and EU judicial system for alleged breaches of domestic and EU Law, mainly in order to request the annulment of the measure in question. These legal actions are based on different legal rules of reference and, therefore, the subject matter may vary depending on the forum chosen by the investor.[83] Then, a number of issues remain open regarding the mutual exclusiveness clause in FTAs after Opinion 1/17.[84] Even if the CJEU has considered the ISDS envisaged in CETA compatible with EU legal order, the relationship between the domestic and the international jurisdictional mechanism needs to be further examined in relation to the possible inconsistences that may arise due to forum-shopping. Other fork-in-the-road (FITR) clauses could be illustrative of the problems arising in the interpretation and application of certain requirements analogous to that embodied in the mutual exclusiveness clause of the CETA. In practical terms, it has even been suggested that the idea of mutual exclusiveness of national courts and ICS Tribunals may not be workable because the differences in remedies and applicable law require investor-claimants to make difficult choices between the protection under domestic or EU law and the protection under international law. In

[80]On problems caused by parallel proceedings and its connection with procedural justice, Gaillard E, Parallell proceedings: Investment arbitration, Max Planck Encyclopedia of International Procedural Law, https://opil.ouplaw.com/home/mpil (last accessed 30 May 2019).

[81]Article 8.22 CETA. See Bungenberg and Reinisch (2018), pp. 77–78.

[82]Article 8.22.1 (f) and (g) in relation to Article 8.22.5 of the CETA. A claim may be submitted by the investor to the CETA Tribunal on condition that the investor previously withdraws or discontinues any existing proceeding or waives its right to initiate any claim or proceeding before a tribunal or court under domestic or international law with respect to a measure alleged to constitute a breach referred to in its claim. This formulation is generally consistent with the approach taken under the ICSID Convention regime. In early drafts of the CETA, the preclusion of parallel proceedings applied only to claims for damages or compensation but not for other remedies, such an annulment of a host State's measure (Hindelang 2015, pp. 56–57).

[83]Opinion of AG Bot delivered on 29 January 2019, ECLI:EU:C:2019:72, para. 168.

[84]Article 8.22 of the CETA is only mentioned once by CJEU, Opinion 1/17, 30 April 2019, ECLI: EU:C:2019:341, para. 135. By the contrary, the AG Bot considers that alternative jurisdiction conferred to the CETA Tribunals does not restrict the substantive rights enjoyed by foreign investors under EU law; nor does it have the effect of limiting the jurisdiction of the CJEU or of the courts and tribunals of the Member states to hear and determine actions brought with a view to ensuring the observance of such rights; and no deprived those courts and tribunals of their status as 'general law' courts within the EU legal order, including their role in any making of references for a preliminary ruling to the CJEU (Opinion of AG Bot, delivered on 29 January 2019, ECLI:EU: C:2019:72, paras 165–172).

addition, the requirement to make such choices "hinders the mutual integration of both legal orders and dispute settlement mechanisms".[85]

The CETA and other EU FTAs include a more general jurisdictional clause on related actions brought before other international dispute settlement mechanisms and bodies under another international agreement.[86] This broader clause can be invoked when there is a potential for overlapping compensation or the other international claim could have a significant impact on the resolution of the claim brought before the ICS Tribunal. In those cases, the ICS Tribunals shall, as soon as possible after hearing the disputing parties, stay its proceedings or otherwise ensure that proceedings brought pursuant to another international agreement are taken into account in its decision, order or award. This is a very flexible clause which could be used by ICS Tribunal to promote indirect judicial dialogue with other international courts and tribunals. But the application of the rules on "related actions" to the dialogue between the ICS Tribunals and the CJEU creates many legal uncertainties.

3.2 Determination of the Respondent

If the investor decides to bring a claim for compensation before the CETA Tribunals, a mandatory mechanism is provided that allows the EU to decide internally who is the party that will appear as the respondent in the dispute.[87] It contributes both to the aim of legal certainty and the guarantee of the autonomy of EU Law. Accordingly, the autonomy and constitutional functions of the CJEU are preserved since the CETA Tribunals are not called on to rule on the internal division of competences and responsibility between the EU and its Member States as regards the matters governed by the provisions of this agreement.[88]

In this way CETA embraces, with a more refined technique than UNCLOS,[89] the proceduralization approach,[90] as a better solution than those consisting of a declaration of competences corresponding to the EU and its Member States or the

[85]Schill SW (2016), The European Commission's proposal of an "Investment Court System" for TTIP: stepping stone or stumbling block for multilateralizing international investment law? https://www.asil.org/insights/volume/20/issue/9/european-commissions-proposal-investment-court-system-ttip-stepping (last accessed 1 June 2020).

[86]Article 8.24 CETA. See Lévesque and Newcombe (2013), pp. 108–110.

[87]Article 8.21 of the CETA.

[88]Opinion 1/17 of 30 April 2019, ECLI:EU:C:2019:341, paras 77 and 132; Opinion 2/13 (Accession of the Union to the ECHR) of 18 December 2014, EU:C:2014:2454, paras 224–231. Opinion of AG Bot, delivered on 29 January 2019, ECLI:EU:C:2019:72, para. 161.

[89]Treves (2014).

[90]Heliskoski (2001), pp. 157–208.

application of the joint responsibility rule.[91] The EU-Singapore,[92] the EU-Vietnam[93] and the Mexico[94] agreements have similar provisions. In the event of the multilateralization of ICS, it has been suggested that the EU should be considered as the appropriate respondent.[95]

According to the CETA rules, if the dispute cannot be settled within 90 days of the submission of the request for consultations and the investor intends to submit a claim, the investor must deliver to the EU a notice requesting a determination of the respondent and identifying the measures against which they intend to submit the claim.[96] After making a determination, the EU shall inform the investor as to whether EU or a Member State shall be the respondent.[97] The possibility of multiple respondents is not expressly envisaged in CETA. In the event that the investor has not been informed of the determination of the respondent within the time period of 50 days, the subsidiary rules provide for the determination of the respondent by considering if the measures identified in the notice are exclusively measures of a member state or include measures of the EU.[98] The CETA Tribunals shall be bound by the determination made by the EU or by the application of the subsidiary rules.[99] When these subsidiary rules apply, the EU and its member states may not assert the inadmissibility of the claim, lack of jurisdiction of the Tribunal or otherwise object to the claim or award on the ground that the respondent was not properly determined.[100] On this point, it seems more doubtful whether the determination of the respondent actually conforms to the autonomy principle in the light of the CJEU position in its Opinion 2/13.[101] Then, some dysfunctions could arise with regards to

---

[91]The declarations of competence externalises or exports the problem to the international level and much room for interpretation would be left to the international court or tribunal charged with applying them. See Contartese and Pantaleo (2018), p. 417; Delgado Casteleiro (2012), pp. 502–503; Govaere (2010), p. 204.

[92]Article 3.5 of the EUSFTA.

[93]Article 3.32 of the EUVFTA.

[94]Article 5 of the EUMTA.

[95]Bungenberg and Reinisch (2018), p. 90.

[96]Article 8.21.1 and 8.21.2 of the CETA.

[97]Article 8.21.3 of the CETA.

[98]Article 8.21.4 of the CETA.

[99]Article 8.21.7 of the CETA.

[100]Article 8.21.6 of the CETA; Article 3.32.5 of the EUVFTA.

[101]In that occasion, the CJEU stated that the ECHR, in ascertaining the plausibility of a request of the EU or the Member States to intervene as co-respondents "would be required to assess the rules of EU law governing the division of powers between the EU and its Member States as well as the criteria for the attribution of their acts or omissions, in order to adopt a final decision in that regard which would be binding both on the Member States and on the EU". Then, it concludes that "[s] uch a review would be liable to interfere with the division of powers between the EU and its Member States' (CJEU, Opinion 2/13, 18 December 2014, ECLI:EU:C:2014:2454, paras 224–225). Mayr (2017), p. 276.

the determination of the respondent, the application of the Regulation 912/2014[102] and judicial review by CJEU on this matter.

The issue of the representation of the parties in international judicial proceedings is usually regulated in very general and flexible terms.[103] The CJEU has interpreted that even if Article 335 TFEU exclusively concerns the representation of the EU in national legal proceedings, it reflects the general principle that the EU has legal capacity[104] and provides a basis for representation of the EU by the European Commission both before national and international courts and tribunals.[105] However, the question of the definition of the EU position in international judicial proceedings is more complex. Even if the WTO design should serve as a model, both political and institutional conflicts may arise. This was the case when the Council of the EU sought the annulment of the decision of the European Commission to submit a written statement on behalf of the EU in advisory proceeding before ITLOS in Case No 21.[106] On that occasion, the CJEU stated that neither Article 16 (1) of the TUE nor Article 218 (9) of the TFUE are applicable to the participation of the EU in international adjudication.[107] In addition, by starting that "the principle of sincere cooperation requires the Commission to consult the Council beforehand if it intends to express positions on behalf of the European Union before an international court",[108] the CJEU brought new dimensions to the principle of unity of EU external representation.[109] Hence, prior information and consultation among institutions is required by virtue of Article 13 (2) of the TFUE, as well as a concert action at an international level between the EU and its Member States on the basis of Article 4 (3) of the TUE.[110]

---

[102]OJ 2014 L 257: EU Regulation, No. 912/2014 of the European Parliament and of the Council establishing a framework for managing financial responsibility linked to investor-to-state dispute settlement tribunals established by international agreements to which the European Union is party.

[103]Amerasinghe (2003), pp. 34–40. Regarding multilaterlization of ICS, see Bungenberg and Reinisch (2018), p. 102.

[104]CJEU, case C-73/14, *Council v. Commission*, EU:C:2015:663, para. 58; CJEU, case C-131/03 P, *Reynolds Tobacco and Others v. Commission*, EU:C:2006:541, para. 94.

[105]CJEU, case C-73/14, *Council v. Commission*, EU:C:2015:663, para. 59.

[106]The Council of the European Union seeked the annulment of the decision of the European Commission of 29 November 2013 to submit the "Written statement by the European Commission on behalf of the European Union" to the International Tribunal for the Law of the Sea ("ITLOS") in Case No 21. CJEU case C-73/14, *Council v. Commission*, EU:C:2015:663. See Ojinaga (2016).

[107]CJEU, case C-73/14, *Council v. Commission*, EU:C:2015:663.

[108]CJEU, case C-73/14, *Council v. Commission*, EU:C:2015:663, para. 86.

[109]Opinion 1/94 (WTO Agreement), EU:C:1994:384, XIX.

[110]CJEU, case C-266/03, *Commission v. Luxembourg*, EU:C:2005:341; CJEU, case C-433/03, *Commission v. Germany*, EU:C:2005:462.

3.3 Jurisdiction and Applicable Law

The compatibility of ISDS with the EU legal order is mainly preserved by autonomy safeguards regarding the jurisdiction of the CETA Tribunals and applicable law. The jurisdiction of CETA Tribunals is confined to review the compatibility of the measures adopted by the Parties with CETA substantive investment protections,[111] with a view to granting compensation to investors suffering losses due to acts found to be incompatible with the investment agreement. When rendering its decision, these Tribunals shall apply CETA as interpreted in accordance with the Vienna Convention on the Law of Treaties on 23 May 1969 and other rules and principles of international law applicable between the Parties.[112] Therefore, the CETA Tribunals do not have jurisdiction to determine the legality of a measure under domestic law[113] while the rules of law applicable to ISDS neither include domestic law nor EU Law. Nevertheless, when determining the consistency of a measure with CETA, these Tribunals may still consider domestic law as a matter of fact.[114] In doing so, they "shall follow the prevailing interpretation given to the domestic law by the courts or authorities of that Party and any meaning given to domestic law by the Tribunal shall not be binding upon the courts or the authorities of that Party".[115] These mandates as regarding how domestic and EU Law must be construed seems to bring solutions to the problems deriving from the autonomy of the international courts and tribunals in general international law; in particular, by commiting the international tribunal in question to respect the primacy of EU Law.[116] But, the effect of these rules in EU legal order are not clear. For example, could the domestic courts of EU Member

[111] Article 8.18.5 of the CETA.

[112] Article 8.31.1 of the CETA.

[113] Article 8.31.2 of the CETA. This is in line with the exclusive jurisdiction of the CJEU to invalidate secondary EU law. See CJEU, Joined cases C-143/88 and C-92/89, Zuckerfabrik Süderdithmarschen AG v Hauptzollamt Itzehoe and Zuckerfabrik Soest GmbH v Hauptzollamt Paderborn., ECLI:EU:C:1991:65, para. 17; CJEU, case C-6/99, Association Greenpeace France and Others v Ministère de l'Agriculture et de la Pêche and Others, ECLI:EU:C:2000:148, para 54; CJEU, case C-344/04, The Queen, a instancia de International Air Transport Association y European Low Fares Airline Association contra Department for Transport, ECLI:EU:C:2006:10, para. 27; CJEU, case C-366/10, Air Transport Association of America and Others v Secretary of State for Energy and Climate Change, ECLI:EU:C:2011:864, para. 47.

[114] Article 8.28 (2) of the CETA. This view appears to reflect a general principle of international law expressed by Permanent Court of International Justice in the Certain German Interests in Polish Upper Silesia Judgment on Merits, 25 May 1926, PCIJ Series A, No 6, p. 20. The explicit consideration of manifest error in the appreciation of the facts, including the appreciation of relevant domestic law as one of the grounds for appeal in CETA, talks about the importance of issues involved in this approach to domestic and EU law and seems, in fact, to be the main reason for a divergence with the WTO system, were appeal is limited to questions of law. By contrast, Article 13 (1) Chap. 8, Sec. 3 of the EUVFTA and Article 3.10 (1) of the EUSFTA when considering appeals from the awards remain silent with regard to the grounds of the appellation.

[115] Article 8.31.2 of the CETA.

[116] Eckes (2019), p. 19.

States refuse the recognition and enforcement of CETA Tribunals decisions by claiming they are not binding on them or that they are in violation of EU law and thus against the "ordre public"?[117]

On the other side, even the direct effect of CETA rules is expressly excluded,[118] the indirect efect and overall impact of the interpretation of CETA rules by CETA Tribunals in the EU legal order, in particular in the interpretation of secundary EU Law, is to some extent uncertain.[119] In any case, it could play an important role in order to avoid the EU being repeatedly compelled to pay damages to the claimant investors.[120]

The CJEU noted that examination of domestic and EU Law as matter of fact cannot be equivalent to an interpretation an application of that law.[121] However, since investor-State tribunals interpret and apply investment treaty obligations in a highly self-referential manner,[122] it is difficult to know when an arbitral tribunal interprets domestic law and when it merely applies it as facts to the case.[123] In any case, the CETA Tribunals will be, to some extent, compelled to interpret the effect of the contested measures and will not necessarily be able to rely on an interpretation of EU Law previously provided by the CJEU. The workability of these formal guarantees to the autonomy of EU Law should then be tested in future practice;[124] for example, in cases where the termination of a contract is at issue in order to determine whether any rights susceptible to expropriation exist; or when deciding if the expropriation was done under due process of law;[125] or when considering a possible misapplication of EU Law which may amount to a denial of justice in breach of CETA.[126] It could be noted that the interpretation and determination of the legal effects of a measure under EU Law can be considered as the very matter of prejudicial competence eventually conferred to the CJEU in its relation with international investment tribunals or other international courts and tribunals. So, we agree

[117] Lavranos (2019), p. 14.

[118] Article 8.30.6 of the CETA.

[119] In its Opinion 1/91 the CJEU stated that: "[W]here, however, an international agreement provides for its own system of courts, including a court with jurisdiction to settle disputes between the Contracting Parties to the agreement, and, as a result, to interpret its provisions, the decisions of that court will be binding on the Community institutions, including the Court of Justice." (CJEU, Opinion 1/91, 14 December 1991, ECLI:EU:C:1991:490, para. 39). Lenk H (2019), The EU investment court system. A viable reform initiative?, https://gupea.ub.gu.se/bitstream/2077/60266/1/gupea_2077_60266_1.pdf (last accessed 1 June 2020), pp. 189–202.

[120] Hindelang (2015), p. 74; Pernice (2014), pp. 146–149.

[121] CJEU, Opinion 1/17, 30 April 2019, ECLI:EU:C:2019:341, para. 131. Lavranos (2019), pp. 14–15.

[122] Schill (2012), p. 591; Gáspar-Szilágyi (2016), p. 26.

[123] Arbitration regarding the Iron Rhine ("Ijzeren Rijn") Railway (The Kingdom of Belgium and The Kingdom of the Netherlands), Award of the Arbitral Tribunal (24 May 2005) XXVII RIAA 35.

[124] Hepburn (2016), pp. 366–367.

[125] Article 8.12(1)(b) of the CETA.

[126] Article 8.10 (2)(a) of the CETA.

with the view that "for the interest of the legal certainty, a preliminary reference procedure should have been welcome".[127] In particular, the power of the CETA Appeals Tribunal to review whether the CETA Tribunal has manifestly erred in the appreciation of facts, including the appreciation of relevant domestic law,[128] would require the involvement of the CJEU.[129]

In practice, the Joint Committee CETA could also play a significative role in the adopting joint binding interpretations CETA and its harmonization with domestic and EU Law.[130]

3.4 *Disconnection or Judicial Dialogue?*

In Opinion 1/17 the CJEU stated that, from the perspective of EU constitutional law, it is possible to establish a judicialized ISDS mechanism without prior involvement or preliminary ruling procedures for judicial dialogue between the CETA Tribunals and the CJEU. In particular, the CJEU concludes that:

> Since the CETA Tribunal and Appellate Tribunal stand outside the EU judicial system and since their powers of interpretation are confined to the provisions of the CETA in the light of the rules and principles of international law applicable between the Parties, it is, moreover, consistent that the CETA makes no provision for the prior involvement of the Court that would permit or oblige that Tribunal or Appellate Tribunal to make a reference for a preliminary ruling to the Court[131]

In the light of the strictly dualistic conception on which the CETA autonomy safeguards are designed, the CJEU reasoning could be undermined by their somewhat formalistic approach. Admittedly, due account must be taken of the fact that such a preliminary ruling mechanism would be difficult to negotiate in FTAs with third states being in mind the requirements of the principle of reciprocity governing the mutual relations of parties.[132] But, even considering the need to grant the same privilege to the highest courts of the EU FTAs treaty partners, it has been noted that "a preliminary reference system could forge a coalition between the ISDS mechanism and the highest courts of the respective host State in controlling government

[127] Gáspar-Szilágyi (2016), p. 34.

[128] Article 8.28(2) (b) of the CETA.

[129] Ankersmit (2019), p. 336.

[130] Ankersmit (2019), p. 336. On problems regarding joint binding interpretations with retroactive effects, not expressly excluded by article 8.31.2 of the CETA, see Opinion 1/17 of 30 April 2019, ECLI:EU:C:2019:341, paras. 236–237. Lavranos (2019), pp. 14–15.

[131] Opinion 1/17 of 30 April 2019, ECLI:EU:C:2019:341, para. 134. See para. 78.

[132] "It is therefore impossible to examine whether the autonomy of EU law is sufficiently preserved by the CETA unless account is taken of that reciprocal aspect of the desired substantive and procedural protection" (Opinion of AG Bot, delivered on 29 January 2019, ECLI:EU:C:2019:72, para. 84 and paras. 179–182).

conduct".[133] Perhaps, the position of CJEU in this regard could be strengthened in a multilateral framework as UNCITRAL by asserting its specific role both as a domestic and an international court.[134]

The procedure of referral is envisaged in the new generation of EU Association Agreements,[135] but many doubts have been expressed about the necessity and effectiveness of extending it beyond the limits of that integration-oriented agreements where the EU Law is part of the applicable law.[136] Nevertheless, the issue has been examined by commentators regarding both the BITs investment arbitral tribunals[137] and the ICS Tribunals.[138]

In practice, the recourse to this mechanism by international arbitral tribunals was rejected by the CJEU in the *MOX Plant* Case, but in a case concerning disputes between Member States.[139] More recently, in the *Achmea* case, the CJEU also explicitly rejected the recourse to the preliminary rulling procedure as regards the investment arbitral tribunals in intra-EU BITs.[140]

Nevertheless, taking into account the possible outcome of the ongoing process of ISDS reform at the UNCITRAL and the current trend towards judicialization of international adjudication, new legal approaches may become necessary for the promotion of judicial dialogue and cooperation between the CJEU and other international jurisdictional structures.

---

[133]Schill (2015), p. 386.

[134]Odermatt (2014), p. 718.

[135]Association Agreements between the EU and its member States and Ukrain, Moldova and Georgia concluded in 2014. See Eckes (2019), p. 18; Geneva Jean Monnet Working Papers 27/2016, Contartese C (2016), The procedures of prior involvement and referral to the CJEU as a means for judicial dialogue between the CJEU and international jurisdictions, https://www.ceje.ch/files/3914/8094/2575/contartese-27-final.pdf (last accessed 1 June 2020), pp. 8–11.

[136]This is in line with Draft Agreement on the European and Community Patents Court and Draft Statute, that was however declared incompatible with the EU Treaties by the CJEU because of the impact it would have on the role of EU Member States domestic courts and tribunals as 'ordinary' judges within the EU legal order. Opinion 1/09 of 8 March 2011, EU:C:2011:123, para. 80.

[137]Fischer-Lescano A and Horst (J 2014), The limits of EU and constitutional law for the Comprehensive Economic and Trade Agreement between the EU and Canada (CETA), https://blog.campact.de/content/uploads/2014/12/Gutachten_CETA_engl_final_27112014.pdf (last accessed 1 June 2020), pp. 14–15; Lee (2018), p. 150.

[138]Burgstaller (2014), p. 569; Gáspar-Szilágyi (2016), pp. 32–35. Lenk H (2019), The EU investment court system. A viable reform initiative?, https://gupea.ub.gu.se/bitstream/2077/60266/1/gupea_2077_60266_1.pdf (last accessed 1 June 2020), pp. 202–206. Schill (2015), pp. 386–387. A comparable preliminary ruling before the Multilateral Investment Court, through which rulings on the interpretation of international investment law could be requested by the first-instance courts, has been suggested. See Schill (2016).

[139]CJEU, case C-459/03, *Commission v. Ireland*, ECLI:EU:C:2006:345, para 155–156. Award of the Arbitral Tribunal in the Arbitration regarding the Iron Rhide ("Izjeren Rijn") Railway, para. 103.

[140]CJEU, case C-284/16, *Slovak Republic v. Achmea BV*, ECLI:EU:C:2018:158, para. 46. Opinion of AG Wathelet, delivered on 19 September 2017, ECLI:EU:C:2017:699, para. 85.

4 Conclusions

The EU is leading the systemic structural reform of ISDS in a very fluid and fragmented scenario. The initial EU proposal for the creation of a MIC has been deconstructed through its special feature, the "Open Architecture". This action has been crucial in order to make the proposal flexible and inclusive for strategic partners.

All the reform options are imperfect and cannot be categorized by themselves but only considering the context of their application. For that reason, a combination of different dispute settlement options under a common institutional structure seems to be the most efficient way to improve the current ISDS system. Nonetheless, this alternative could give rise to a complex scenario of dispute settlement procedures and bodies, with different competences and levels of legitimacy.

By establishing such a mechanism in its FTAs, the EU intends to satisfy a demand for neutrality and speciality in the resolution of disputes between investors and States, and to address some of the criticism of the ad hoc arbitration of traditional ISDS mechanisms. The EU leader role in the creation of a Multilateral Investment Court has been strengthened by CJEU's Opinion 1/17 on the compatibility of the ICS in CETA with the autonomy of the EU legal order. Notwithstanding, the CJEU reasoning regarding jurisdictional autonomy could need further development and adjustment. In particular, the current articulation of ICS in CETA as an alternative jurisdictional mechanism equipped with techniques that ensure the ISDS disconnection from EU Law and its judicial system, could be theoretically supplemented with mechanisms for judicial dialogue and cooperation between the CJEU and other international jurisdictional structures.

At any rate, the EU could actually take the opportunity not only to drive the ISDS judicialization but to improve the current normative framework, both in general international law and in EU constitutional law, as regards its participation in international dispute settlement.

References

Amerasinghe CF (2003) Jurisdiction of international tribunals. Kluwer, The Hague

Ankersmit L (2019) An incoherent approach towards Aarush and CETA: the commission and external oversight mechanism. In: Govaere I, Garben S (eds) The interface between EU and international law. Hart, Oxford, pp 321–340

Boisson de Chazournes L (2017) Plurality in the fabric of international courts and tribunals: the threads of a managerial approach. Eur J Int Law 28(1):13–72

Bungenberg N, Reinisch A (2018) From bilateral arbitral tribunals and investment courts to a multilateral investment court. Springer Open, Berlin

Burgstaller M (2014) Dispute settlement in EU international investment agreements with third states: three salient problems. J World Investment Trade 15:551–569

Cai C (2018) Balanced investment treaties and the BRICS. Am J Int Law Unbound 112:217:217–217:222

Contartese C, Pantaleo L (2018) Division of competences, EU autonomy and the determination of the respondent party: proceduralisation as a possible way-out? In: Neframi E, Gatti M (eds) Constitutional issues of EU external relations law. Nomos, Baden-Baden, pp 409–446

Cutler C (2018) The judicialization of private transnational power and authority. Indiana J Glob Leg Stud 25(1):61–95

Delgado Casteleiro A (2012) EU declarations of competence to multilateral agreements: a useful reference base? Eur Foreign Aff Rev 17(4):491–509

Eckes C (2019) EU powers under external pressure. How the EU's external actions alter its internal structures. Oxford University Press, Oxford

Gáspar-Szilágyi S (2016) A standing investment court under TTIP from the perspective of the CJEU. J World Investment Trade 17(5):701–742

Govaere I (2010) Beware of the Trojan horse: dispute settlement in (mixed) agreements and the autonomy of the EU legal order. In: Hillion C, Koutrakos P (eds) Mixed agreements revisited. The EU and its member States in the world. Hart, Oxford

Heliskoski J (2001) Mixed agreements as a technique for organizing the international relations of the European Community and its member states. Martinus Nijhoff, Leiden

Hepburn J (2016) Applicable law in TTP investment disputes. Melb J Int Law 17:349–368

Herranz-Surrallés A (2020) 'Authority Shifts' in global governance: intersecting politicizations and the reform of investor – state arbitration. Polit Gov 8(1):336–347

Hindelang S (2015) Repellent forces: the CJEU and investor – state dispute settlement. Archiv des Völkerrechts 53(1):68–89

Hoffmeister F, Alexandru G (2014) A first glimpse of light on the emerging invisible EU model BIT. J World Invest Trade 15:379–401

Lavranos N (2019) CJEU opinion 1/17: keeping international investment law and EU law strictly apart. Eur Invest Law Arbitr Rev Online 4(1):240–259

Lee J (2018) The empire strikes back: case note of the CJEU decision in Slovak Republic v. ACHMEA BV. Contemp Asia Arbitr J II(1):137–152

Lenk H (2015) Challenging the notion of coherence in EU foreign investment policy. Eur J Leg Stud 8(2):6–20

Lévesque C, Newcombe A (2013) Canada. In: Brown C (ed) Commentaries on selected model investment treaties. Oxford University Press, Oxford, pp 108–110

Liu R (2019) Adopting and adjusting to the development of the investor-State dispute settlement mechanism in China's recent bilateral investment treaty negotiations with the European Union. Hast Int Comp Law Rev 42(1):261–285

Mayr S (2017) CETA, TTIP, TiSA, and their relationship with EU law. In: Griller S, Obwexer W, Vranes E (eds) Mega-regional trade agreements: CETA, TTIP, and TiSA: new orientations for EU external economic relations. Oxford University Press, Oxford, pp 246–278

Mohamadieh K (2019) The future of investor-State dispute settlement deliberated at UNCITRAL: unveiling a dichotomy between reforming and consolidating the current regime. South Centre Investment Policy Brief No. 16

Ning H, Qi T (2018) Multilateral investment court: the gap between the EU and China. Chinese J Glob Gov 4:154–175

Odermatt J (2014) The Court of Justice of the European Union: international or domestic court? Cambridge J Int Comp Law 3(3):696–718

Odermatt J (2018) The principle of autonomy: an adolescent disease of EU external relations law. In: Cremona M (ed) Structural principles in EU external relations law. Hart, Oxford, pp 291–316

Ojinaga R (2016) La Unión Europea y los estados miembros en los procedimientos de arreglo jurisdiccional de controversias en la CNUDM. Revista de Derecho Comunitario Europeo 55:977–1018

Pernice I (2014) Study on international investment protection agreements and EU law. In: Kuijper PJ, Pernice I, Hindelang S, Kinnear M, Schwarz M, Investor- State Dispute Settlement (ISDS) Provisions in the EU's International Investment Agreements, Directorate- General for External Policies of the Union, vol. 2, pp 132–164

Puig S, Shaffer G (2018) Imperfect alternatives: institutional choice and the reform of investment law. Am J Int Law 112:361–409
Roberts A (2018a) Incremental, systemic, and paradigmatic reform of investor – state arbitration. Am J Int Law 112(3):410–432
Roberts A (2018b) Symposium on the BRICS approach to the investment treaty system. Investment treaties: the reform matrix. Am J Int Law Unbound 112(191):187–190
Rosas A (2007) The European Court of Justice in context: forms and patterns of judicial dialogue. Eur J Leg Stud 1(2):1–16
Rosas A (2018) The EU and international dispute settlement. Europe World 1(1):1–29
Ruiz Fabri H, Paine J (2019) The procedural cross-fertilization pull. Max Planck Institute Luxembourg for Procedural Law, Research Paper Series 6
Schill SW (2012) Deference in investment treaty arbitration: re-conceptualizing the standard of review. J Int Disput Settl 3(3):577–607
Schill SW (2015) Opinion 2/13 – The end for dispute settlement in EU trade and investment agreements? J World Invest Trade 6(3):379–388
Schill SW, Vidigal G (2020) Designing investment dispute settlement à la Carte: insights from comparative institutional design analysis. Law Pract Int Courts Tribunals 18:311–341
Sornarajah M (2018) The unworkability of "Balanced Treaties" and the importance of diversity of approach among the BRICS. Am J Int Law Unbound 112(191):223–227
Titi C (2014) The right to regulate in international investment law. Nomos, Baden-Baden
Titi C (2015) International investment law and the European Union: towards a new generation of international investment agreements. Eur J Int Law 6(3):639–661
Titi C (2018) Procedural multilateralism and multilateral investment court. In: Fahey E (ed) Institutionalisation beyond the nation State: transatlantic relations – data privacy and trade law. Springer, Heidelberg, pp 149–164
Treves T (2014) Union Européenne et règlement des différends dans le cadre de la Convention des Nations Unies sur le droit de la mer. Aspects récents. In: Doumbé-Billé S, Thouvenin J-M (eds) Droit international de la mer et droit de l'Union Européenne: Cohabitation, confrontation, cooperation? Pédone, Paris, pp 339–346
Wessel R (2013) Between the authority of international law and the autonomy of EU law. In: Diez-Hochleitner J (ed) Últimas tendencias en la jurisprudencia del Tribunal de Justicia de la Unión Europea (Recent trends in the case law of the Court of Justice of the European Union). La Ley-Grupo Wolters Kluwer, Madrid, pp 759–765

Rosario Ojinaga Ruiz is Associate Professor on Public International Law and Jean Monnet Chair Holder at the University of Cantabria (Spain). Director of the Jean Monnet Module "European Union in the World: International Law and Politics" (2017–2020) and the Post-Grade Course of Specialization on EU Law and External Action. She has acted as counsel in cases before the International Tribunal for the Law of the Sea.

Maria Lina Leiva is PhD Candidate in the Doctorate in Legal and Business Science of University of Cantabria. She is an Argentinian lawyer and holds a Master in Internationalization from the University of Barcelona. She has over 6 years of experience in international trade in the private sector.

Compulsory Optionality: International Standardizing Bodies as Transnational Actors in International Investment Law

Eleni-Amalia Giannakopoulou and Marios Tokas

Contents

1 Introduction 46
2 The Definition of International Standards 47
  2.1 The Classification of International Standardizing Bodies 47
  2.2 The Six Core Principles of International Standard-Setting 48
3 International Standards and WTO Law 49
  3.1 The Scope and Extent of the Normativity Loan Contained in the TBT and the SPS Agreements 50
  3.2 The Evidentiary Pertinence of International Standards in WTO Law 51
4 IIAs Containing Direct References to International Standards 54
5 Interpretation and Application of IIA Clauses with Direct References to International Standards 56
  5.1 International Standards and the Definition of "Investment" in IIAs 56
  5.2 International Standards and the "Fair and Equitable Treatment" Clauses in IIAs 59
  5.3 International Standards and Non-discrimination Clauses in IIAs 62
6 International Standards and the Assessment of Contributory Fault in Investment Arbitration 67
7 Conclusions 69
References 70

Abstract From a traditional public international law perspective, a standard is either binding or it is not: there is no in-between. The emergence of international standards as a key component of modern international public policy, however, has

---

The authors would like to thank Dr. Anastasios Gourgourinis and Prof. Axel Marx for our fruitful discussions on the matter, as well as N. Mouzoula and K. Daskalopoulou for their insightful comments. The opinions expressed and any/all errors or omissions are only attributable to the authors.

E.-A. Giannakopoulou
School of Law, National and Kapodistrian University of Athens, Athens, Greece

M. Tokas (✉)
Graduate Institute of International and Development Studies, Geneva, Switzerland
e-mail: marios.tokas@graduateinstitute.ch

A. Gourgourinis (ed.), *Transnational Actors in International Investment Law*, European Yearbook of International Economic Law,
https://doi.org/10.1007/978-3-030-60679-4_3

proven that normativity does not have such a binary notation. The voluntary instruments described as international standards have acquired growing influence in the field of World Trade Organization law. This chapter argues that international investment law has not escaped these developments. Accordingly, the purpose of the present chapter is to identify the role of international standardization bodies as transnational actors of international investment law, by determining their influence on the interpretation and application of rights and obligations under international investment agreements.

1 Introduction

International standardizing bodies have become more and more influential in the international economic law regime. In many instances, the practical implications of the adoption of a new standard surpasses the conventional examination of sources of international law. This is evinced in the present sanitary crisis where World Health Organization ("WHO") recommendations and standards are the driving force behind domestic and international responses to the coronavirus spread, irrespective of their formal legal status and normativity.[1]

Adjudicators and academics have gradually started to recognize the relevance of international standards in the interpretation and application of domestic law.[2] World Trade Organization ("WTO") Members have formally decided that international standards play a decisive role in international trade and have directly incorporated them in the Technical Barriers to Trade ("TBT") Agreement and the Agreement on the Sanitary and Phytosanitary Measures ("SPS").[3]

International investment law has not escaped this development, as evinced by International Investment Agreement ("IIA") treaty-making, where international standards are directly employed for the determination of treaty rights and obligations. Nevertheless, what we put forward in this chapter is that the relevance of international standards is not limited to such instances of direct incorporation in the treaty text. Accordingly, the present chapter focuses its attention on the role of international standardization in the interpretation and application of typical IIA clauses or customary rules of international law, and argues that international standardizing bodies constitute an overlooked transnational actor of international investment law.

[1] WHO, Country & Technical Guidance Coronavirus disease (COVID-19), https://www.who.int/emergencies/diseases/novel-coronavirus-2019/technical-guidance, (last accessed 23 April 2020).

[2] See generally: Basedow (2008), Hall and Biersteker (2002), Mattli and Büthe (2005), Mattli (2001) and Glinski (2007).

[3] Desta (2012).

2 The Definition of International Standards

The working definition of standardization adopted for the purposes of the present chapter is rather wide. We shall examine standardization as the process of developing and adopting voluntary "best practices", outside of the strict governmental regulatory reach.[4] The best practices examined usually take the form of codified technical knowledge that enables the development of processes and products, and prescribes the quality or performance of a given procedure, practice or product.[5]

Nevertheless, our definition of an international standard is not output oriented—it does not identify the principal characteristics of a best practice per se. Rather, the definition is concentrated on the fora in which international standards are developed, and the procedures observed for their development. For this reason, our definition of an international standard is focused on identifying two factors. First, the actor, i.e. the international standardizing body. Second, the decision-making processes that are expected to produce a best practice outcome.

2.1 The Classification of International Standardizing Bodies

Various definitions and theoretical frameworks have been put forward so as to examine the phenomenon of international standardization.[6] Notably, Mattli and Büthe introduce a four-way distinction on different standardizing processes based upon the presence of two characteristics, i.e. whether the institutional setting is public or private, and whether the selection mechanism is market-based or a non-market-based.[7] In specific, their typology takes into account two factors. First, whether the development of the standard is set upon a private or public setting. Second, whether there is a single dominant body that leads in the development of a particular kind of international standards, or whether there is competition in that area of standard setting.

Based upon their framework, we will examine the following:

- public non-market standardization, i.e. formal intergovernmental collaborations. Examples of such standardization processes are the Basel Committee on Banking Supervision,[8] or International Labor Organization ("ILO") when adopting

[4]Kerwer (2005), pp. 611–612. This is similar but not exactly the same as the term "standard" in Annex 1.2 TBT Agreement.

[5]Delimatsis (2018), p. 275; Büthe and Mattli (2011), p. 17.

[6]For different types of classification and definitions see: Pauwelyn (2014); Kerwer (2005); Mattli and Seddon (2015), pp. 182–183.

[7]Büthe and Mattli (2011), p. 19.

[8]Fratianni (2006) and Goodhart (2011).

Recommendations[9] or the International Telecommunications Union's ("ITU") Telecommunications Standardization Sector.[10]

- public standard-setting institutions with no universal dominance where we notice different agencies and standard-setting bodies competing for global "normative dominance",[11] such as the Codex Alimentarius Commission, that set permissive food safety standards and the Cartagena Protocol of the Convention on Biological Diversity.[12] The overlap is identified in the regulation of living modified organisms as the Cartagena Protocol introduces more stringent standards than the Codex Alimentarius.[13]
- non-market private "rule-makers". Examples of such organizations are the International Standardization Organization ("ISO"),[14] the International Electrotechnical Commission ("IEC")[15] and the International Accounting Standards Board ("IASB").[16]

2.2 *The Six Core Principles of International Standard-Setting*

The definition of international standards is correlated to a "trust in the process" principle. It derives from the confidence that standard-setting decision making procedures adhering to some core procedural principles produce outcomes with "deference entitling" properties. The definition of an international standard is construed inside-out: any instrument that is the outcome of this procedure is deemed to be a "best practice" which is not to be second-guessed in its substance.

In this sense, our definition of international standards will necessarily include certain core principles that guarantee a "best practice" outcome, which is widely interrelated with the legitimacy of the standard and its recognition in the international sphere. In this regard, inspiration can be drawn from the current scrutinizing trend towards the assessment of internal requirements of international

---

[9]International Labour Organization (2019), Rules of the game: An introduction to the standards-related work of the International Labour Organization, https://www.ilo.org/wcmsp5/groups/public/%2D%2D-ed_norm/%2D%2D-normes/documents/publication/wcms_672549.pdf, (last accessed 23 April 2020).

[10]Büthe and Mattli (2011), p. 27.

[11]Büthe and Mattli (2011), pp. 23–25.

[12]Dupuy and Viñuales (2018), pp. 235–237; WHO and FAO (2018), Codex Alimentarius: Understanding Codex, http://www.fao.org/3/CA1176EN/ca1176en.pdf, (last accessed 23 April 2020).

[13]Dupuy and Viñuales (2018), pp. 240–242; Büthe (2009).

[14]ISO (2010), Good Standardization Practices, https://www.iso.org/files/live/sites/isoorg/files/store/en/PUB100440.pdf, (last accessed 23 April 2020); Lindahl (2015); Delimatsis (2015); Büthe and Mattli (2011).

[15]Larouche and van Overwalle (2015).

[16]Mattli and Büthe (2005).

standardization in the WTO regime.[17] This means that the products of international standardizing bodies identified above may not be taken at their face value. The further warranted scrutiny relates to the fundamental concerns of equal and substantive participation in the decision-making process.[18]

To that end, the standard setting processes with which we are concerned here would have to observe six core principles: transparency, openness, impartiality and consensus, relevance and effectiveness, coherence and developing country interests.[19] Accordingly, there must be adequate time and opportunities for written comments on each stage of the standard development; meaningful opportunities for participation; democratic foundations based on increased voting majorities; involvement of science and technology experts; avoidance of duplication or overlap with other standardizing bodies.[20]

3 International Standards and WTO Law

In the WTO context, international standards have mainly been used for the purposes of harmonization and prevention of unnecessary regulatory diversity. International standards have been used as proxies for instituting convergence of national policies, with a view of deflating compliance costs for manufacturers, enhancing market access and achieving inter-operability and global compatibility.[21]

Nevertheless, in the context of the general agreements—the General Agreement on Tariffs and Trade 1994 ("GATT 1994") and the General Agreement on Trade in Services ("GATS")—harmonization through the use of international standards has been nothing more than wishful thinking.[22] Despite the fact that both Agreements explicitly recognize their importance, they do not attribute normativity to international standards.[23] In fact, in the regulation of services there is no WTO provision requiring their use by regulators.[24]

[17] In this regard, see Delimatsis (2015, 2019) and Pauwelyn (2014).

[18] Delimatsis (2019), Pauwelyn (2014) and Mavroidis and Wolfe (2017).

[19] WTO Committee on Technical Barriers to Trade, 21 January 2012, WTO Doc. G/TBT/1/Rev.12, Decision of the Committee on Principles for the Development of International Standards, Guides and Recommendations with relation to Articles 2, 5 and Annex 3 of the Agreement, pp. 47–49; International Organization for Standardization (2019), ISO Publications on Good Standardization Practices, https://www.iso.org/publication/PUB100440.html (last accessed 22 April 2020), pp. 63–88.

[20] Delimatsis (2018), pp. 273–325.

[21] Mavroidis (2012), pp. 670–678.

[22] E.g. GATT 1994, Art. XXXVIII:2(e); GATS Article VII:5, Annex A:7(a).

[23] Marceau and Trachtman (2014), p. 393.

[24] Hoekman B and Mavroidis P (2015), A Technical Barriers to Trade Agreement for Services?. EUI Working Paper RSCAS 2015/25, https://papers.ssrn.com/sol3/papers.cfm?abstract_id=2625640 (last accessed 22 April 2020), pp. 3–7; Marchetti (2015), pp. 137–159.

By contrast, the TBT and the SPS Agreements do not merely envision harmonization as a remote goal. The adoption of international standards for the regulation of trade in goods constitutes a hard law obligation under both of the Agreements.[25] By their very terms, the TBT and the SPS delegate regulatory authority to international standardizing bodies and explicitly lend normativity to international standards.[26]

In view of this glaring difference, the following questions seem to be exceptionally apposite for the purposes of the present chapter: what is the relevance of international standards when applying WTO provisions that do not explicitly accord them any normative value? Could the choice of the WTO Member not to "normativize" a "best practice" be interpreted as ipso facto excluding its evidentiary power?

3.1 The Scope and Extent of the Normativity Loan Contained in the TBT and the SPS Agreements

The normativity loan to international standards in the TBT and the SPS Agreements takes place in two ways. In the first instance, Article 2.4 of the TBT Agreement and Article 3.1 of the SPS Agreement oblige national governments to use international standards as a basis for their technical regulations and SPS measures respectively.

In the second instance, under Article 2.5 of the TBT and Article 3.2 of the SPS Agreement, when a measure is in accordance with relevant international standards, this creates a rebuttable presumption of conformity with WTO obligations. In particular, there is a presumption that international standards constitute the least trade restrictive option.[27] Measures conforming to relevant international standards are presumed to be permitted under Article 2.2 of the TBT Agreement, which prohibits unnecessary obstacles to trade.[28] The presumption of consistency under Article 3.2 of the SPS goes even further: the conforming measure is deemed to be consistent with the entirety of the SPS Agreement and the GATT 1994.[29]

The scope and extent of these two types of normativity loans are qualified by a key consideration: the degree of the required conformity of the measures with the relevant international standards. The conceptual similarities between the

---

[25]Tamiotti (2007), pp. 221–226; Landwehr (2007), pp. 415–422; Büthe (2008), pp. 231–238.

[26]See TBT, Art. 2.4 and 2.5; SPS, Art. 3.1 and 3.2.

[27]Hoekman B and Mavroidis P (2015), A Technical Barriers to Trade Agreement for Services?. European University Institute Working Paper RSCAS 2015/25, https://papers.ssrn.com/sol3/papers.cfm?abstract_id=2625640 (last accessed 22 April 2020), p. 3; Marceau and Trachtman (2014), pp. 386–393.

[28]Tamiotti (2007), p. 226; Panel Report, *Australia – Certain Measures Concerning Trademarks, Geographical Indications and Other Plain Packaging Requirements Applicable to Tobacco Products and Packaging*, para. 7.402, WTO Docs. WT/DS435/R, WT/DS441/R WT/DS458/R, WT/DS467/R (adopted August 27, 2018).

[29]Landwehr (2007), p. 422; Büthe (2008), pp. 223–226.

corresponding provisions of the TBT and the SPS allows for a common answer. A juxtaposition of the relevant terms used in each of the corresponding provisions makes it clear that the degree of conformity required under Article 2.4 of the TBT Agreement and Article 3.1 of the SPS Agreement is not the same as the one envisaged under Article 2.5 of the TBT and Article 3.2 of the SPS Agreement.[30]

While the degree of the required conformity in Article 2.5 of the TBT and Article 3.2 of the SPS Agreement amounts to a full adoption of the international standard,[31] the conformity requirement in Article 2.4 of the TBT Agreement and Article 3.1 of the SPS Agreement is substantially lower.[32] As interpreted by the Appellate Body, the obligation under Article 2.4 of the TBT and 3.1 of the SPS Agreement merely requires the use of the international standard "as a constituent basis" for the measure.[33]

3.2 *The Evidentiary Pertinence of International Standards in WTO Law*

Under traditional public international law thinking, normativity and State consent go hand-in-hand. In the absence of State consent, no international instrument can produce normative effects.[34] It could be argued that this is also the case with international standards: their normativity derives from the normativity loans provided by explicit references in the texts of the TBT and the SPS Agreements and does not go any further than that. Nevertheless, the pertinence of international standards in WTO law is not limited to (or, rather, dependent on) explicit treaty references.[35]

---

[30] Appellate Body Report, *European Communities – Measures Concerning Meat Products (Hormones)*, paras 163–167, WTO Docs, WT/DS26/AB/R (adopted February 13, 1998); Appellate Body Report, *European Communities – Trade Restrictions on Sardines*, paras 241–244, WTO Doc. WT/DS231/AB/R (adopted September 26, 2002).

[31] Tamiotti (2007), p. 226; Landwehr (2007), p. 422.

[32] Appellate Body Report, *European Communities – Measures Concerning Meat Products (Hormones)*, paras 163–167, WTO Docs, WT/DS26/AB/R (adopted February 13, 1998); Appellate Body Report, *European Communities – Trade Restrictions on Sardines*, paras 241–244, WTO Doc. WT/DS231/AB/R (adopted October 23, 2002).

[33] Appellate Body Report, *European Communities – Measures Concerning Meat Products (Hormones)*, paras 163–166, WTO Docs, WT/DS26/AB/R (adopted February 13, 1998); Appellate Body Report, *European Communities – Trade Restrictions on Sardines*, para. 245, WTO Doc. WT/DS231/AB/R (adopted October 23, 2002).

[34] Pauwelyn (2014), pp. 748–751.

[35] In this respect see Pauwelyn (2014).

The Panel in *Australia – Tobacco Plain Packaging* has explicitly rejected the idea that Article 2.5 of the TBT Agreement—or any other similar provision—is the only avenue for an instrument to shape WTO obligations.[36] The Panel in that case saw no basis to dismiss ex ante the evidentiary relevance of the Framework Convention on Tobacco Control ("FCTC") guidelines on the sole ground that they did not fall within the narrow contours of the normativity loan contained in Article 2.5 TBT. Indeed, it would be unreasonable to assume that an internationally recognized best practice, reflecting the international consensus among the scientific community and 180 FCTC parties,[37] would be stripped of its probative value in the absence of a specific provision warranting its use. The evidentiary pertinence of international standards has been demonstrated in the following instances under WTO law: the assessment of "necessity", "justifiability" of interference and "justifiability" of discrimination.

The FCTC Guidelines were determinative for the Panel in *Australia – Tobacco Plain Packaging* to conclude that the tobacco plain packaging measures were "necessary" under Article 2.2 of the TBT Agreement. The FCTC guidelines were used as a proxy for the effectiveness of the alternative measures proposed by the complainants. In particular, the Panel rejected the alternative measures relating to the increase of the minimum legal age for the purchase of tobacco products,[38] the increase of tobacco taxation[39] and the improvement of social marketing campaigns[40] based on the fact that they are all recognized in the FCTC as part of a *comprehensive* tobacco control policy and could not be thus effectively implemented as individual measures. The pre-vetting mechanism suggested by the complainants was also dismissed on the premise that it is not recognized in the FCTC as an effective tobacco control policy, and could not thus constitute a substitute to the tobacco

[36]Panel Reports, *Australia – Certain Measures Concerning Trademarks, Geographical Indications and Other Plain Packaging Requirements Applicable to Tobacco Products and Packaging*, paras 7.404–7.417, WTO Docs WT/DS435/R, WT/DS441/R WT/DS458/R, WT/DS467/R (adopted August 27, 2018).

[37]Panel Reports, *Australia – Certain Measures Concerning Trademarks, Geographical Indications and Other Plain Packaging Requirements Applicable to Tobacco Products and Packaging*, para. 7.416, WTO Docs WT/DS435/R, WT/DS441/R WT/DS458/R, WT/DS467/R (adopted August 27, 2018).

[38]Panel Reports, *Australia – Certain Measures Concerning Trademarks, Geographical Indications and Other Plain Packaging Requirements Applicable to Tobacco Products and Packaging*, para. 7.1457, WTO Docs WT/DS435/R, WT/DS441/R WT/DS458/R, WT/DS467/R (adopted August 27, 2018).

[39]Panel Reports, *Australia – Certain Measures Concerning Trademarks, Geographical Indications and Other Plain Packaging Requirements Applicable to Tobacco Products and Packaging*, paras 7.1509, 7.1531, WTO Docs. WT/DS435/R, WT/DS441/R WT/DS458/R, WT/DS467/R (adopted August 27, 2018).

[40]Panel Report, *Australia – Certain Measures Concerning Trademarks, Geographical Indications and Other Plain Packaging Requirements Applicable to Tobacco Products and Packaging*, para. 7.1594, 7.1531, WTO Docs. WT/DS435/R, WT/DS441/R WT/DS458/R, WT/DS467/R (adopted August 27, 2018).

plain packaging measures. On the same conceptual grounds, the Panel also found that the tobacco plain packaging measures were not an "unjustifiable" encumbrance of intellectual property rights under Article 20 of the Agreement on Trade Related aspects of Intellectual Property Rights.

In the context of necessity valuation, in *United States – Clove Cigarettes* the Panel reaffirmed its finding that the banning of clove cigarettes was in full conformity with Article 2.2 of the TBT, by stating that a ban of flavoured cigarettes is recommended in the WHO Partial Guidelines for the application of the FCTC.[41] Similarly, the Dominican Republic in *Dominican Republic – Import and Sale of Cigarettes*, also cited the FCTC in support of its argument on the international recognition of tax stamps as a legitimate method to prevent the smuggling of cigarettes and tax evasion. By reference to the FCTC, the Panel agreed that, in principle, tax stamps constitute a useful tool to monitor tax collection,[42] notwithstanding the fact that both parties agreed that the FCTC was not legally binding on them.[43]

Finally, in *Argentina – Financial Services*, the Financial Action Task Force constituted the drive for the Appellate Body to disqualify Argentina's measure under the chapeau of Article XIV of the GATS. Although the Appellate Body made no direct reference to the particular instrument, it made a finding that reflected the Financial Action Task Force Guidelines.[44] The Appellate Body had already agreed with Argentina that imposing penalty taxes on financial transactions with "non-cooperative countries" was a necessary measure.[45] Nevertheless, in the context of assessing "arbitrary or unjustifiable discrimination" the Appellate Body had to take a closer look at how countries were listed as "cooperative" or "non cooperative" by Argentina.[46] Against the backdrop of preventing money laundering and the financing of terrorism, the proxy used for the justifiability of the distinction was the availability of tax information; a proxy that clearly reflected the Financial Action Task Force Guidelines. It was this proxy that Argentina had failed to observe by listing countries with no available tax information as "cooperative", and led the Apellate Body to find that there was "arbitrary discrimination".

[41] Panel Report, *United States – Measures Affecting the Production and Sale of Clove Cigarettes*, paras 7.427–7.428, WTO Doc. WT/DS406/R (adopted April 24, 2012).

[42] Panel Report, *Dominican Republic – Measures Affecting the Importation and Internal Sale of Cigarettes*, paras 7.216–7.217, WTO Doc. WT/DS302/R (adopted May 19, 2005).

[43] Panel Report, *Dominican Republic – Measures Affecting the Importation and Internal Sale of Cigarettes*, para. 4.314, WTO Doc. WT/DS302/R (adopted May 19, 2005).

[44] Delimatsis and Hoekman (2018), pp. 283–288.

[45] Appellate Body Report, *Argentina – Measures Relating to Trade in Goods and Services*, para. 6.197, WTO Doc. WT/DS453/AB/R (adopted May 9, 2016).

[46] Panel Report, *Argentina – Measures Relating to Trade in Goods and Services*, paras 7.751–7.753, WTO Doc. WT/DS453/R (adopted May 9, 2016).

4 IIAs Containing Direct References to International Standards

In a manner similar to the TBT and the SPS Agreements, there are some instances in modern IIA treaty-making where normativity loans to international standards have been recorded. Drawing inspiration from the TBT – SPS model of operation, the purpose of this section is to classify direct references to international standards in IIAs, to identify their typology and to determine their normative value in shaping the scope of the substantive investment protection. It is important to note that, for the purposes of the present section, the analysis will not be limited to IIAs that contain an investor-State dispute settlement mechanism. Rather, it shall also involve any agreements that regulate State activity interfering with the operations of foreign direct investment.

The first type of direct references to international standards consists of clauses that require their use by the host State. The obligatory effect of those clauses—similarly to Article 2.4 of the TBT Agreement and 3.1 of the SPS[47]—does not amount to a requirement for positive integration. Accordingly, there is no obligation for the contracting parties to adopt international standards every time that they are concluded. Rather, the obligation for adopting international standards only comes into play when the State unilaterally decides to regulate on an area covered by an international standard.

Typically, this class of clauses comes with the title “right to regulate”.[48] Contrary to standard IIAs, these provisions do not vaguely define the State’s right to regulatory intervention. Instead of a generic qualification, such as “fair and equitable treatment”, these clauses make a specific determination of the permissible regulatory interference by reference to international standards, thus, substituting normative flexibility with normative precision.

In some of these clauses, there are direct references to specific international standards. For example, Article 8.3 of the Ecuador—European Free Trade Agreement (“EFTA”) Free Trade Agreement (“FTA”) qualifies state inteference with investors’ rights only in cases of compliance with among others, the Declaration of the United Nations Conference on the Human Environment of 1972, the ILO Declaration on Fundamental Principles and Rights at Work and its Follow-up of 1998, the Ministerial Declaration of the United Nations Economic and Social Council on Full and Productive Employment and Decent Work of 2006. Similarly, in Article 8(4) of the Kazakhstan - Singapore BIT, exceptions to free capital transfers are only permitted “in accordance with the international standards of the Financial Action Task Force to prevent money laundering, terrorism and proliferation financing”.

[47] Mavroidis (2012), p. 679.

[48] EFTA States – Indonesia Economic Partnership Agreement, Art. 8.2; Ecuador – EFTA States FTA, Art. 8.3; EU – Japan Economic Partnership Agreement, Art. 8.3.

By contrast, other clauses of this type give obligatory effect to relevant "international standards" without any further specification. In these cases, our analysis on the definition of a best practice finds immediate traction. A very illustrative example would be the Economic Partnership Agreement between the EU and its member States, and the South African Development Community States. Article 9, titled "Right to regulate and levels of protection" reads:

> 1. The Parties recognise the right of each Party to establish its own levels of domestic environmental and labour protection, and to adopt or modify accordingly its relevant laws and policies, consistently with internationally recognised standards and agreements to which they are a party.

The second type of direct references consists of clauses obliging the use of international standards by investors. The new developments in investment arbitration have generated a new wave of IIAs that recognize the obligation of strong market players for self-regulation. Interestingly, these obligations are directly defined by international standards on Corporate Social Responsibility ("CSR").[49] As a result, they may form the legal premise for the defence of post establishment illegality, or the substantive basis for the filing of a counter-claim.

For instance, the modern Brazilian Investment Cooperation and Facilitation Agreements contain CSR clauses with relatively strong wording,[50] while, notably, Article 18 of the Morocco – Nigeria Bilateral Investment Treaty ("BIT"), entitled "Post establishment obligations" stands out for the explicit imposition of CSR obligations to investors:

> [...] Companies in areas of resource exploitation and high-risk industrial enterprises shall maintain a current certification to ISO 14001 or an equivalent environmental management standard. Investments shall uphold human rights in the host State. Investors and investments shall act in accordance with core labour standards as required by the ILO Declaration on Fundamental Principles and Rights of Work, 1998. [...]

The third type of direct references consists of IIA clauses explicitly permitting measures which are in accordance with international standards. This kind of references to international standards could be assimilated to Article 2.5 of the TBT Agreement and Article 3.2 of the SPS. They do not establish a positive obligation for host States to regulate in conformity with existing international standards. In this sense, they do not rule out other regulatory possibilities of the host State, which remains free to opt for different measures to address a specific situation. Yet, they effectively incentivize the observance of relevant international standards by explicitly allowing the taking of measures which are in accordance with the latter, as is the case in certain IIA clauses regarding taxation.[51] For example, under Annex 11-I of the investment chapter of the Australia – Korea FTA the consistency of a taxation

[49]See also on CSR: Marx (2014) and Dimopoulos (2015).

[50]See, Brazil – Malawi BIT, Art. 9; Brazil – Ecuador BIT, Art. 14. Cf. also the references to CSR in Canada – Burkina Faso BIT, Art. 16; Australia – Hong Kong Investment Agreement, Art. 16; Belarus – India BIT, Art. 12; Argentina – Japan BIT, Art. 17.

[51]See for example, Kazakhstan – Singapore BIT, Art. 21; Armenia – Korea BIT, Annex II.

measure with internationally recognized tax policies, principles, and practices renders it non-expropriatory in character:

> The determination of whether a taxation measure, in a specific fact situation, constitutes an expropriation requires a case-by-case, fact-based inquiry that considers all relevant factors relating to the investment, including the factors listed in Annex 11-B and the following considerations: [. . .] (b) a taxation measure that is consistent with internationally recognised tax policies, principles, and practices should not constitute an expropriation.

5 Interpretation and Application of IIA Clauses with Direct References to International Standards

Notwithstanding the instances of normativity loans to international standards in modern IIA treaty-making, the vast majority of IIAs in force lack such or similar clauses. Nevertheless, it is the typical generic wording of standard IIA clauses which constitutes an indicator that international standards may be useful either for the purposes of their interpretation or for their fact-intensive application.

Taking WTO law as a paradigm, the purpose of the present section is to display the potential usefulness of international standards as part of the practice of treaty interpretation or as an objective point of reference in fact-intensive determinations, either under IIA clauses or customary rules of international law.

5.1 International Standards and the Definition of "Investment" in IIAs

International standards become highly relevant for a treaty interpreter when examining the ordinary meaning of term. In specific, according to Article 31(1) of the Vienna Convention on the Law of Treaties, a term should be examined in light of its ordinary meaning.[52] The common practice is to identify this ordinary meaning in dictionaries.[53]

---

[52]Kasikili/Sedudu Island (Botswana v Namibia) (Judgment) [1999] ICJ Rep 1045, para. 18; Oil Platforms (Islamic Republic of Iran v United States of America) (Judgment) [1996] ICJ Reports 161, para. 41; *Romak S.A. (Switzerland) v. The Republic of Uzbekistan*, UNCITRAL, PCA Case No. AA280, Award, 26 November 2009, para. 159; *Wintershall Aktiengesellschaft v. Argentine Republic*, ICSID Case No. ARB/04/14, Award, 8 December 2008, para. 77; *Burlington Resources Inc. v. Republic of Ecuador*, ICSID Case No. ARB/08/5, Decision on Jurisdiction, 2 June 2010, para. 104.

[53]Dörr (2018), p. 542; Weeramantry (2012), pp. 49–50; Gardiner (2017), pp. 186–187; Alasdair Ross Anderson et al v. Republic of Costa Rica, ICSID Case No. ARB(AF)/07/3, Award, 19 May 2010, paras 48, 57; *Aguas del Tunari, S.A. v. Republic of Bolivia*, ICSID Case No. ARB/02/3, Decision on Jurisdiction, 21 October 2005, paras 227, 229, 231, and 232; *Ronald S. Lauder v. The Czech Republic*, UNCITRAL, Final Award, 3 September 2001, para. 221.

Yet, according to the International Court of Justice, the ordinary meaning of the term in question is found by reference to "the most commonly used criteria in international law and practice, to which the parties have referred".[54] On this note, international tribunals have started to examine the ordinary meaning of a term in other international instruments, whether international agreements or soft law instruments.[55]

In this context, WTO case law has corroborated in many instances that the search of the ordinary meaning is a contemporary scavenger hunt of the usage of the term.[56] Most relevant to our examination are the findings in *EC – Biotech*. The Panel explicitly reasoned that:

> in addition to dictionaries, other relevant rules of international law may in some cases aid a treaty interpreter in establishing, or confirming, the ordinary meaning of treaty terms in the specific context in which they are used. Such rules would not be considered because they are legal rules, but rather because they may provide evidence of the ordinary meaning of terms in the same way that dictionaries do. They would be considered for their informative character.[57]

The Panel examined different materials such as "reference works, glossaries, official documents of the relevant international organizations, including conventions, standards and guidelines" that were provided by the parties and other international organizations such as the Convention on Biological Diversity Secretariat.[58]

Similarly, the Panel in *Mexico – Telecoms* interpreted the term "anti-competitive practices" in light of domestic competition law of WTO Members, the United Nations Set of Multilaterally Agreed Equitable Principles and Rules for the Control of Restrictive Business, Organization for Economic Co-operation and Development ("OECD") Recommendations and the WTO Working Group on the Interaction between Trade and Competition Policy.[59] The Panel in *Australia – Tobacco Plain*

[54] *Kasikili/Sedudu Island (Botswana v Namibia)* (Judgment) [1999] ICJ Rep 1045, paras 21, 27.

[55] *Application of the International Convention on the Elimination of All Forms of Racial Discrimination (Georgia v Russian Federation)* (Provisional Measures) [2008] ICJ Report 2011, para. 29; Rantsev v. Cyprus and Russia, App. no. 25965/04 (ECtHR, 7 January 2010), paras 272–282 and 137–185.

[56] E.g. Appellate Body Report, *United States – Tax Treatment for "Foreign Sales Corporations" Recourse to Article 21.5 of the DSU by the European Communities*, para. 141, WTO Doc. WT/DS108/AB/RW (adopted January 29, 2002); Appellate Body Report, *United States – Import Prohibition of Certain Shrimp and Shrimp Products*, paras 128, 130–131, WTO Doc. WT/DS58/AB/R, (adopted November 6, 1998).

[57] Panel Reports, *European Communities – Measures Affecting the Approval and Marketing of Biotech Products*, WTO Docs WT/DS291/R, WT/DS292/R, WT/DS293/R, (adopted November 21, 2006), paras 7.92, 7.94–7.96.

[58] Panel Reports, *European Communities – Measures Affecting the Approval and Marketing of Biotech Products*, WTO Docs WT/DS291/R, WT/DS292/R, WT/DS293/R, (adopted November 21, 2006), paras 7.92, 7.94–7.96.

[59] Panel Report, *Mexico – Measures Affecting Telecommunications Services*, paras 7.235–7.236, WTO Doc. WT/DS204/R, (adopted June 1, 2004).

Packaging was quite explicit in reasoning that international standards may inform the interpretation of specific provisions under a covered agreement.[60]

In investment arbitration, the *Methanex v USA* tribunal considered that issues should not be strictly considered in their literal meaning, i.e. on a purely semantic basis,[61] while the tribunal in *Bayindir v Pakistan* made references to a comparative study of BITs in order to confirm its interpretation of the term "investment".[62]

In this regard, the possibility for *lex mercatoria* or other non-binding instruments to be considered in the process of determining the ordinary meaning of a term has also been supported by Gazzini.[63]

As such, international standards should be considered relevant evidence of the ordinary usage of a term.[64] As described by N. Koenig, one of the forefathers of the Codex Alimentarius, standards are "especially important in providing buyers and sellers with a common language for local and long-distance trading".[65]

Such standardizing practices could be considered as highly relevant when examining the exact scope of the definition of investment in an IIA. This could be exemplified by taking a look at the *Postova v Greece* case.[66] In specific, the tribunal had to examine whether Government Bonds are covered by the definition of investment in the Greek-Slovakia BIT. Claimants argued that Government Bonds can be classified either as "loans, claims to money or to any performance under contract having a financial value", or "shares in and stock and debentures of a company and any other form of participation in a company".[67]

The tribunal utilized general dictionaries such as the Merriam Webster, examined the text of third-party BITs (as interpreted by other tribunals) and provided some general comments on the particular nature of governmental bonds.[68] Yet, notwithstanding the validity and persuasiveness of the award, it is undoubtable that the

---

[60]Panel Reports, *Australia – Certain Measures Concerning Trademarks, Geographical Indications and Other Plain Packaging Requirements Applicable to Tobacco Products and Packaging*, paras 7.412, 7.1531, WTO Docs. WT/DS435/R, WT/DS441/R WT/DS458/R, WT/DS467/R (adopted August 27, 2018).

[61]*Methanex Corporation v the United States of America*, UNCITRAL, Partial Award, 7 August 2002, para. 136.

[62]*Bayindir Insaat Turizm Ticaret Ve Sanayi AS v Islamic Republic of Pakistan*, ICSID Case No. ARB/03/29, Decision on Jurisdiction, 14 November 2005, para. 113; Weeramantry (2012), paras 3.32–3.51.

[63]Gazzini (2016), p. 214.

[64]Also proposed by Pauwelyn (2014), p. 757.

[65]Koenig (1964), p. 335.

[66]*Poštová banka, a.s. and ISTROKAPITAL SE v. Hellenic Republic*, ICSID Case No. ARB/13/8, Award, 9 April 2015.

[67]*Poštová banka, a.s. and ISTROKAPITAL SE v. Hellenic Republic*, ICSID Case No. ARB/13/8, Award, 9 April 2015, paras 248–350.

[68]*Poštová banka, a.s. and ISTROKAPITAL SE v. Hellenic Republic*, ICSID Case No. ARB/13/8, Award, 9 April 2015, paras 313–324.

tribunal could have been more robust, if it had utilized the tools provided by the Vienna Convention on treaty interpretation differently.

In specific, instead of examining the text of third-party BITs and their subsequent interpretation by tribunals, which is academically disputed,[69] the tribunal could have examined the common usage of the term described in the BIT by taking a look at international glossaries and standards. In specific, the Basel Committee has an extensive glossary on financial instruments where details definitions on terms like "debt instrument", "loan", "financial claim" or "financial asset" can be found.[70] Similarly, the OECD holds a detailed Glossary Glossary of Foreign Direct Investment Terms and Definitions[71] while similarly the International Monetary Fund ("IMF") has published its own Glossary of Foreign Direct Investment Terms.[72] Lastly, the Tribunal could have sought guidance from relevant international standards such as the ISO 10962:2019[73] on *Securities and related financial instruments – Classification of financial instruments code* that provides the basis for classifying financial negotiated internationally as well as to domestic instruments.

These examples are a mere illustration of the usefulness of international standards and glossaries that, practically speaking, provide the basis of the international understanding of economic, financial and commercial transactions. No one can deny the fact that the understanding of the Basel Committee on banking regulation and transactions, or the understanding of the International Chamber of Commerce on documentary credits, or even the understanding of the International Institute for the Unification of Private Law on commercial contracts or leasing, reflects the common and predominant understanding of the terms at the international level. As such, the ordinary meaning of the economic activities encapsulated in the definition of "investment" should constitute the reflection of international harmonization and unification as depicted in such international instruments, standards, and glossaries.

5.2 *International Standards and the "Fair and Equitable Treatment" Clauses in IIAs*

International standards may definitely provide for an objective point of reference for evaluating "fair and equitable treatment". Their existence may be particularly

[69]E.g. Mitchell and Munro (2017); Weeramantry (2012), paras 5.35–5.37.

[70]Basel Committee, Glossary, https://www.bis.org/statistics/glossary.html, (last accessed 23 April 2020).

[71]OECD, Glossary Glossary of Foreign Direct Investment Terms and Definitions, https://www.oecd.org/daf/inv/investment-policy/2487495.pdf, (last accessed 23 April 2020).

[72]IMF, Report on the Survey of Implementation of Implementation of Methodological Standards for Direct Investment–Appendix II: Glossary of Foreign Direct Investment Terms, https://www.imf.org/external/np/sta/di/glossary.pdf, (last accessed 23 April 2020).

[73]At that time ISO 10962:2015. Available at: https://www.iso.org/obp/ui/#iso:std:iso:10962:ed-4:v1:en.

relevant in two instances: the evaluation of legitimate expectations and arbitrariness or unreasonableness.

International standards can provide for the frame of the investor's legitimate expectations. Being the outcome of a transparent standardization process, an international standard is by definition readily available to the investor as a potential regulatory change. The fact that the investors themselves might have taken place in the standardization process further reiterates the idea that the adoption of an international standard could not easily frustrate any legitimate expectations.[74]

This notion was confirmed in the *Philip Morris v Uruguay* case. There, the tribunal examined the investor's legitimate expectations in the light of the widely accepted articulations of international concern on the harmful effect of tobacco, as reflected in the FCTC and the guidelines adopted thereunder.[75] The obvious international regulatory concerns with regard to tobacco plain packaging, could only lead the tribunal to a single conclusion: that "the expectation could only have been of progressively more stringent regulation of the sale and use of tobacco products".[76]

International standards are also highly relevant for the assessment of the standards of "arbitrariness" or "unreasonableness". In clarifying the standards, the tribunals in *Saluka v Czech Republic* and *Micula v Romania* explained that a measure is reasonable when it "bears a reasonable relationship to some rational policy" and the pursuit of this policy takes into account the consequences that may bring upon the investors.[77] The tribunal in *Occidental v Ecuador* concluded that a decision is arbitrary if it is "founded on prejudice or preference rather than on reason and fact",[78] while the tribunal in *Cystallex v Venezuela* considered that the reasonableness of a measure needs to be examined in its scientifically evidenced justification.[79]

It follows that the requirement for "reasonableness" and "non-arbitrariness" is closely interrelated to a requirement of suitability; there must be a reasonable relationship between the means employed and the ends sought to be achieved.[80] This reasonable causal relationship is the outcome of science backed assumptions—

[74]See generally: Palombino (2018), pp. 96–121; Potestà (2013).

[75]*Philip Morris Brands Sàrl, Philip Morris Products s.a. and Abal Hermanos s.a. v. Uruguay*, ICSID Case No. ARB/10/7, Award, 8 July 2016.

[76]*Philip Morris Brands Sàrl, Philip Morris Products s.a. and Abal Hermanos s.a. v. Uruguay*, ICSID Case No. ARB/10/7, Award, 8 July 2016, para. 430.

[77]*Saluka Investment BV v. Czech*, UNCITRAL, Partial Award, 17 March 2006, para. 460; *Ioana Micula at al. v. Romania*, ICSID Case No. ARB/05/20, Final Award, 11 December 2013, para. 525; *AES Summit Generation Limited and AES-Tisza Erömü Kft v. The Republic of Hungary*, ICSID Case No. ARB/07/22, Award, 10 September 2010, para. 10.3.7.

[78]*Occidental Exploration and Production Company v. Ecuador*, UNCITRAL/LCIA Case No. UN 3467, Final Award, 1 July 2004, para. 162; *Link-Trading Joint Stock Company v. Department for Customs Control of the Republic of Moldova*, Final Award, UNCITRAL, Final Award, 18 April 2002, para. 501.

[79]*Crystallex International Corporation v. Venezuela*, ICSID Case No. ARB (AF)/11/2, Award, 4 April 2016, paras 591, 594.

[80]Heiskanen (2008); Paparinskis (2014), pp. 218–259; Dolzer and Schreuer (2012), pp. 193–195.

that, in general, the measure taken by the host State is scientifically expected to reach a certain result.[81]

This reasonable relationship was founded by the *Philip Morris v Uruguay* tribunal on the basis of the FCTC guidelines. The tribunal rejected the claimant's argument that there was not enough scientific evidence to suggest that the 80/80 packaging rule would achieve the purported results. In specific it deemed:

> For a country with limited technical and economic resources, such as Uruguay, adhesion to the FCTC and involvement in the process of scientific and technical cooperation and reporting and of exchange of information represented an important if not indispensable means for acquiring the scientific knowledge and market experience needed for the proper implementation of its obligations under the FCTC and for ensuring the fulfilment of its tobacco control policy.[82]

In the tribunal's view, the international standard provided in the FCTC guidelines constituted by definition a sufficient evidentiary basis for the reasonableness of the tobacco control policy. There was no need for Uruguay to perform additional scientific studies or to gather further evidence in support of the 80/80 packaging rule. The FCTC guidelines provided par excellence the required scientific justification for the implementation of the measures.[83] The FCTC guidelines were explicitly used by the tribunal as an objective point of reference as per the required reasonableness.[84]

In a similar manner, the tribunal in *Chemtura v Canada* examined the legality of Canada's cancellation of Chemtura's authorization to produce certain lindane-based pesticides that have been environmentally damaging.[85] The tribunal examined the measure in light of the international practice on banning lindane usage such as the Aarhus Protocol on Persistent Organic Pollutants of the Convention on Long-range Transboundary Air Pollution and the Stockholm Convention on Persistent Organic Pollutants, and found that even if the measures adopted could have been stricter than necessary, it constituted a legitimate exercise of its right to regulate.[86] As a result, the tribunal rejected a FET violation under North American Free Trade Agreement ("NAFTA").

In its analysis, the Tribunal agreed with the parties that it does not have the capacity to "second-guess the correctness of the science-based decision-making of highly specialized national regulatory agencies"; yet, it could not disregard "the fact

---

[81] Similar analysis is made in Kurtz (2016), pp. 136–167.

[82] *Philip Morris Brands Sàrl, Philip Morris Products s.a. and Abal Hermanos s.a. v. Uruguay*, ICSID Case No. ARB/10/7, Award, 8 July 2016, para. 393.

[83] *Philip Morris Brands Sàrl, Philip Morris Products s.a. and Abal Hermanos s.a. v. Uruguay*, ICSID Case No. ARB/10/7, Award, 8 July 2016, para. 396.

[84] *Philip Morris Brands Sàrl, Philip Morris Products s.a. and Abal Hermanos s.a. v. Uruguay*, ICSID Case No. ARB/10/7, Award, 8 July 2016, para. 401.

[85] *Chemtura Corporation v. Government of Canada*, UNCITRAL (formerly Crompton Corporation v. Government of Canada), Award, 2 August 2010.

[86] *Chemtura Corporation v. Government of Canada*, UNCITRAL (formerly Crompton Corporation v. Government of Canada), paras 131, 135–136, 192, 266–267; Dupuy and Viñuales (2018), p. 464.

that lindane has raised increasingly serious concerns both in other countries and at the international level since the 1970s".[87] Accordingly, the tribunal accepted a further degree of deference to the host State based on the fact that the measure at issue was a domestic manifestation of an international concern and an international law-making practice towards restriction. It follows that adherence to international standards by the host state creates a presumption of legality - thus ascribing them a de facto abrogatory effect similar to that contained explicitly in Articles 2.5 of the TBT and 3.2 of the SPS Agreement.

5.3 International Standards and Non-discrimination Clauses in IIAs

Our next example on the relevance of international standards in international investment arbitration is the examination of "like circumstances" in non-discrimination clauses, i.e. Most Favoured Nation ("MFN") and National Treatment.

Notwithstanding the textual differences or even the silence on the matter, tribunals have consistently examined the "likeness" of the circumstances or situations as a prerequisite for establishing "less favourable treatment" in MFN and National Treatment clauses.[88] In their examinations, the tribunals have adopted a variety of different tests[89] such as the "competition criterion",[90] the "economic sector criterion"[91] and the "regulatory framework criterion".[92] In most of the instances, Tribunals seem to examine all three of the criteria without a specific consistent methodology; yet, they also seem to agree that the overall legal context in which

---

[87] *Chemtura Corporation v. Government of Canada*, UNCITRAL (formerly Crompton Corporation v. Government of Canada), Award, 2 August 2010, paras 133–143.

[88] Diebold (2011), p. 841; Nikièma (2017), The Most-Favoured Nation clause in Investment Treaties, https://www.iisd.org/sites/default/files/publications/mfn-most-favoured-nation-clause-best-practices-en.pdf, (last accessed 23 April 2020), p. 19; Dolzer and Schreuer (2012), p. 199; *Consortium RFCC v. Morocco*, ICSID Case No. ARB/00/6, Award, 22 December 2003, para. 53; *Parkerings-Compagniet AS v. Republic of Lithuania*, ICSID Case No. ARB/05/8, Award, 11 September 2007, para. 369.

[89] The criteria can be found in academia with different names: Sarzo (2018), pp. 383–391; Diebold (2011), pp. 835–845; Bjorklund (2008), pp. 38–48.

[90] *Sergei Paushok, CJSC Golden East Company and CJSC Vostokneftegaz Company v. Government of Mongolia*, UNCITRAL, Award on Jurisdiction and Liability, 28 April 2011, para. 315; *S.D. Myers v. Canada*, UNCITRAL, Partial Award, 13 November 2000, para. 250.

[91] *Archer Daniels Midland Co. v. Mexico*, ICSID Case No. ARB (AF)/04/5, Award, 21 November 2007, para. 198; *Marvin Roy Feldman Karpa v. Mexico*, ICSID Case No. ARB (AF)/99/1, Award, 16 December 2002, paras 171–172; *Grand River Enters. Six Nations Ltd. v. United States*, UNCITRAL, Award, 12 January 2011, para. 165.

[92] *Apotex Holdings Inc. v. United States*, ICSID Case No. ARB(AF)/12/1, Award, 25 August 2014, para. 8.15; *Pope & Talbot v. Canada*, NAFTA/UNCITRAL, Award on the Merits, Phase 2, 10 April 2001, paras 83–95.

the measure at issue is placed has to be considered.[93] In this regard, a proper examination of international standardizing practices could bridge the possible difference in the methodology or application of the different test, especially since international standards may not only reflect regulatory concerns but may also have a bearing into the competitiveness of the operators at issue.

In sum, the "competition criterion" focuses on the competitive relation between the investors or investments in comparison, i.e. whether "the producers of like products which were directly competitive were in like circumstances as regards a measure designed expressly for the purpose of affecting that competition".[94] The "economic sector criterion" examines whether the investors operate in the same business, economic sector or industry.[95] Lastly, the "regulatory framework criterion" places at the centre of the "likeness" analysis the relevant applicable regulatory framework.[96] The tribunal in *Merill v Canada* exemplifies this approach by stating that "the proper comparison is between investors which are subject to the same regulatory measures under the same jurisdictional authority".[97]

Within all these approaches, which even the tribunals that utilized them considered as insufficient or not decisive,[98] we can find some common threads that can be harmoniously knitted together. In specific, we have seen the case law infuse the regulatory considerations when utilizing the economic sector or competition criteria.[99]

The tribunal in *SD Myers v Canada* accepted that "like circumstances" exist within the same economic or business sector. It noted though, without specifically applying it, that "the assessment of 'like circumstances' must also take into account

[93]Dolzer and Schreuer (2012), p. 200.

[94]*Corn Products International Inc v. United Mexican States,* ICSID Case No. ARB(AF)/04/1, Decision on Responsibility, 15 January 2008, paras 137, 120; *Paushok Sergei Paushok, CJSC Golden East Company and CJSC Vostokneftegaz Company v. Government of Mongolia,* UNCITRAL, Award on Jurisdiction and Liability, 28 April 2011, para. 315.

[95]*Occidental Exploration and Production Company v. Ecuador*, LCIA Case No. UN3467, Final Award, 1 July 2004, para. 173; *Pope & Talbot v. Canada*, NAFTA/UNCITRAL, Award on the Merits, Phase 2, 10 April 2001, para. 78; *Champion Trading Company and Ameritrade International, Inc v. Arab Republic of Egypt*, ICSID Case No. ARB/02/9, Award, 27 October 2006, para. 130; *Archer Daniels Midland Co. v. Mexico*, ICSID Case No. ARB (AF)/04/5, Award, 21 November 2007, paras 197–201; S.D. Myers v. Canada, NAFTA/UNCITRAL, Partial Award, 13 November 2000, para. 250.

[96]*Pope & Talbot v. Canada*, NAFTA/UNCITRAL, Award on the Merits, Phase 2, 10 April 2001, paras 83–95; DiMascio and Pauwelyn (2008).

[97]*Merrill & Ring Forestry LP v. Government of Canada*, UNCITRAL/ICSID Administrated, Award, 31 March 2010, para. 89.

[98]*Champion Trading Company and Ameritrade International, Inc v. Arab Republic of Egypt, ICSID Case No. ARB/02/9, Award, 27 October 2006*, para. 154; *Railroad Development Corporation v Republic of Guatemala, ICSID Case No ARB/07/23 Award, 29 June* 2012, para. 153; Molinuevo (2012), p. 119.

[99]*Merrill & Ring Forestry LP v. Government of Canada*, UNCITRAL/ICSID Administrated, Award, 31 March 2010, para. 88.

circumstances that would justify governmental regulations that treat them differently in order to protect the public interest".[100] In this sense, it proclaimed as relevant certain environmental considerations adopted by the NAFTA parties and the practice of OECD countries as enshrined in the OECD Declaration on International and Multinational Enterprises.[101] Accordingly, any examination for discrimination in international investment law, would resemble the examination of "arbitrary or unjustifiable discrimination" in the context of the WTO. However, this acceptance by the tribunal was left at the level of pronouncements since the analysis of the tribunal did not really focus on the aforementioned instruments and considerations.

In a different instance, the tribunal in *Parkerings v Lithuania* examined whether the claimant, Parkerings, and Pinues Proprius, a Dutch investor operated in like circumstances. The tribunal utilized the economic sector criterion with a slight differentiation. In specific, the tribunal infused in its analysis of the economic sector and the size of the projects of each investor,[102] regulatory considerations. It found decisive the fact that Claimant's investment extended significantly more in the culturally sensitive are of old town of Vilnius, which is a protected cultural heritage under the United Nations Educational, Scientific and Cultural Organization.[103] Hence, the tribunal found the investors not to operate in "like circumstances" due to non-economic values and considerations, even though the analysis was based upon the economic sector criterion.

Similarly, the tribunal in *Levy v Peru* examined whether Banco Nuevo Mundo operated in "like circumstances" as the second largest domestic bank or as certain other smaller domestic banks.[104] The analysis of the tribunal initiated by examining the relevant economic sector and moved on to examine the specific market circumstances within the sector, which it considered as "a sensitive area for any country, there are marked differences between the various banks operating in it". The tribunal considered in its examination issues of competitiveness such as the "segment [of a bank] and the number of individuals affected, its market share, and other similar factors".[105] What was decisive was the fact that claimant did not consistently demonstrate whether Banco Nuevo Mundo classified as a small or as a systemic bank.[106] The market strength of an undertaking or a company should normally be

[100] *S.D. Myers v. Canada*, NAFTA/UNCITRAL, Partial Award, 13 November 2000, para. 250.

[101] *S.D. Myers v. Canada*, NAFTA/UNCITRAL, Partial Award, 13 November 2000, paras 247–248.

[102] *Parkerings-Compagniet AS v. Republic of Lithuania*, ICSID Case No. ARB/05/8, Award, 11 September 2007, para. 391.

[103] *Parkerings-Compagniet AS v. Republic of Lithuania*, ICSID Case No. ARB/05/8, Award, 11 September 2007, paras 381–396.

[104] *Renée Rose Levy De Levi v. The Republic of Peru*, ICSID Case No. ARB/10/17, Award, 26 February 2014.

[105] *Renée Rose Levy De Levi v. The Republic of Peru*, ICSID Case No. ARB/10/17, Award, 26 February 2014, para. 397.

[106] *Renée Rose Levy De Levi v. The Republic of Peru*, ICSID Case No. ARB/10/17, Award, 26 February 2014, para. 401.

considered irrelevant for the economic sector criterion.[107] Yet, the examination of the tribunal was upon the examination of the consequences of a bank's failure-liquidation. As such, a purely economic analysis of the circumstances is affected by the general policy consideration attached to the different systemic consequences caused by the insolvency of a bank as considered small or systemic.

This jurisprudential example clearly illustrates our point on the relevance of international standards. Indeed, the explanation followed by the tribunal would have been much more convincing if they utilised standards such as the Basel Committee's standards on global systemically important banks[108] the Basel Committee's framework on International Convergence of Capital Measurement and Capital Standards[109] and ISO's 03.060 standards on Finance, Banking and Monetary Systems.[110] Each of those set of standards could provide the objective point of reference on the specific characteristics of banking operators, especially in relation to the systemic significance which was considered important by the tribunal.

Such considerations could be further expanded into an analysis of the adherence of investors to the ISO standards 13.020 on environmental protection[111] or 27.015 on energy efficiency,[112] or other corporate social responsibility standards such as "The Equator Principles"[113] or the OECD Guidelines for Multinational Enterprises.[114] The

[107] *International Thunderbird Gaming Corporation v. United Mexican States*, NAFTA/UNCITRAL, Arbitral Award, 26 January 2006, paras 175–183; *Corn Products International Inc v. United Mexican States*, ICSID Case No. ARB(AF)/04/1, Decision on Responsibility, 15 January 2008, para. 267.

[108] Basel Committee on Banking Supervision, July 2013, Global systemically important banks: updated assessment methodology and the higher loss absorbency requirement, https://www.bis.org/publ/bcbs255.pdf, (last accessed 23 April 2020).

[109] Basel Committee on Banking Supervision, June 2011, Basel III: A global regulatory framework for more resilient banks and banking systems, https://www.bis.org/publ/bcbs189.pdf, (last accessed 23 April 2020); Basel Committee on Banking Supervision, June 2006, International convergence on capital measurements and capital standards, https://www.bis.org/publ/bcbs128.pdf, (last accessed 23 April 2020).

[110] ISO, 03.060: Finance, Banking, Monetary Systems, Insurance, https://www.iso.org/ics/03.060/x/, (last accessed 23 April 2020).

[111] ISO, 13.020: Energy Efficiency, Energy Conservation in General, https://www.iso.org/ics/13.020/x/, (last accessed 23 April 2020).

[112] ISO, 27.015: Environmental Protection, https://www.iso.org/ics/27.015/x/, (last accessed 23 April 2020).

[113] The Equator Principles, A financial industry benchmark for determining, assessing and managing environmental and social risk in projects, https://equator-principles.com/wp-content/uploads/2020/01/The-Equator-Principles-July-2020.pdf, (last accessed 23 April 2020); Wörsdörfer (2015).

[114] OECD, Guidelines for Multinational Enterprises, https://read.oecd-ilibrary.org/taxation/oecd-transfer-pricing-guidelines-for-multinational-enterprises-and-tax-administrations-2017_tpg-2017-en#page1, (last accessed 23 April 2020).

adoption of standards by market operators constitute a market-based manifestation of policy considerations.[115]

In this sense, the tribunal in *Bilcon v Canada* could have reached a decision that "core community values" constituted the basis to distinguish between investors.[116] Indeed, should Canada adhere to an international standard that reflected those "core community values", then the tribunal could have only concluded that the circumstances between projects that satisfy international standards and those that do not, are not situated in "like circumstances". To reach such a result, it would be required to show whether the international standard truly reflected the considerations of the local community. The latter requires an analysis on whether the standards satisfies the criteria that we set: transparency, effectiveness, participation and scientific rigorousness.

Our proposition becomes more vivid in instances where the IIA introduces a list of relevant considerations for the determination of "likeness". For example, Article 17 of the Investment Agreement for the COMESA Common Investment Area (2007) reads:

> For greater certainty, references to 'like circumstances' in paragraph 1 of this Article requires an overall examination on a case-by-case basis of all the circumstances of an investment including, inter alia: (a) its effects on third persons and the local community; ... (e) the regulatory process generally applied in relation to the measure concerned; and (f) other factors directly relating to the investment or investor in relation to the measure concerned; and the examination shall not be limited to or be biased towards any one factor[117]

It is evident that international standards on environmental protection, responsible finance, labour protection and other policy related international best practices are more than relevant in an IIA that provides for such an elaborate list of relevant considerations. In this sense, adherance to international standards may even become de facto obligatory when deciding reasonable distinctions between investors or investments.

[115]References are made, for example, to legitimate expectations of consumers: Glinski (2007), pp. 122 et seq.; or reasonable reliance of market actors: Beckers (2018), p. 366; or means for overcoming information asymmetries: Büthe and Mattli (2011).

[116]*Bilcon of Delaware et al v. Government of Canada*, PCA Case No. 2009-04, Award on Jurisdiction and Liability, 17 March 2015.

[117]Investment Agreement for the COMESA (Common Market for Eastern and Southern Africa) Common Investment Area.

6 International Standards and the Assessment of Contributory Fault in Investment Arbitration

Investment tribunals are often called upon to determine the existence of investor's contributory fault; in other words, whether the investor has materially contributed to the injury it sustained by an internationally wrongful act of the host State. To the extent not explicitly provided otherwise in an IIA, the default position is that the assessment of contributory fault takes place in accordance with the customary secondary rules enshrined in Article 39 of the International Law Commission Articles on State Responsibility. International standards are could have a role to play in this respect.

Acts provoking a breach are sufficient for a finding of contributory fault.[118] Not every action or omission which contributes to the damage suffered is relevant for this purpose. The actions or omissions to be taken into consideration under Article 39 may only be those which can be considered as wilful or negligent, "those that manifest a lack of due care".[119] Against this backdrop, any assessment of negligence would prove itself to be extremely difficult. The absence of a precise legal standard for the evaluation of negligence, arguably, allows for too much space for adjudicatory opinion or even imagination. This might prove to be even worse when it comes to instances of investment reprisal due to the indirect causality of the action or omission on the eventual loss. How should an international adjudicator assess the wrongfulness of the investor's conduct in those cases?

The assessment of the wrongfulness has been a relatively straightforward exercise in cases of illegal investors' actions. Typical examples would be the cases in *Occidental v Ecuador, Copper Mesa v Ecuador* and *Goetz v Burundi*. In all those cases, the action that prompted the disproportionate sanction by the host State was illegal, and, thus, a finding of a contributory fault did not face any particular difficulties. In *Occidental v Ecuador*, the investor violated the terms of the concession agreement by transferring certain rights without Ecuador's consent.[120] In *Goetz v Burundi,* the revocation of the investor's operating license was caused by a breach of the certificate's conditions.[121] Much more, in *Copper Mesa v Ecuador*, the investor was guilty of directing violent acts, using armed men, firing guns and

[118] *Occidental Petroleum Corp, Occidental Exploration and Production Company v. Ecuador*, ICSID Case No. ARB/06/11, ICSID ARB/06/11, Award, 5 October 2012, para. 687.

[119] United Nations, International Law Commission (2001), Draft articles on Responsibility of States for Internationally Wrongful Acts, with commentaries, https://legal.un.org/ilc/texts/instruments/english/commentaries/9_6_2001.pdf, (last accessed 23 April 2020), pp. 109–110.

[120] *Occidental Petroleum Corp, Occidental Exploration and Production Company v. Ecuador*, ICSID Case No. ARB/06/11, ICSID ARB/06/11, Award, 5 October 2012, para. 679.

[121] *Goetz and others v. Burundi*, ICSID Case No. ARB/95/3, Award, 10 February 1999, paras 296–299.

spraying mace at civilians, which were all in violation of the Ecuadorian criminal law.[122]

Nevertheless, the cases of contributory fault have not been limited to instances of illegality. In *South American Silver v Bolivia*, the tribunal confirmed this thesis. In that case, a severe social conflict among Bolivia's indigenous communities, marches, demonstrations, physical violence and deaths were all caused by the investor's failure to implement an indigenous community relations program.[123] As a response to this situation, Bolivia revoked the investor's mining concessions, and subsequently pleaded contributory negligence. Indeed, the conflict among the indigenous communities had its genesis in the investor's project. Nevertheless, the investor emphasized that the respondent could not invoke contributory negligence since there was no regulatory framework in Bolivia defining any obligation for the implementation of a community relations program.[124] The tribunal departed from the reasoning of previous case law,[125] and rejected the claimant's argument.[126]

The *Yukos v Russian Federation* case offers a quite similar example. There, the underlying reason for the investment's expropriation was the investor's tax optimization arrangements of the investor, which allowed it to avoid paying significant amounts of taxes to Russia. The tribunal emphasized that there was no evidence in the record suggesting that this tax minimization scheme was illegal.[127] However, the tribunal deemed that it was an "abuse"[128] and "questionable".[129] Particular instances of misconduct were not violations of the law, but rather an abuse of Russian corporate law and *"principles of corporate governance"*.[130]

Still, measuring misconduct as the *Yukos* tribunal did is not unproblematic. Indeed, there is no textbook definition of "abusive" or "questionable"—and, certainly—many diametrically different opinions may exist as to whether a particular,

[122] *Copper Mesa Mining Corporation v. Republic of Ecuador*, PCA No. 2012-2, Award (Redacted), 15 March 2016, paras 6.99–6.100.

[123] *South American Silver Limited v. Bolivia*, UNCITRAL, PCA Case No. 2013-15, Award, 22 November 2018, paras 472–491.

[124] *South American Silver Limited v. Bolivia*, UNCITRAL, PCA Case No. 2013-15, Award, 22 November 2018, para. 757.

[125] On the other side of the spectrum see *Abengoa S.A. y COFIDES S.A. v. United Mexican States*, ICSID Case No. ARB(AF)/09/2, Award, 18 April 2013, paras 653–673; *Bear Creek Mining Corporation v. Republic of Peru*, ICSID Case No. ARB/14/21, Award, 30 November 2017, paras 565–569.

[126] *South American Silver Limited v. Bolivia*, UNCITRAL, PCA Case No. 2013-15, Award, 22 November 2018, para. 491.

[127] *Yukos Universal Limited (Isle of Man) v. The Russian Federation*, UNCITRAL, PCA Case No. 2005-04/AA227, Final Award, 18 July 2014, para. 1611.

[128] *Yukos Universal Limited (Isle of Man) v. The Russian Federation*, UNCITRAL, PCA Case No. 2005-04/AA227, Final Award, 18 July 2014, para. 1612.

[129] *Yukos Universal Limited (Isle of Man) v. The Russian Federation*, UNCITRAL, PCA Case No. 2005-04/AA227, Final Award, 18 July 2014, para. 1634.

[130] *Yukos Universal Limited (Isle of Man) v. The Russian Federation*, UNCITRAL, PCA Case No. 2005-04/AA227, Final Award, 18 July 2014, paras 1283–1290.

otherwise legal, conduct constitutes an abuse or is of questionable morality. Nor is imposing an "illegality" requirement for the finding of contributory fault a veritable solution, since this would allow investors to benefit from legal systems that are still developing to regulate negative externalities of investments, that may be yet unknown. More importantly, it would allow multinational enterprises—with significant experience on the various regulations on their activities—to benefit from the inexperience of developing host States that might not have identified the precise risks of their investment activities. Some form of self-regulation of multi-national enterprises, which would then become the benchmark for the evaluation of contributory fault, is necessitated.[131]

This benchmark may well be provided by international standards. The OECD Guidelines for multinational enterprises, the ILO Tripartite Declaration of Principles Concerning Multinational Enterprises and Social Policy, the United Nations Global Compact, as well as industry driven standards on CSR such as the ISO 26000[132] and ISO 14001 constitute landmark standardisation efforts on key issues of international public policy which are suitable to be taken into consideration in contributory fault analysis.

7 Conclusions

The present chapter sought to demonstrate why and how international standardizing bodies function as transnational actors of international investment law, given the important role of international standardization in the interpretation and application of IIA clauses and rules of public international law. International standards, as defined in the present chapter, enjoy a significant interpretative and evidentiary utility in the context of the determining rights and obligations in international investment law. It should be noted, though, that the instances past or potential resort to international standards provided in the present chapter are not exhaustive. Additional arguments can also be raised on the effects of CSR standards on the lawfulness and reasonableness of the conduct of the investor,[133] while international standards may be considered a de facto obligatory effect in the operation of the FET standard, in manner similar to the claim in *Peter Allard v Barbados*.[134] To this end, it is beyond the shadow of doubt that international standardizing bodies today have grown to

[131]For more: Yilmaz Vastardis and Chambers (2018).

[132]See Bijlmakers and van Calster (2015), pp. 275–310.

[133]Similarly: Bonnitcha and McCorquodale (2017) and Fasterling (2017).

[134]Claimant tried to substantiate a claim of violation of FET on the basis of alleged violations of commitments made by Barbados under international environmental treaties. *Peter A. Allard v. The Government of Barbados*, PCA Case No. 2012-06. Award, 27 June 2016, paras 33–52, 164–165, 170.

become a highly influential actor of international investment law, in a way that it may even appear to challenge traditional approaches to normativity.

References

Basedow J (2008) The State's private law and the economy: commercial law as an amalgam of public and private rule-making. Am J Comp Law 56(3):703–721

Beckers A (2018) Enforcing corporate social responsibility codes on global self-regulation and national private law; on global self-regulation and national private. Hart Publishing, Oxford

Bijlmakers S, van Calster G (2015) You'd be surprised how much it costs to look this cheap! A case study of ISO 26000 on social responsibility. In: Delimatsis P (ed) The law, economics and politics of international standardization. Cambridge University Press, Cambridge, pp 275–310

Bjorklund AK (2008) National treatment. In: Reinisch A (ed) Standards of investment protection. Oxford University Press, Oxford, pp 29–58

Bonnitcha J, McCorquodale R (2017) The concept of 'due diligence' in the UN guiding principles on business and human rights. Eur J Int Law 28:899–919

Büthe T (2008) The globalization of health and safety standards: delegation of regulatory authority in the SPS Agreement of the 1994 Agreement Establishing the World Trade Organization. Law Contemp Probl 71:219–255

Büthe T (2009) The politics of food safety in the age of global trade: the Codex Alimentarius Commission in the SPS agreement of the WTO. In: Coglianese C, Finkel AM, Zaring D (eds) Import safety: regulatory governance in the global economy. University of Pennsylvania Press, Pennsylvania, pp 88–109

Büthe T, Mattli W (2011) The new global rulers: the privatization of regulation in the world economy. Princeton University Press, Oxford

Delimatsis P (2015) 'Relevant international standards' and 'recognised standardisation bodies' under the TBT Agreement. In: Delimatsis P (ed) The law, economics and politics of international standardization. Cambridge University Press, Cambridge, pp 104–136

Delimatsis P (2018) Global standard-setting 2.0: how the WTO spotlights ISO and impacts the transnational standard-setting process. Duke J Comp Int Law 28:273–325

Delimatsis P (2019) International trade law and technical standardization. In: Contreras J (ed) The Cambridge handbook of technical standardization law. Cambridge University Press, Cambridge, pp 7–27

Delimatsis P, Hoekman B (2018) National tax regulation, voluntary international standards, and the GATS: Argentina–Financial Services. World Trade Rev 17(2):265–290

Desta MG (2012) GATT/WTO law and international standards: an example of soft law instruments hardening up? In: International investment law and soft law. Edward Elgar Publishing, Cheltenham, Northampton, pp 148–191

Diebold NF (2011) Standards of non-discrimination in international economic law. Int Comp Law Q 60(4):831–865

DiMascio N, Pauwelyn J (2008) Nondiscrimination in trade and investment treaties: worlds apart or two sides of the same coin? Am J Int Law 102(1):48–89

Dimopoulos A (2015) Standards of responsible investment and international investment law. In: Delimatsis P (ed) The law, economics and politics of international standardization. Cambridge University Press, Cambridge, pp 338–364

Dolzer R, Schreuer C (2012) Principles of international investment law, 2nd edn. Oxford University Press, Oxford

Dörr O (2018) Article 31. In: Dörr O, Schmalenbach K (eds) Vienna Convention on the Law of Treaties. Springer, Berlin, Heidelberg, pp 557–616

Dupuy PM, Viñuales JE (2018) International environmental law, 2nd edn. Cambridge University Press, Cambridge

Fasterling B (2017) Human rights due diligence as risk management: social risk versus human rights risk. Bus Hum Rights J 2:225–247

Fratianni M (2006) Central bank cooperation at the bank for international settlements, 1930–1973. J Econ Hist 66(1):268–270

Gardiner RK (2017) Treaty interpretation, 2nd edn. Oxford University Press, Oxford

Gazzini T (2016) Interpretation of international investment treaties. Hart Publishing, Oxford, Portland, Oregon

Glinski C (2007) Corporate codes of conduct: moral or legal obligation?. In: McBarnet D, Voiculescu A, Campbell T (eds) New corporate accountability: corporate social responsibility and the law. Clarendon/Oxford University Press, Oxford, pp 119–147

Goodhart C (2011) The Basel Committee on banking supervision: a history of the early years, 1974–1997. Cambridge University Press, Cambridge

Hall RB, Biersteker TJ (eds) (2002) The emergence of private authority in global governance. Cambridge University Press, Cambridge

Heiskanen V (2008) Arbitrary and unreasonable measures. In: Reinisch A (ed) Standards of investment protection. Oxford University Press, Oxford, pp 87–110

Kerwer D (2005) Rules that many use: standards and global regulation. Gov: Int J Policy Adm Inst 18(4):611–632

Koenig N (1964) A new vital influence in international food standards. Food Drug Cosmet Law J 19:326–336

Kurtz J (2016) The WTO and international investment law: converging systems. Cambridge University Press, Cambridge

Landwehr O (2007) Article 3 SPS. In: Wolfrum R, Stoll PT, Seibert-Fohr A (eds) WTO-technical barriers and SPS measures. Koninklijke Brill NV, Leiden, pp 412–427

Larouche P, van Overwalle G (2015) Interoperability standards, patents and competition policy. In: Delimatsis P (ed) The law, economics and politics of international standardisation. Cambridge University Press, Cambridge, pp 367–393

Lindahl H (2015) ISO standards and authoritative collective action: conceptual and normative issues. In: Delimatsis P (ed) The law, economics and politics of international standardisation. Cambridge University Press, Cambridge, pp 42–57

Marceau GZ, Trachtman J (2014) A map of the World Trade Organization law of domestic regulation of goods: the technical barriers to trade agreement, the sanitary and phytosanitary measures agreement, and the general agreement on tariffs and trade. J World Trade 48 (2):351–432

Marchetti J (2015) Technical standard-setting in the financial sector. In: Delimatsis P (ed) The law, economics and politics of international standardization. Cambridge University Press, Cambridge, pp 137–159

Marx A (2014) Legitimacy, institutional design, and dispute settlement: the case of eco-certification systems. Globalizations 11(3):401–416

Mattli W (2001) The politics and economics of international institutional standards setting: an introduction. J Eur Public Policy 8(3):328–344

Mattli W, Büthe T (2005) Global private governance: lessons from a national model of setting standards in accounting. Law Contemp Probl 68(3/4):225–262

Mattli W, Seddon J (2015) The power of the penholder: the missing politics in global regulatory governance analysis. In: Delimatsis P (ed) The law, economics and politics of international standardisation. Cambridge University Press, Cambridge, pp 367–393

Mavroidis PC (2012) Technical barriers to trade. In: Mavroidis P (ed) Trade in Goods. Oxford University Press, Oxford, pp 668–743

Mavroidis PC, Wolfe R (2017) Private standards and the WTO: reclusive no more. World Trade Rev 16(1):1–24

Mitchell AD, Munro J (2017) Someone else's deal: interpreting international investment agreements in the light of third-party agreements. Eur J Int Law 28(3):669–695

Molinuevo M (2012) Protecting investment in services: investor-State arbitration versus WTO dispute settlement. Kluwer Law International, Alphen aan den Rijn

Palombino FM (2018) Fair and equitable treatment and the fabric of general principles. T.M.C. Asser Press, The Hague

Paparinskis M (2014) The international minimum standard and fair and equitable treatment. Oxford University Press, Oxford

Pauwelyn J (2014) Rule-based Trade 2.0? The rise of informal rules and international standards and how they may outcompete WTO treaties. J Int Econ Law 17:739–751

Potestà M (2013) Legitimate expectations in investment treaty law: understanding the roots and the limits of a controversial concept. ICSID Rev 28:88–122

Sarzo M (2018) The national treatment obligation. In: Gattini A, Tanzi A, Fontanelli F (eds) General principles of law and international investment arbitration. Brill Nijhoff, Leiden, pp 378–397

Tamiotti L (2007) Article 2 TBT. In: Wolfrum R, Stoll PT, Seibert-Fohr A (eds) WTO-technical barriers and SPS measures. Koninklijke Brill NV, Leiden, pp 210–234

Weeramantry JR (2012) Treaty interpretation in investment arbitration, 1st edn. Oxford University Press, Oxford

Wörsdörfer M (2015) The equator principles and human rights due diligence – towards a positive and leverage-based concept of corporate social responsibility. Philos Manage 14:193–218

Yilmaz Vastardis A, Chambers R (2018) Overcoming the corporate veil challenge: could investment law inspire the proposed business and human rights treaty? Int Comp Law Q 67 (2):389–423

Eleni-Amalia Giannakopoulou is an LL.B. candidate at the School of Law National and Kapodistrian University of Athens, a minor student of Finance at Deree, the American College of Greece, and a research trainee at the Athens Public International Law Center (Athens PIL).

Marios Tokas works as an interantional trade intern at White and Case LLP and is a candidate for the Master's in international law at the Graduate Institute of International and Development Studies. He is an associate research fellow and trade programe coordinator at the Centre for International Sustainable Development Law and works as a data analyst for Arbitrator Intelligence.

New Actors in Investment Arbitration: The Legitimate Government

Krystle Baptista

Contents

1 Introduction 74
2 The Venezuelan Situation: The Co-existence of Two Governments 74
 2.1 Context 74
 2.2 The Appointment of the "*Procurador Especial*" 78
 2.3 ICSID Arbitrations 79
3 Jurisdiction of ICSID Arbitral Tribunals and Annulment Committees to Determine the Legitimate Representative of a Respondent-State 81
 3.1 Jurisdiction Under the ICSID Rules 81
 3.2 Jurisdiction Under the ICSID Additional Facility Rules 92
4 Possible Practical Solutions 99
5 Conclusion 102
References 102

Abstract This chapter explores the penetration in investment arbitration of a new actor: the legitimate government of the Respondent-State, in competition with the de facto government, for the representation of the State before investment tribunals. The chapter addresses whether ICSID and ICSID Additional Facility arbitral tribunals have jurisdiction to determine who is the legitimate government of the respondent State, and thus, who is the proper representative of the State. It concludes that such decision escapes the tribunal's jurisdiction and advocates, inter alia, that the decision should be taken at the political level by the State Members of the World Bank.

Thanks to Sofia de Sampaio Jalles, Francisca Seara Cardoso, Edward Thorn, Adam Jankowski and Sofia Kurtis de Alzaga for your help in editing this paper.

K. Baptista (✉)
International Law & Arbitration, Madrid, Spain
e-mail: kbs@kbarbitration.com

A. Gourgourinis (ed.), *Transnational Actors in International Investment Law*,
European Yearbook of International Economic Law,
https://doi.org/10.1007/978-3-030-60679-4_4

1 Introduction

On 23 January 2019, Juan Guaidó, the head of the Venezuelan National Assembly, invoked a mechanism in Venezuela's constitution to declare himself the country's interim president, initially calling on Nicolás Maduro, the incumbent head of State, to either step aside or hold new elections. Hours later, US President Donald Trump issued a statement recognizing Guaidó as Venezuela's legitimate president and rejecting the authority of the Maduro government. Several countries across South America and Europe recognized Guaidó's government in the following days and weeks.

On 27 March 2019, Guaidó's appointed Special Attorney General notified the International Centre for Settlement of Investment Disputes ("ICSID" or the "Centre") that it should not "entertain any submission or petition presented by lawyers allegedly acting on behalf of Nicolás Maduro" in the arbitrations before the Center. There are close to 20 investment cases pending against Venezuela in ICSID.

The analysis in the present chapter starts with a brief factual background of the situation in Venezuela in order to address whether an investment arbitral tribunal subject to ICSID Rules or the ICSID Additional Facility Rules is the proper forum to decide on the legitimacy of governments. The analysis leads to a negative answer and to the proposition that political decisions ought to be made by politicians. The chapter offers several practical solutions for arbitral tribunals confronted with the situation before concluding the analysis.

2 The Venezuelan Situation: The Co-existence of Two Governments

2.1 Context

In May 2018, presidential elections took place in Venezuela, resulting in the reelection of Nicolás Maduro for the period of 2019–2025.[1] The opposition parties

[1]Maduro parece deslegitimado luego de su dudoso triunfo electoral. La Capital, 22 May 2018, www.lacapital.com.ar/el-mundo/maduro-parece-deslegitimado-luego-su-dudoso-triunfo-electoral-n1610559.html (last accessed 24 August 2020).

refused to participate[2] and many countries,[3] international organizations[4] and NGOs[5] refused to recognize the process and its outcome[6] due to the lack of transparency and irregularities in the call for elections.

On 23 January 2019, the President of the Venezuelan National Assembly, Juan Guaidó, proclaimed himself the Interim President of the Bolivarian Republic of Venezuela[7] in accordance with Article 233 of the Venezuelan Constitution.[8]

[2]La Asamblea Nacional en Venezuela desconoce el segundo mandato de Nicolás Maduro. RT, 5 January 2019, www.actualidad.rt.com/actualidad/301160-asamblea-nacional-venezuela-desconocer-mandato-maduro (last accessed 24 August 2020); AD, PJ y VP no participarán en elecciones presidenciales. El Nacional, 20 February 2018, www.elnacional.com/venezuela/politica/participaran-elecciones-presidenciales_223759/ (last accessed 24 August 2020).

[3]Catena P, Gobierno apuesta a endurecer postura por Venezuela en reunión con Grupo de Lima. La Tercera, 2 May 2018, www.latercera.com/politica/noticia/gobierno-apuesta-endurecer-postura-venezuela-reunion-grupo-lima/151678 (last accessed 24 August 2020); Villalobos P, Costa Rica apoya resolución que censura convocatoria prematura de elecciones en Venezuela. Amelia Rueda, 23 February 2018, www.ameliarueda.com/nota/costa-rica-resolucion-desconoce-convocatoria-prematura-eleccion-venezuela(last accessed 24 August 2020); Dobson P, VIII Americas Summit: Cuba & Bolivia Stand by Venezuela amid US Threats. Venezuela Analysis, 16 April 2018, www.venezuelanalysis.com/news/13768 (last accessed 24 August 2020); Gobierno de los Países Bajos no reconoce elecciones venezolanas. El Nacional, 23 May 2018, www.elnacional.com/mundo/europa/gobierno-los-paises-bajos-reconoce-elecciones-venezolanas_236734/ (last accessed 24 August 2020); Russia Criticizes Calls to Boycott Venezuela's Elections, US Plans for Regime Change. TeleSUR, 4 May 2018, www.telesurenglish.net/news/Russia-Criticizes-Calls-to-Boycott-Venezuelas-Elections-US-Plans-for-Regime-Change-20180504-0003.html (last accessed 24 August 2020).

[4]La OEA aprobó resolución que declara ilegítimo el nuevo Gobierno de Nicolás Maduro. El Universal, 10 January 2019, www.eluniversal.com/politica/30186/la-oea-aprueba-resolucion-que-declara-ilegitimo-gobierno-de-venezuela (last accessed 24 August 2020); Estados Unidos y la OEA desconocen el gobierno de Nicolás Maduro. Expansión, 10 January 2019, www.expansion.mx/mundo/2019/01/10/estados-unidos-y-la-oea-desconocen-el-gobierno-de-Nicolás-maduro (last accessed 24 August 2020); La CIDH instó a Venezuela a convocar "otras" elecciones con "sufragio libre". El Universal, 19 May 2018, www.eluniversal.com/politica/9783/st-condiciones-de-publicacion.html (last accessed 24 August 2020); Grupo de Lima rechaza elecciones presidenciales de Venezuela. TeleSUR, 13 February 2018, www.telesurtv.net/news/Grupo-de-Lima-rechaza-elecciones-presidenciales-de-Venezuela-20180213-0062.html (last accessed 24 August 2020).

[5]MUD no participará en elecciones presidenciales del 22-A. El Nacional, 21 February 2018, www.elnacional.com/oposicion/mud-participara-elecciones-presidenciales-del-22-a_224001 (last accessed 24 August 2020); La MUD anuncia que no participará en las presidenciales de Venezuela y Maduro dice que quiere "megaelección" que incluya parlamentarias y locales. BBC Mundo, 21 February 2018, www.bbc.com/mundo/noticias-america-latina-43148830 (last accessed 24 August 2020).

[6]Maduro parece deslegitimado luego de su dudoso triunfo electoral. La Capital, 22 May 2018, www.lacapital.com.ar/el-mundo/maduro-parece-deslegitimado-luego-su-dudoso-triunfo-electoral-n1610559.html (last accessed 24 August 2020).

[7]Juan Guaidó jura como presidente de Venezuela ante miles de opositores. El Comercio, 23 January 2019, www.elcomercio.pe/mundo/venezuela/venezuela-vivo-oposicion-marcha-miercoles-23-enero-Nicolás-maduro-directo-23e-noticia-600055 (last accessed 24 August 2020); Vinogradoff L, Maduro se convierte en presidente "ilegítimo" de Venezuela, aislado por la comunidad internacional. ABC, 11 January 2019, www.abc.es/internacional/abci-comienza-toma-posesion-maduro-no-reconocida-comunidad-internacional-201901101634_noticia.html (last accessed 24 August 2020).

[8]Art. 233 of the Venezuelan Constitution: There will be absolute absence of the President of the Republic in the case of: death, resignation, (...) as well as the popular revocation of his mandate.

Guaidó's proclamation is based on a reading of the Venezuelan Constitution which would give Guaidó democratic legitimacy,[9] as opposed to Maduro's claim to power, which relies on elections widely held to have been irregular.[10]

Since his proclamation, Guaidó has been recognized as the legitimate Venezuelan President[11] by approximately 60 States.[12] The US government was the first country to recognize Guaidó, only a few minutes after his proclamation.[13] However, Guaidó lacks effective power since Maduro has refused to step down and holds de facto control over key institutions, including the army.[14] Guaidó does not have control

---

While the new president is elected and takes office, the President of the National Assembly' will be in charge of the Presidency of the Republic. (Free translation from the author).

[9]Cambio histórico en Venezuela: La oposición gana las elecciones parlamentarias. RT, 7 December 2015, www.actualidad.rt.com/actualidad/193510-venezuela-oposicion-lidera-elecciones-parlamentarias (last accessed 24 August 2020).

[10]Venezuela election: Fourteen ambassadors recalled after Maduro win. BBC News, 22 May 2018, www.bbc.com/news/world-latin-america-44204632 (last accessed 24 August 2020).

[11]Recognition has been granted with different consequences for his representatives. See Paddeu F, Dunkelberg A, Recognition of Governments: Legitimacy and Control Six Months after Guaidó. Opinio Juris, 18 July 2019, www.opiniojuris.org/2019/07/18/recognition-of-governments-legitimacy-and-control-six-months-after-guaido (last accessed 24 August 2020).

[12]Torres A, 'Here is a list of countries recognizing Juan Guaidó as Venezuela's interim president. ABC Local 10, 13 March 2019, www.local10.com/news/venezuela/here-is-list-of-countries-recognizing-juan-guaido-as-venezuela-s-interim-president (last accessed 24 August 2020); The last recognition seems to be from Greece: Ministry of Foreign Affairs announcement on the recognition of J. Guaido as President a.i. of Venezuela. Ministry of Foreign Affairs, 12 July 2019, https://www.mfa.gr/en/current-affairs/statements-speeches/ministry-of-foreign-affairs-announcement-on-the-recognition-of-guaido-as-president-ai-of-venezuela.html (last accessed 24 August 2020).

[13]The White House, Statement from President Donald J. Trump Recognizing Venezuelan National Assembly President Juan Guaido as the Interim President of Venezuela. The White House, 23 January 2019, www.whitehouse.gov/briefings-statements/statement-president-donald-j-trump-recognizing-venezuelan-national-assembly-president-juan-guaido-interim-president-venezuela (last accessed 24 August 2020); Wadhams N, Rosati A, Talev M, Maduro Squeezed as Trump Recognizes Guaido and Protests Expand. Bloomberg, 23 January 2019, www.bloomberg.com/news/Art.s/2019-01-23/trump-said-to-intend-to-recognize-guaido-as-venezuela-president (last accessed 24 August 2020).

[14]Sanderson C and Jones T, ICSID committee challenged in Venezuela row. Global Arbitration Review, 17 April 2020, https://globalarbitrationreview.com/article/1225799/icsid-committee-challenged-in-venezuela-row (last accessed 24 August 2020); Crystallex International Corp v. Bolivarian Republic of Venezuela, USCA, (3rd Cir. 2019), Transcript of the oral hearing, 15 April 2019, p. 178:8–12, https://www.italaw.com/sites/default/files/case-documents/italaw10518.pdf (last accessed 24 August 2020); Crystallex International Corp v. Bolivarian Republic of Venezuela, USCA, (3rd Cir. 2019) Opinion of the Court, 29 July 2019, fn. 2, https://www.italaw.com/sites/default/files/case-documents/italaw10704.pdf (last accessed 24 August 2020).

over at least some of the territory, but arguably does have habitual obedience of a majority of the population and a reasonable prospect of permanence.[15]

On 5 February 2019, pursuant to Article 333 of the Venezuelan Constitution, the Venezuelan National Assembly enacted the Statute that Governs the Transition to Democracy to Reestablish the Full Force and Effect of the Constitution of the Bolivarian Republic of Venezuela (the "Estatuto"), in order to regulate the political change undertaken in the country. Such Estatuto was annulled[16] a few days later, on 8 February 2019, by the Constitutional Chamber of the Republic's Supreme Court of Justice, which is widely held to be under complete control of Maduro,[17] rather than an independent body of the Venezuelan State. For example, the US Government has included the judges that rendered the decision annulling the Estatuto on the Specially Designated Nationals and Blocked Persons List (SDN), since they are considered to be responsible for rulings that have usurped the authority of the democratically elected National Assembly.[18]

---

[15]Lee Anderson J, Venezuela's Two Presidents Collude. The New Yorker, 3 June 2019, https://www.newyorker.com/magazine/2019/06/10/venezuelas-two-presidents-collide (last accessed 24 August 2020); Faiola A, Juan Guaidó promised to save Venezuela. Now the flame he lit is petering out, and his U.S. backers are weighing their options. Washington Post, 17 December 2019, https://www.washingtonpost.com/world/the_americas/juan-guaido-promised-to-save-venezuela-a-year-later-the-flame-he-lit-is-petering-out-his-us-backers-are-weighing-their-options/2019/12/17/48a18186-1495-11ea-80d6-d0ca7007273f_story.html (last accessed 24 August 2020); Long G, Aides to Venezuela's Guaidó quit over plan to topple Maduro. Financial Times, 11 May 2020, https://www.ft.com/content/a3bfd388-222e-4f4e-96b3-0a0ad3bee911 (last accessed 24 August 2020); Lafuente J, Juan Guaidó: "We need a solution in Venezuela no matter what." El Pais, 17 December 2019, https://english.elpais.com/elpais/2019/12/16/inenglish/1576491263_356074.html (last accessed 24 August 2020); The battle for Venezuela's future. The Economist, 2 February 2019, https://www.economist.com/leaders/2019/02/02/the-battle-for-venezuelas-future (last accessed 24 August 2020).

[16]El TSJ de Venezuela declara nulo el Estatuto de la Transición aprobado por el Parlamento. Notimerica, 11 February 2019, www.notimerica.com/politica/noticia-tsj-venezuela-declara-nulo-estatuto-transicion-aprobado-parlamento-20190211121618.html (last accessed 24 August 2020).

[17]Fiscal pide anular designación de magistrados y responsabiliza al Gobierno por seguridad de su familia. Informe21, 12 June 2017, www.informe21.com/politica/fiscal-luisa-ortega-pide-anular-la-designacion-de-33-magistrados-del-tsj (last accessed 1 August 2020); Federación Nacional de Abogados emite nota de protesta ante sentencias del TSJ (+Pronunciamiento). Versión Final, 1 April 2017, www.versionfinal.com.ve/politica-dinero/federacion-nacional-de-abogados-emite-nota-de-protesta-ante-sentencias-del-tsj-pronunciamiento (last accessed 24 August 2020); Designados nuevos magistrados del TSJ. El Nacional, 23 December 2015, www.elnacional.com/venezuela/politica/designados-nuevos-magistrados-del-tsj_38324/ (last accessed 24 August 2020); Acceso a la Justicia califica al TSJ como politizado y parcializado. Runrun, 12 January 2017, www.runrun.es/nacional/292643/acceso-a-la-justicia-califica-al-tsj-como-politizado-y-parcializado (last accessed 24 August 2020).

[18]Department of the Treasury's Office of Foreign Assets Control (OFAC) designated eight Venezuelan government officials pursuant to Executive Order 13692. Authenticated U.S. Government Information, 8 March 2015, https://www.treasury.gov/resource-center/sanctions/Programs/Documents/13692.pdf (last accessed 24 August 2020).

2.2 *The Appointment of the* "Procurador Especial"

One of Guaidó's announced priorities has been to safeguard Venezuela's international interests. With that aim, on 27 February 2019, he appointed José Ignacio Hernández, a Venezuelan lawyer and administrative and constitutional law professor, as "Procurador Especial"[19] (Special Attorney General).[20]

The National Assembly has also repudiated the General Attorney named by Nicolás Maduro, who is considered a usurper without the power to represent the State. Notably, on 19 March 2019, the National Assembly confirmed the lack of legal authority of Mr. Reinaldo Muñoz Pedroza to act as Attorney General of the Republic, explaining that:

- Any and all acts and contracts executed by Reinaldo Muñoz Pedroza are to be considered inexistent pursuant to Article 138 of the Venezuelan Constitution, and thus, such acts and contracts cannot be attributed to the State;[21]
- The judicial and extrajudicial representation of Venezuela falls exclusively in the mandate of the Procurador Especial appointed by Guaidó and in the lawyers designated by him.[22]

The Procurador Especial has sought to intervene in numerous arbitrations and court proceedings in which the State and its national oil company, Petróleos de Venezuela, S.A. (PDVSA), are involved in order to "defend and represent the rights and interests of the Republic, state companies and other decentralized public entities outside Venezuela."[23] In particular, after the US President officially recognized

---

[19]Legislative Gazzette N° 4, 20 February 2019, http://www.asambleanacional.gob.ve/gacetas (last accessed 24 August 2020).

[20]Art. 15 (b) of the Statute that Governs the Transition to Democracy to Reestablish the Full Force and Effect of the Constitution of the Bolivarian Republic of Venezuela (the "**Estatuto**", a statute approved by the Venezuela National Assembly in accordance with Art. 333 of the Venezuelan Constitution, meant to regulate the "unprecedented and imminent" political change affecting the country).

[21]Art. 1 to the National Assembly's Agreement, 19 March 2019: Ratify that all acts and contracts adopted or signed by Reinaldo Muñoz Pedroza, invoking his status as Attorney General of Republic, must be considered non-existent, in accordance with article 138 of the Constitution of the Bolivarian Republic of Venezuela, and that therefore, such acts and contracts will not be attributable to the State. (Free translation from the author), https://www.asambleanacional.gob.ve/actos/detalle/acuerdo-ratificacion-usurpacion-procurador-general-de-la-republica-y-en-apoyo-del-procurador-especial (last accessed 24 August 2020).

[22]Art. 2 to the National Assembly's Agreement: Ratify that the judicial and extrajudicial representation of the Venezuelan State, including in international arbitrations, rests exclusively with the *Procurador Especial* appointed in accordance with article 15 of the Statute that governs the transition to democracy to restore the validity of the constitution of the Bolivarian Republic of Venezuela, or in the attorneys appointed by him. (Free translation from the author), 19 March 2019, www.asambleanacional.gob.ve/actos/detalle/acuerdo-ratificacion-usurpacion-procurador-general-de-la-republica-y-en-apoyo-del-procurador-especial (last accessed 24 August 2020).

[23]Art. 15(b) of the Statute: (. . .) the President in charge of the Republic may designate whoever acts as special attorney [*procurador especial*] for the defense and representation of the rights and

Guaidó, the *Procurador Especial* has presented motions in at least two cases before the US District Courts:[24] the enforcement procedure of the *Crystallex v. Venezuela* 2016 ICSID Award[25] and the *Red Tree Investment v. PDVSA* case.[26] The Procurador Especial has also sought to intervene in the cases pending against Venezuela at ICSID. Although the US Courts have been willing to abide by the US government's view of the legitimacy of Guaidó, the situation in ICSID has been different.

2.3 ICSID Arbitrations

On 27 March 2019, the Procurador Especial sent a letter to ICSID's Secretary General, Ms. Meg Kinnear, informing of his appointment as Special Attorney General and requesting that:[27]

- The Centre decline to process any request signed or sent by individuals acting on behalf of Nicolás Maduro or the office of the General Attorney of Venezuela, and
- Any communication from ICSID to the Republic of Venezuela should be addressed to the Procurador Especial, and not to Mr. Muñoz Pedroza, who lacks authority to represent the Republic.

---

interests of the Republic, State companies and other international decentralized entities of the Public Administration. The *procurador especial* shall have the capacity to appoint legal representatives, including in international arbitration proceedings, and shall exercise the powers mentioned in numerals 7, 8, 9 and article 13 of the Organic Law and the Office of the Attorney General of the Republic, with the limitations derived from article 84 and this Statute. Such representation will be especially oriented to ensure the protection, control and recovery of State assets abroad, as well as to execute any action that is necessary to safeguard the rights and interests of the State. The *procurador* appointed in this way will have the power to execute any action and exercise all the rights that the *Procurador General* would have, with respect to the assets mentioned here. For such purposes, he must comply with the same conditions that the Law requires to become the [Procurador General de la República] Attorney General of the Republic.

[24] Sondra Faccio, New Developments in Proceedings Involving Venezuela: Interim President Guaidó Intervenes Before US Courts. Kluwer Arbitration Blog, November 24 2019, http://arbitrationblog.kluwerarbitration.com/2019/11/24/new-developments-in-proceedings-involving-venezuela-interim-president-guaido-intervenes-before-us-courts/ (last accessed 24 August 2020).

[25] Crystallex International Corp v. Bolivarian Republic of Venezuela, USCA (3rd Cir. 2019), Opinion of the Court, 29 July 2019, fn. 2, https://www.italaw.com/sites/default/files/case-documents/italaw10704.pdf (last accessed 24 August 2020).

[26] Memorandum of Law in Support of Defendants' Motion for Stay, https://www.courtlistener.com/recap/gov.uscourts.nysd.512231/gov.uscourts.nysd.512231.10.0.pdf (last accessed 24 August 2020).

[27] See tweet by the Special General Attorney, showing the letter sent to ICSID. www.twitter.com/ignandez/status/1110989446189645825 (last accessed 24 August 2020).

The letter was delivered to the arbitral tribunals or annulment committees sitting in proceedings against Venezuela pending at the Centre.[28]

On 29 April 2019, Mr. Hernández wrote again to the Centre, requesting that the Centre *itself* determine who can legitimately represent Venezuela in the cases initiated against it.[29] The Procurador Especial argued that the issue was not merely a procedural question within the power of each individual tribunal and that leaving the decision to each tribunal created the risk of contradictory decisions on the same issue.[30] Almost one year later, on 30 March 2020, Mr. Hernández reiterated the risks derived from ICSID's recognition of the Maduro government in a letter sent to the President of the World Bank, Mr. David Malpass.[31]

Despite the plea of the Procurador Especial, each arbitration tribunal or annulment committee has addressed the issue individually and all of them have decided on maintaining the status quo: maintaining the representation that was acting at the time the decision was made. This means in plain terms that the representative designated by Maduro has continued to represent the State.[32] There is little public information available on the decisions issued by arbitral tribunals and annulment committees, therefore, the cases commented below are some of the few for which there is public information.

The *Favianca* committee was the first panel to decide the issue of Venezuela's representation. The committee found that, taking into account considerations of fairness to both parties and efficiency, the evidence on the record did not justify a change in the status quo.[33] The situation in other ICSID cases against Venezuela is

[28]Jones T, Perry S, ICSID Committee Rebuffs Guaidó. Global Arbitration Review, 10 May 2019, www.globalarbitrationreview.com/Art./1192627/icsid-committee-rebuffs-guaido (last accessed 24 August 2020).

[29]Jones T, Perry S, Guaidó calls on ICSID to take sides. Global Arbitration Review, 2 May 2019, www.globalarbitrationreview.com/Art./1190944/guaido-calls-on-icsid-to-take-sides (last accessed 24 August 2020).

[30]Jones T, Perry S, Guaidó calls on ICSID to take sides. Global Arbitration Review, 2 May 2019, www.globalarbitrationreview.com/Art./1190944/guaido-calls-on-icsid-to-take-sides (last accessed 24 August 2020); Mr. Hernández' Letter to ICSID dated 29 April 2019.

[31]Gobierno Legítimo de Venezuela advierte al Banco Mundial sobre riesgos de reconocer al régimen de Maduro. Centro de comunicación nacional, 31 March 2020, https://presidenciave.com/presidencia/gobierno-legitimo-de-venezuela-advierte-al-banco-mundial-sobre-riesgos-de-reconocer-al-regimen-de-maduro/ (last accessed 24 August 2020).

[32]Sanderson C, Jones T, ICSID committee challenged in Venezuela row. Global Arbitration Review, 17 April 2020, https://globalarbitrationreview.com/article/1225799/icsid-committee-challenged-in-venezuela-row (last accessed 24 August 2020).

[33]Jones T, Perry S, ICSID Committee Rebuffs Guaidó. Global Arbitration Review, 10 May 2019 www.globalarbitrationreview.com/Art./1192627/icsid-committee-rebuffs-guaido (last accessed 24 August 2020).

unclear, although a decision in *Valores*[34] and in the *ConocoPhillips*[35] has been reported.

3 Jurisdiction of ICSID Arbitral Tribunals and Annulment Committees to Determine the Legitimate Representative of a Respondent-State

After the intervention of the Procurador Especial, the preliminary issue before the arbitral tribunals and annulment committees deciding an investment case against Venezuela seems to have been whether the tribunal or committee had jurisdiction to determine who the legitimate representative of the Respondent State is (the "Issue").

According to the ICSID Search Cases Database, Venezuela is listed as respondent under 16 pending cases in the Centre.[36] Six are subject to the Additional Facility Arbitration Rules ("AF Rules") and the other ten are held under the ICSID Arbitration Rules ("ICSID Rules"). Half of the proceedings under the ICSID Rules are being heard by annulment committees.

Thus, for the purposes of the present analysis, the issue of jurisdiction must be analyzed under both sets of rules. Accordingly, this section will analyze whether the arbitral tribunals or committees have jurisdiction to determine the legitimate representative of a State: first, under the ICSID Rules and then, under the AF Rules.

3.1 Jurisdiction Under the ICSID Rules

3.1.1 Parties' Representatives Under the ICSID Rules

The ICSID Rules devote Rule 18 to the Representation of Parties. The Rule:[37]

[34]Valores Mundiales, S.L. and Consorcio Andino S.L. v. Bolivarian Republic of Venezuela, ICSID Case No. ARB/13/11.

[35]ConocoPhillips Petrozuata BV, ConocoPhillips Hamaca B.V. and ConocoPhillips Gulf of Paria BV v Bolivarian Republic of Venezuela (ICSID Case No. ARB/07/30); Sanderson C and Jones T, ICSID committee challenged in Venezuela row. Global Arbitration Review, 17 April 2020, https://globalarbitrationreview.com/article/1225799/icsid-committee-challenged-in-venezuela-row (last accessed 24 August 2020).

[36]ICSID, Advanced Search, https://icsid.worldbank.org/en/Pages/cases/AdvancedSearch.aspx (last accessed 24 August 2020).

[37]ICSID Arbitration Rules, Rule 18: (1) Each party may be represented or assisted by agents, counsel or advocates whose names and authority shall be notified by that party to the Secretary-General, who shall promptly inform the Tribunal and the other party. (2) For the purposes of these Rules, the expression "party" includes, where the context so admits, an agent, counsel or advocate authorized to represent that party.

- acknowledges an absolute right of the parties to be represented by agents and/or counsel of their own choosing, and
- establishes a basic procedure for the notification of the appointment of representatives.

The right to be represented by chosen agents and/or counsel is recognized in Article 42 of the Statute of the International Court of Justice and as a right to a fair trial in Article 6(3)(c) of the European Convention on Human Rights.[38]

The Rule allows any party to be either represented or assisted by "agents", "counsel" or "advocates", but it does not require such representation or assistance. This means that parties may represent themselves before ICSID tribunals or may authorize someone to represent them.[39] However, in the case of countries, representation by agents or counsel is necessary due to the nature of State entities.

ICSID Rules do not provide further details as to the meaning of the terms "representation" or "assistance". The ordinary meaning of the words suggests that the difference between the two concepts lies on the scope of power granted to the person that represents or assists. A representative has the power to speak for and engage the designating party, whereas an assistant to the party will aid in its defense before the arbitral tribunal. In any case, the scope of authority will have to be determined by the designating party.[40]

In disputes between States, these are frequently represented before the arbitral tribunal by agents—in the case of Venezuela, the Procurador General—who are assisted by counsel—the designated law firm. The agents are the full and official representatives of the party, who manage and control the case, and instruct counsel.[41]

The procedure for notification and appointment established under the Rule is quite simple. The names and authority of agents, counsel or advocates must be notified to the Secretary General, who will, in turn, inform the tribunal and the opposing party.

3.1.2 The Authority to Represent a Party Under the ICSID Rules

ICSID Rule 18 does not differentiate between the authority of an agent and that of counsel, or an advocate. Therefore, the designating party must specify in its desig-

---

[38] Baptista and Riofrío Piché (2019), para. 22.69.
[39] Baptista and Riofrío Piché (2019), para. 22.70.
[40] Baptista and Riofrío Piché (2019), para. 22.71.
[41] Baptista and Riofrío Piché (2019), para. 22.72.

nation the scope of authority of the persons designated as agents, counsel or advocates.

Rule 18 does not establish a general requirement for an agent or counsel representing a party to provide a power of attorney or any other proof of authority. However, the ICSID Secretariat, and certainly the arbitral tribunal, have an implied power to request such proof of authority when appropriate.[42]

In usual practice, the party itself or its counsel informs the ICSID Secretariat on its legal representation and attaches a power of attorney. If no power of attorney is provided, the ICSID Secretariat requests that an authorization be provided, which may take the form of a simple letter. Representation is rarely contested in ICSID arbitration, but when it has been, the matter was usually addressed by the arbitral tribunal.[43]

The proper representation of the parties—and especially of States—is crucial, because Article 52(1) of the ICSID Convention states that each party may request the annulment of an award on the grounds that:

- the tribunal was not properly constituted;[44]
- there was a serious departure from a fundamental rule of procedure;[45] or
- the tribunal manifestly exceeded its powers.[46]

An ICSID tribunal could be held as not 'properly constituted' if the person that purported to appoint one of its members had no power to do so under the relevant national law.[47] In principle, Guaidó's Procurador has only sought to represent the State as of 5 February 2019, while the constitution of the tribunals appointed by the Maduro government has not been disputed. It is premature to evaluate whether this could be interpreted as an implicit acceptance of the authority of the Venezuelan representatives, or if an annulment argument could be made based on the improper constitution of the arbitral tribunals.

The proper representation of a party lies in the core of the party's right to present its case, which is a fundamental due process right. The situation in the case of Venezuela, however, is rare and atypical, because it is not an issue of state

---

[42]Interocean Oil Development Company and Interocean Oil Exploration Company v. Federal Republic of Nigeria, ICSID Case No. ARB/13/20, Procedural Order No 5, 15 October 2016, paras 55, 65, 95, 96(a); Baptista and Riofrío Piché (2019), para. 22.81.

[43]Baptista and Riofrío Piché (2019), para. 22.82; Generation Ukraine, Inc. v. Ukraine, ICSID Case No. ARB/00/9, Award, 16 September 2003, para. 16.1.; Scimitar Exploration Limited v. Bangladesh and Bangladesh Oil, Gas and Mineral Corporation, ICSID Case No. ARB/92/2, Award, 5 April 1994, paras 7–8, 21, 25, 29; Interocean Oil Development Company and Interocean Oil Exploration Company v. Federal Republic of Nigeria, ICSID Case No. ARB/13/20, Procedural Order No 5, 15 October 2016, paras 50(a), 52.

[44]Art. 52(1)(a) of the ICSID Convention.

[45]Art. 52(1)(d) of the ICSID Convention.

[46]Art. 52(1)(b) of the ICSID Convention.

[47]Art. 42(1) of the ICSID Convention: The arbitral tribunals must decide a dispute in accordance with such rules of law as may be agreed by the parties.

succession—the Respondent continues to be the Venezuelan State—or even, government succession, but rather of the presence of two competing governments portraying to represent the State. In theory, the State's interest should remain unchanged or could be properly represented by any of the Procuradores. However, the political difference between the governments is so profound that the legal strategy of each government might be very different. Two different governments are requesting to represent the State. If the State is not represented by its legitimate government, can it present its case properly? The argument could certainly be developed to challenge the awards against the State.

Finally, there is a crucial issue regarding the scope of power granted to the arbitral tribunal to control a party's representation, which will be addressed in detail in the following subsection. For now, it suffices to say that arbitral tribunals do not have the power to determine the legitimate government of Venezuela.

3.1.3 The Tribunal's Power to Control a Party's Representation Under the ICSID Arbitration Rules

ICSID Rule 18 leaves very important questions unanswered:

- Is the parties' right to select representatives of their own choosing unrestricted?
- Do ICSID tribunals and annulment committees have the power to exclude an agent or counsel?
- And—more on point with the case of Venezuela—do ICSID tribunals and annulment committees have the power to determine who is the legitimate agent of a State? And, if so, under what circumstances?

The ICSID Convention and the Rules do not explicitly give the power to the tribunal to exclude an agent or counsel. If tribunals assume an authority to which they are not clearly entitled, there is a risk that their award may be annulled on the ground that they have exceeded the scope of their power.[48] To what extent can a tribunal be deemed to have the power to exclude an agent or counsel, or to determine who is the legitimate agent, where such authority is not expressly available?

C. Schreuer confirms that tribunals have an inherent power to take measures to preserve the integrity of the proceedings in the following terms:[49]

> An ICSID tribunal's power to close gaps in the rules of procedure is declaratory of the inherent power of any tribunal to resolve procedural questions in the event of lacunae. In exercising this power, the tribunal may not go beyond the framework of the Convention, the Arbitration Rules and the parties' procedural agreements but must, first of all, attempt to close any apparent gaps through the established methods of interpretation for treaties and other legal documents. But the tribunal is free of the constraints of procedural law in any national legal system of law, including that of the tribunal's seat (see also paras. 3.20 supra). ICSID tribunals have exercised their procedural discretion by formulating general rules for

[48] Art. 52(1)(b) of the ICSID Convention.

[49] Schreuer (2001), p. 683.

the proceedings before them or by making specific decisions. They have done this earlier in the form of procedural orders or informally.

Such inherent power is legally grounded in Article 44 of the Convention, which grants tribunals a gap filling power to address "any question of procedure" which is not covered by the Convention, the ICSID Rules or any rules agreed by the parties.[50] Article 44 is complemented by Rule 19, which provides that the tribunal shall make the orders required for the proceeding.[51]

The more pertinent question then becomes whether the determination of who is the appropriate agent or counsel is a procedural matter.

As mentioned supra, prior ICSID case law dealing with the representation of the parties suggests that the tribunal has jurisdiction to determine a party's representation.

The following cases serve as an example:

In *Generation Ukraine v. Ukraine*, the respondent raised a jurisdictional objection at the final hearing based on an alleged deficiency in the formal appointment of the claimant's counsel by the Board of Directors of Generation Ukraine. The tribunal dismissed the objection as belated, but clarified that even if this had not been so, the tribunal would dismiss it as 'hypertechnical and unmeritorious' because the continuous presence of the sole shareholder of Generation Ukraine at the hearings left no doubt that the corporation chose to be represented by the counsel who appeared on its behalf.[52]

In *Scimitar v. Bangladesh*, the tribunal dismissed the case for lack of jurisdiction under Article 41(5) of the ICSID Rules. The tribunal accepted the respondent's challenge to the tribunal's jurisdiction, based on the fact that the request for arbitration had been introduced by persons not properly authorized and that there was no subsequent authorization under the law of the British Virgin Islands.[53]

More recently in *Interocean v. Nigeria*, the claimant requested that the tribunal direct the State to produce an instrument authorizing an English law firm—who had initially been engaged by the respondent 'to act as Co-counsel along with Counsel already on record'—to act as counsel to the respondent. The tribunal found that there were inconsistencies, ambiguities and contradictions in the manner in which respondent had addressed the authority of its counsel, and ordered the respondent to submit

---

[50]Art. 44 of the ICSID Convention: Any arbitration proceeding shall be conducted in accordance with the provisions of this Section and, except as the parties otherwise agree, in accordance with the Arbitration Rules in effect on the date on which the parties consented to arbitration. If any question of procedure arises which is not covered by this Section or the Arbitration Rules or any rules agreed by the parties, the Tribunal shall decide the question.

[51]Commission and Moloo (2018), para. 1.17.

[52]Generation Ukraine, Inc. v. Ukraine, ICSID Case No. ARB/00/9, Award, 16 September 2003, para. 16.1.

[53]Scimitar Exploration Limited v. Bangladesh and Bangladesh Oil, Gas and Mineral Corporation, ICSID Case No. ARB/92/2, Award, 5 April 1994, paras 7–8, 21, 25, 29.

a letter from the Attorney General confirming that the law firm was validly appearing on behalf of the respondent in the proceedings.[54]

Other cases have dealt more closely with the tribunal's power to exclude counsel. The following issues have arisen in cases regarding the existence of conflicts of interests: Counselor- arbitrator conflicts and counsel-party conflicts.

For example, the emergence of a conflict of interest between counsel and one of the arbitrators arose through the nomination of counsel after the constitution of the arbitral tribunal,[55] which could imperil the tribunal's status or legitimacy. In *Hrvatska* and *Rompetrol*, the tribunal recognized the fundamental principle that parties are free to organize their representation, and acknowledged that ICSID tribunals have no explicit power to exclude counsel.[56] Yet, in *Hrvatska*, the tribunal excluded counsel[57] based on the immutability of properly constituted tribunals enshrined in Article 56(1) of the Convention.[58] In *Rompetrol*, although the tribunal remained silent over whether it had power to exclude counsel, it did hold that if such power existed, it would be one "to be exercised only rarely and in compelling circumstances",[59] and it refrained from interfering with claimant's choice of counsel.

[54]Interocean Oil Development Company and Interocean Oil Exploration Company v. Federal Republic of Nigeria, ICSID Case No. ARB/13/20, Procedural Order No 5, 15 October 2016, paras 50(a), 52.

[55]Hrvatska Elektroprivreda d.d. v. Republic of Slovenia, ICSID Case No. ARB/05/24, Order Concerning the Participation of Counsel, 6 May 2008; Rompetrol Group N.V. v. Romania, ICSID Case No. ARB/06/3, Decision of the Tribunal on the Participation of a Counsel, 14 January 2010.

[56]Hrvatska Elektroprivreda d.d. v. Republic of Slovenia, ICSID Case No. ARB/05/24, Order Concerning the Participation of Counsel, 6 May 2008, para. 24.; Rompetrol Group N.V. v. Romania, ICSID Case No. ARB/06/3, Decision of the Tribunal on the Participation of a Counsel, 14 January 2010, para. 20.

[57]In *Hrvatska* the claimant challenged a counsel appointed by the respondent on the ground that he was a barrister at the same chambers as the president of the tribunal. The claimant was notified of the participation of the barrister only shortly before the hearing. The tribunal found that, although the respondent was free to select its legal team as it saw fit prior to the constitution of the tribunal, it was not entitled to subsequently amend the composition of its legal team in such a fashion as to imperil the tribunal's status or legitimacy. The tribunal concluded that a fundamental principle (such as that of a party's right to choose its representative) must give way to overriding exceptions. In that case, such overriding exception was that of the immutability of properly constituted tribunals enshrined in Art. 56(1) of the Convention. In light of the fundamental rule determined in Art. 56(1) of the Convention and given its inherent procedural powers confirmed by Art. 44 of the Convention, the tribunal concluded that it had the power to exclude counsel and that the circumstances of the case required so.

[58]Hrvatska Elektroprivreda d.d. v. Republic of Slovenia, ICSID Case No. ARB/05/24, Order Concerning the Participation of Counsel, 6 May 2008, para. 25.

[59]Rompetrol Group N.V. v. Romania, ICSID Case No. ARB/06/3, Decision of the Tribunal on the Participation of a Counsel, 14 January 2010, para. 18.

3.1.4 The Situation Created by Venezuela's Dual Government

However, none of the cases deal with the situation created by Venezuela's dual government, and hence such tribunals did not decide whether they had jurisdiction to determine who is the legitimate agent or representative of a State party for the specific case.[60]

The above-mentioned cases decided:

- whether a party was represented by the counsel on record, and thus accept without a doubt that they had the power to decide such procedural issue for the case;[61] or
- whether the involvement of new counsel imperiled the proceedings, in which case, they admitted that they had no express power to exclude counsel, yet under the circumstances of the case acted to protect a competing fundamental principle[62] or not.[63]

However, those tribunals were not put in a position where they would have to choose between two competing agents of the same State and determine the legitimate one.

The determination of who the legitimate government of a State is, is a highly political question. In fact, "there is probably no other subject in the field of international relations in which law and politics appear to be more closely interwoven."[64]

Political issues are clearly outside the scope of ICSID arbitral tribunals, both under the BITs and the ICSID Convention.

If one were to analyze the BITs signed by Venezuela—or any BIT—it would be shocking to find a provision giving investment arbitral tribunals jurisdiction to determine any political matter. In general, the jurisdiction granted to investment tribunals by BITs is limited to:

- disputes arising between a Contracting Party and an investor of the other Contracting Party
- related to the fulfillment of any of the treaty's dispositions
- as regards an investment of the investor.

---

[60]Of course, the author recognizes the principle of *kompetenz-kompetenz* enshrined in Art. 41(1) of the ICSID Convention, and thus, has no doubt that the Tribunal shall be the judge of its own competence. In this case, only to find that it is not within its jurisdiction to determine who is the legitimate representative of the Respondent State for that case, much less in general.

[61]Generation Ukraine, para. 16.1; Scimitar Exploration paras 7–8, 21, 25, 29; Interocean Oil, paras 50(a), 52.

[62]Hrvatska Elektroprivreda d.d. v. Republic of Slovenia, ICSID Case No. ARB/05/24, Order Concerning the Participation of Counsel, 6 May 2008.

[63]Rompetrol Group N.V. v. Romania, ICSID Case No. ARB/06/3, Decision of the Tribunal on the Participation of a Counsel, 14 January 2010.

[64]Crawford (2012), p. 144. (Crawford was referring to the recognition of States, but the recognition of governments is addressed by the author in the same chapter and he is of the opinion that recognition of government and state is closely related, although not identical.)

For example, the BIT between Venezuela and Uruguay, which is the basis of one of the many ICSID cases against Venezuela, limits the jurisdiction of the arbitral tribunals to:[65]

> Any dispute arising between an investor of a contracting state and the other contracting state over the latter's fulfilment of the provisions of the present Agreement related to the former's investment, and which cannot be resolved amicably, shall be submitted to the courts of the contracting state or to arbitration, at the investor's choice. [Free translation]

The same is true of the ICSID Convention, which limits the jurisdiction of the Centre to legal disputes arising directly out of investments between a Contracting State an a national of another Contracting State:

> Article 25(1) The jurisdiction of the Centre shall extend to any legal dispute arising directly out of an investment, between a Contracting State (or any constituent subdivision or agency of a Contracting State designated to the Centre by that State) and a national of another Contracting State, which the parties to the dispute consent in writing to submit to the Centre. When the parties have given their consent, no party may withdraw its consent unilaterally.

The determination of the legitimate representative of a State is a political dispute, not a legal one arising directly out of an investment.[66]

The decision to recognize a government is a discretionary and sovereign act. The United Nations acknowledges this principle, stating that such decisions fall within the sovereign power of states themselves: "The recognition of a new State or government is an act that only other States and governments may grant or withhold."[67]

Thus, the inevitable conclusion is that ICSID arbitration tribunals or annulment committees have no jurisdiction to decide which of the Venezuelan *Procuradores* is the rightful representative of the State.[68] If they did have jurisdiction, however, they would have to analyze the issue both under international law and under domestic law.[69]

---

[65] Art. 9 of the Venezuela-Uruguay BIT, https://investmentpolicy.unctad.org/international-investment-agreements/treaty-files/2382/download (last accessed 24 August 2020).

[66] ICSID Arbitration Rules, Rule 53: The provisions of these Rules shall apply mutatis mutandis to any procedure relating to the interpretation, revision or annulment of an award and to the decision of the Tribunal or Committee.

[67] About UN Membership. United Nations, www.un.org/en/sections/member-states/about-un-membership/index.html (last accessed 24 August 2020); European Parliament Resolution on Recognition of Palestine Statehood. (2014/2964(RSP), 17 December 2014, www.europarl.europa.eu/doceo/document/TA-8-2014-0103_EN.html (last accessed 24 August 2020). The European Parliament takes the same position, as evidenced by its 2014 resolution on the recognition of the Palestinian State: "the recognition of the State of Palestine falls in the competence of the Member States."

[68] Valores Mundiales, S.L. and Consorcio Andino S.L. v. Bolivarian Republic of Venezuela, ICSID Case No. ARB/13/11, Procedural Order No. 2, 29 August 2019, para. 31.

[69] Art. 42(1) of ICSID Convention: (...) In the absence of such agreement, the Tribunal shall apply the law of the Contracting State party to the dispute and such rules of international law as may be applicable.

3.1.5 Decisions Made by Annulment Committees on Venezuela's Representation

Despite this, at least three arbitral tribunals and one annulment committee have addressed the issue and have decided that there was no need to change the status quo (rejecting the participation of the Procurador Especial and maintaining Maduro's Procurador as Venezuela's legitimate representative in the case). The publicly available resources in this regard are very limited, and include e.g. the *Valores* decision and reports of the *Favianca* and *ConocoPhillips* decisions, so, any conclusions reached are preliminary and based on these sources.

The Favianca[70] annulment committee noted that under the ICSID Convention and the BIT, "the State, as such" is the respondent party in the proceeding. It observed that until now the State has been represented by the people appointed to that end by the Attorney General's Office, as required by Venezuelan law.[71] The committee found that, taking into account considerations of fairness to both parties and efficiency, the evidence on the record did not justify a change in the status quo and, thus, only allowed the Maduro government to represent the State.[72]

In *Valores*, the annulment committee also found that Maduro's Procurador ought to continue representing Venezuela in the arbitration.[73] The committee analyzed the issue pursuant to national and international law:

- Pursuant to international law, the committee found that there had not been a change in government under international law. The committee explained that the State's representation is held by the government, that is to say, the individual with effective control over the territory. The committee decided that the Procurador Especial was unable to prove that the President of the National Assembly, Mr. Guaidó, effectively holds control of the Republic, even if recognized as the legitimate government by many States.[74]
- Based on Venezuelan law, the committee pointed out that the Estatuto and the designation of Mr. Guaidó as president were voided by the Venezuelan Supreme

[70]Fábrica de Vidrios Los Andes, C.A. and Owens-Illinois de Venezuela, C.A. v. Bolivarian Republic of Venezuela, ICSID Case No. ARB/12/21.

[71]Jones T, Perry S, ICSID committee rebuffs Guaidó. Global Arbitration Review, 10 May 2019, www.globalarbitrationreview.com/Art./1192627/icsid-committee-rebuffs-guaido (last accessed 24 August 2020).

[72]Jones T, Perry S, ICSID committee rebuffs Guaidó. Global Arbitration Review, 10 May 2019, www.globalarbitrationreview.com/Art./1192627/icsid-committee-rebuffs-guaido (last accessed 24 August 2020).

[73]Valores Mundiales, S.L. and Consorcio Andino S.L. v. Bolivarian Republic of Venezuela, ICSID Case No. ARB/13/11, Procedural Order No. 2, 29 August 2019, para. 51. https://jusmundi.com/en/document/decision/es-valores-mundiales-s-l-y-consorcio-andino-s-l-c-republica-bolivariana-de-venezuela-resolucion-procesal-no-2-thursday-29th-august-2019 (last accessed 24 August 2020).

[74]Valores Mundiales, S.L. and Consorcio Andino S.L. v. Bolivarian Republic of Venezuela, ICSID Case No. ARB/13/11, Procedural Order No. 2, 29 August 2019, paras 48–49.

Court, who guards the constitutionality of Venezuelan Laws pursuant to Article 335 of the Venezuelan Constitution.[75]

The *Valores* annulment committee outright acknowledged that it could not decide with an erga omnes effect on who is Venezuela's legitimate government.[76] Thus, to solve the request in a practical way, it narrowed down the issue to a strictly procedural matter, limited to the specific proceeding:[77] deciding who can speak for the State and, thus, who the committee should recognize in the following procedural steps.[78]

The committee distinguished its case from *Heemsen v. Venezuela*[79] and *Longreef v. Venezuela*[80]—where the arbitrators declared themselves incompetent to resolve matters similar to the one raised by the Procurador Especial in *Valores*—on the basis that in those cases the issue was prompted by the claimants who sought a declaration on the validity of the acts performed by Venezuela's representatives.[81] The committee considered that in *Heemsen* and *Longreef*, the request was of a substantive nature, whereas in their case—as in *Favianca* and *Air Canada v. Venezuela*[82]—the issue affected the "normal development of the process".

Whether the issue raised by the appointment of the Procurador Especial is substantive or procedural in nature is debatable, as discussed in the prior sections of this chapter. However, the annulment committee, conscious of the limits of its own jurisdiction, took a pragmatic approach: it shifted the scope of the decision and found a solution to continue with the case. The solution is final since there is no review for decisions taken by annulment committees, and thus, no remedy is available to the State.[83]

In any case, the decision raises the question of whether the analysis of the Committee was appropriate under international law. Arguably the opposite conclu-

[75] Valores Mundiales, S.L. and Consorcio Andino S.L. v. Bolivarian Republic of Venezuela, ICSID Case No. ARB/13/11, Procedural Order No. 2, 29 August 2019, para. 32.

[76] Valores Mundiales, S.L. and Consorcio Andino S.L. v. Bolivarian Republic of Venezuela, ICSID Case No. ARB/13/11, Procedural Order No. 2, 29 August 2019, para. 31.

[77] Valores Mundiales, S.L. and Consorcio Andino S.L. v. Bolivarian Republic of Venezuela, ICSID Case No. ARB/13/11, Procedural Order No. 2, 29 August 2019, para. 32.

[78] Valores Mundiales, S.L. and Consorcio Andino S.L. v. Bolivarian Republic of Venezuela, ICSID Case No. ARB/13/11, Procedural Order No. 2, 29 August 2019, para. 32.

[79] Enrique Heemsen and Jorge Heemsen v. Bolivarian Republic of Venezuela, PCA Case No. 2017-18.

[80] Longreef investments AVV v. Bolivarian Republic of Venezuela, ICSID Case No. ARB/11/5, Annulment Procedure.

[81] Valores Mundiales, S.L. and Consorcio Andino S.L. v. Bolivarian Republic of Venezuela, ICSID Case No. ARB/13/11, Procedural Order No. 2, 29 August 2019, paras 36–37.

[82] Air Canada v. Bolivarian Republic of Venezuela, ICSID Case No. ARB(AF)/17/1.

[83] The only practical recourse would be to raise the issue when opposing execution of the Award, which comes with its own legal challenges.

sion could be reached, because the illegality[84] tainting the effective government is so central to the question of governmental status that international law may justifiably, and exceptionally, treat the non-effective (but representative and independent) government as the legitimate authority of the State.[85]

In addition, under international law, recognition of an authority (most frequently in exile) as a government has been treated by courts as strong, or even, conclusive evidence of the governmental status of such authority;[86] an analysis overlooked by the annulment committee. Indeed, the Guaidó government is not a government in exile, but precisely, its lack of effective control over the country makes it remarkably similar to one. Thus, recognition by many of the world's leading countries could, under international law, lead to the conclusion that indeed, Guaidó ought to be the legitimate representative of the Venezuelan State also before investment tribunals analyzing the State's actions.

Finally, the arbitral tribunal's analysis of Venezuelan law is superfluous.[87] Under Venezuelan law, the Supreme Court lost its original legitimacy when in December 2015, 13 judges and 21 substitute judges were appointed by the then-Maduro-controlled National Assembly in violation of the Constitution and the laws.[88] A few days earlier, the opposition had won the elections to take over the National Assembly, which is the only internationally recognized legitimate State organ. Thus, the appointments were made surreptitiously and without following the prescribed legal terms to ensure the loyalty of the high court to Maduro. The consequence of such loyalty is a clear rupture of the rule of law. As has been internationally recognized, the only legitimate organ of the Venezuelan State is the National Assembly, which has ratified that Maduro's Procurador cannot represent or bind the Venezuelan State with his actions or omissions.[89] Thus, under Venezuela law,

---

[84]For example, by violating human rights, creating a humanitarian crisis, preventing the International community from proving aid to diminish the crisis, and staying in government through fraudulent elections.

[85]Talmon (1999), pp. 499–537. This issue could be the subject of an independent paper on its own, which the author would like to address in the future.

[86]Talmon (1998), pp. 189–190.

[87]Although probably based on the evidence presented by the parties.

[88]A strict analysis over the illegitimacy of the appointment of the judges to the Supreme Court would require a constitutional analysis which escapes the scope of this paper. However, the lack of legitimacy of the Venezuelan Supreme Court has been widely denounced *inter alia* by the Venezuelan Attorney General, the National Federation of Lawyers and the *Procurador Especial* in his role as an administrative law professor. *See* Fiscal pide anular designación de magistrados y responsabiliza al Gobierno por seguridad de su familia. Informe21, 12 June 2017, www.informe21.com/politica/fiscal-luisa-ortega-pide-anular-la-designacion-de-33-magistrados-del-tsj (last accessed 24 August 2020); Federación Nacional de Abogados emite nota de protesta ante sentencias del TSJ. Versión Final, 1 April 2017, www.versionfinal.com.ve/politica-dinero/federacion-nacional-de-abogados-emite-nota-de-protesta-ante-sentencias-del-tsj-pronunciamiento (last accessed 24 August 2020).

[89]National Assembly's Agreement. 19 March 2019, www.asambleanacional.gob.ve/actos/detalle/acuerdo-ratificacion-usurpacion-procurador-general-de-la-republica-y-en-apoyo-del-procurador-especial (last accessed 24 August 2020).

the annulment committee could have found that the *Procurador Especial* was the rightful representative of Venezuela.

The *ConocoPhillips*[90] annulment committee seems to have taken a slightly different approach. In the underlying proceeding, the Republic was represented by De Jesús & Jesús and Curtis Mallet-Prevost Colt & Mosle. However, in the annulment proceeding the Maduro government instructed Gugliemino & Asociados and De Jesús & Jesús, while the *Procurador Especial* instructed Curtis Mallet-Prevost Colt & Mosle. On 3 April 2020, the *ConocoPhillips* committee issued a decision agreeing with other committees and tribunals that it should maintain the status quo of Venezuela's representation—but because both counsel appeared in the underlying arbitration, it found that it would be procedurally fair for both counsel to continue.[91] Thus, in this case counsel instructed by both *Procuradores* would be allowed to plead for the State.

3.2 Jurisdiction Under the ICSID Additional Facility Rules

Venezuela denounced the ICSID Convention in January 2012,[92] and its withdrawal became effective on July 2012. This has inter alia the following relevant implications:

- Venezuela would no longer be subject to the ICSID Convention or be part of the ICSID system;
- Arbitrations against Venezuela based on bilateral investment treaties would have to be pursued under the ICSID AF Rules, other institutional rules, or be ad hoc;
- Venezuela would no longer have a representative at ICSID's Administrative Council.

Since most of Venezuela's BITs provide an opportunity to arbitrate under UNICTRAL Arbitration Rules or ICSID Additional Facility Rules, claims against Venezuela have been submitted under both sets of rules.

[90] ConocoPhillips Petrozuata BV, ConocoPhillips Hamaca B.V. and ConocoPhillips Gulf of Paria BV v Bolivarian Republic of Venezuela, ICSID Case No. ARB/07/30.

[91] Sanderson C, Jones T, ICSID committee Challenged in Venezuela Row. Global Arbitration Review, 17 April 2020, https://globalarbitrationreview.com/article/1225799/icsid-committee-challenged-in-venezuela-row (last accessed 24 August 2020).

[92] Gobierno Bolivariano denuncia ante el Banco Mundial convenio con Ciadi. NJGI, 25 January 2012, www.democracyctr.org/justinvestment_org_es/2012/01/gobierno-venezolano-denuncia-ante-el-banco-mundial-convenio-con-ciadi (last accessed 24 August 2020).

3.2.1 The Distinction Between ICSID and AF Arbitrations

A critical distinction between the two is that while ICSID arbitrations do not have a true seat of arbitration and operate in a self-contained system, independent of domestic procedural law, arbitrations under ICSID's Additional Facility have a true seat and are subject to the domestic procedural law of that seat. Article 20 of the AF Rules calls for the tribunal to determine a "place of arbitration ... after consultation with the parties and the Secretariat" and further requires that "(t)he award shall be made at the place of arbitration."[93] Accordingly, an award under AF Rules would be subject to:[94]

- the appeal or review mechanisms established in the law of the place of arbitration, and
- the rules contained in national laws and applicable treaties.

Article 1 of the AF Rules requires the Tribunal to consider the mandatory law of the seat of the arbitration when resolving procedural disputes:[95]

> Where the parties to a dispute have agreed that it shall be referred to arbitration under the Arbitration (AF) Rules, the dispute shall be settled in accordance with these Rules, save that if any of these Rules is in conflict with a provision of the law applicable to the arbitration from which the parties cannot derogate, that provision shall prevail.

Rules 26[96] and 27[97] of the AF Rules are dedicated to the treatment of party representatives and procedural orders respectively, and they replicate Rules 18 and 19 of the ICSID Rules. Hence, the AF Rules—like the ICSID Rules—are silent as to the procedure to follow when two separate governments purport to represent a party in an arbitration.

In addition, since the ICSID Convention is not applicable, in an AF arbitration, the arbitrator's gap filling powers are derived from Rule 35 of the AF Rules, which expressly grants the arbitral tribunal the power to decide "any question of procedure", which is not covered by the AF Rules or any rules agreed by the Parties.

---

[93] Art. 20(3) of ICSID AF Arbitration Rules.

[94] Schreuer (2001), p. 1244; Overview of Arbitration under the ICSID Additional Facility. www.icsid.worldbank.org/en/Pages/process/Overview-ICSID-Additional-Facility-Arbitration.aspx (last accessed 24 August 2020). Explaining that "(i)n addition to the provisions of the Arbitration (Additional Facility) Rules, the laws of the place of arbitration apply to the proceeding."

[95] Art. 1 of the ICSID AF Arbitration Rules.

[96] Art. 26 of the ICSID AF Arbitration Rules: Representation of the Parties: (1) Each party may be represented or assisted by agents, counsel or advocates whose names and authority shall be notified by that party to the Secretariat, which shall promptly inform the Tribunal and the other party. (2) For the purposes of these Rules, the expression "party" includes, where the context so admits, an agent, counsel or advocate authorized to represent that party.

[97] Art. 27 of the ICSID AF Arbitration Rules: Procedural Orders: The Tribunal shall make the orders required for the conduct of the proceeding.

This leads to the same question raised under the ICSID Rules: whether the determination of who the appropriate agent or counsel is, is a procedural matter. The answer has already been addressed by the author in the negative, with the obvious consequence that the arbitral tribunals under the AF Rules would also have no jurisdiction to decide who is the legitimate government of the Respondent State.

However, in an AF arbitration, if a tribunal considers that it has jurisdiction to decide such issue,[98] the tribunal should consider any mandatory law of the seat of the arbitration to determine who should be recognized as Venezuela's proper party representative.

The concept that an arbitration is governed by the law of the place in which it is held is "well established in both the theory and practice of international arbitration".[99] The seat provides an external source of procedural rules and control over the arbitration and serves as a territorial link between the arbitration itself and the law of the place in which such arbitration is legally situated.[100] The law of the seat of arbitration provides rules that govern the conduct of arbitral proceedings, in particular, in relation to the level of due process to be afforded the parties[101] and the rights of representatives to appear on behalf of parties.[102]

3.2.2 Consequences for the Annulment and Enforcement of Awards

The fact that there is a seat of arbitration also has important implications in relation to the annulment, and recognition and enforcement of the award. In a jurisdiction that follows the UNCITRAL Model law and that is a signatory to the New York

---

[98]Which the author submits that it does not, for the same reasons analyzed supra in the case of ICSID Arbitrations.

[99]Blackaby et al. (2015), p. 172.

[100]Blackaby et al. (2015), p. 173: Stating that "the place, or 'seat', of the arbitration is not merely a matter of geography. It is the territorial link between the arbitration itself and the law of the place in which that arbitration is legally situated: When one says that London, Paris or Geneva is the place of arbitration, one does not refer solely to a geographical location. One means that the arbitration is conducted within the framework of the law of arbitration of England, France or Switzerland or, to use an English expression, under the curial law of the relevant country. The geographical place of arbitration is the factual connecting factor between that arbitration law and the arbitration proper, considered as a nexus of contractual and procedural rights and obligations between the parties and the arbitrators. The seat of an arbitration is thus often intended to be its legal centre of gravity.

[101]Webster and Buhler (2014), p. 344: Stating that "the Tribunal must ensure that the procedure meets the requirements of due process at the place of arbitration, the issue is what those basic requirements are and how they are interpreted in some of the major centers of arbitration."

[102]Born (2015), pp. 599–600.

Convention, the award could be annulled or its enforcement and recognition could be refused if the competent court finds that:

- the party against whom the award is invoked was "unable to present its case."[103]
- or if the award would be contrary to the public policy of the court's country.[104]

On these two points, it is reasonable to sustain that:

- Being represented by an illegitimate government could violate the State's due process rights because, unless the conduct is ratified, it implies that the State has not been properly represented and that
- Recognition of a foreign government is part of a State's public policy, because it concerns a political decision drawn by a myriad of strategic national concerns.

Venezuela is no stranger to these realities and has in the past emphasized the importance of the seat's laws to the conduct of an arbitration. For example, in *Gold Reserve v. Republic of Venezuela*, a case before the U.S. District Court for the District of Columbia, Venezuela opposed recognition and enforcement of an ICSID award issued under the AF Rules, highlighting that the underlying arbitration had been "seated in Paris, France, governed by French arbitration law, and conducted under the judicial supervisory authority of the courts in Paris".[105] Venezuela explained that it had filed a petition to annul the arbitration award before the Paris Court of Appeal, "which has jurisdiction over petitions to set aside arbitration awards seated in Paris".[106] Venezuela also justified that its set-aside petition in France was based, *inter alia*, on the arbitral tribunal's purported denial of Venezuela's "due process under French law through inequitable treatment of the parties", and because the Tribunal had allegedly "disregarded its mandate under French law".[107] Venezuela urged the U.S. court to "not recognize under the

[103]Convention on the Recognition and Enforcement of Foreign Arbitral Awards (New York Convention), opened for signature 10 June 1958, Art V.1(b); UNCITRAL Model Law on International Commercial Arbitration (UNCITRAL Model Law), Art 34.2.a(ii).

[104]New York Convention, Art. V.2.(b); UNCITRAL Model Law, Art. 34.2.b(ii).

[105]Gold Reserve v. Republic of Venezuela, Case I: 14-cv-02014- JEB, Doc. 19, 6 (D.D.C. 12 June 2015), Respondent Bolivarian Republic of Venezuela's Motion to Dismiss Petition and to Deny Recognition of Arbitral Award, or in the Alternative, to Stay Enforcement, with Incorporated Memorandum of points and Authorities, https://www.italaw.com/sites/default/files/case-documents/italaw10196.pdf (last accessed 24 August 2020).

[106]Gold Reserve v. Republic of Venezuela, Case I: 14-cv-02014- JEB, Doc. 19, 6 (D.D.C. 12 June 2015), Respondent Bolivarian Republic of Venezuela's Motion to Dismiss Petition and to Deny Recognition of Arbitral Award, or in the Alternative, to Stay Enforcement, with Incorporated Memorandum of points and Authorities, p. 22/50, https://www.italaw.com/sites/default/files/case-documents/italaw10196.pdf (last accessed 24 August 2020).

[107]Gold Reserve v. Republic of Venezuela, Case I: 14-cv-02014- JEB, Doc. 19, 6 (D.D.C. 12 June 2015), Respondent Bolivarian Republic of Venezuela's Motion to Dismiss Petition and to Deny Recognition of Arbitral Award, or in the Alternative, to Stay Enforcement, with Incorporated Memorandum of points and Authorities, p. 22/50, https://www.italaw.com/sites/default/files/case-documents/italaw10196.pdf (last accessed 24 August 2020).

New York Convention an award that is the result of procedures that violate the law of the seat of the arbitration".[108]

Accordingly, under the AF Rules, the arbitral tribunal ought to consider the law of the seat of arbitration when determining the question of the proper representation of Venezuela in international arbitration proceedings.

3.2.3 Case Study: Seat of Arbitration: Paris, France

For example, if the arbitration is seated in Paris, France, the tribunal would have to take French law into consideration. In France, as in many other countries, the executive branch has exclusive jurisdiction to decide the country's international relations, including whether to recognize a particular government of a foreign state.[109] France's legislative power can, at most, invite the executive to recognize or withdraw recognition of a State or government.[110]

In particular, due to the "Act of Government" doctrine, a decision by the French executive to recognize a foreign government cannot be challenged before French courts. Acts of Government—which include acts concerning international relations, "adopted by the French authorities in the conduct of diplomatic and foreign relations"[111]—enjoy immunity from judicial review.[112] The decision to recognize a government is an act adopted in the conduct of foreign relations. The recognition of a foreign government under French law can therefore only be carried out by the executive branch and is not subject to judicial review.

For present purposes, this means that French courts must abide by the executive's decision to recognize a particular foreign government and its representatives, which relieves them from having to decide the issue. The French Directory of International Law explains it in the following terms:

> (T)he recognition therefore clarifies a highly troubled international situation; it also clarifies it in the internal order of the recognizing State. Indeed, its courts could hesitate to grant the new State the benefit of State prerogatives as long as their government had not recognized it: here again, recognition puts an end to uncertainty.[113]

[108]Gold Reserve v. Republic of Venezuela, Case I: 14-cv-02014- JEB, Doc. 19, 6 (D.D.C. 12 June 2015), Respondent Bolivarian Republic of Venezuela's Motion to Dismiss Petition and to Deny Recognition of Arbitral Award, or in the Alternative, to Stay Enforcement, with Incorporated Memorandum of points and Authorities, p. 32/50, https://www.italaw.com/sites/default/files/case-documents/italaw10196.pdf (last accessed 24 August 2020).

[109]Art. 52 of the French Constitution: (T)he President of the Republic shall negotiate and ratify (international) treaties; French Const. Art. 14: (T)he President of the Republic shall accredit ambassadors and envoys extraordinary to foreign powers; foreign ambassadors and envoys extraordinary shall be accredited to him.

[110]Assemblée Nationale Français, Resolution on Recognition of Palestine Statehood, JI 5, Dec. 2, 2014 "Invit(ing) the French Government to recognize the State of Palestine" http://www.assemblee-nationale.fr/14/ta/ta0439.asp (last accessed 24 August 2020).

[111]Chapus (1990), p. 950.

[112]Conseil d'Etat, No. 120437/120737, Sept. 23, 1992; Conseil d'Etat, No. 171277, Sept. 29, 1995.

[113]Danic (2013), pp. 527–528.

The *Tribunal administratif de Paris* applied this reasoning in a case in which Colonel Gaddafi's government disputed the Libyan National Transitional Council's (NTC) right to act on behalf of Libya's Economic and Social Development Fund. The NTC argued that Gaddafi's government claim was inadmissible because France's decision to recognize the NTC as the holder of Libyan governmental authority was an Act of Government.[114] The *Tribunal administratif de Paris* agreed, considering that:[115]

> (T)he act of legal and political recognition of the National Transitional Council (NTC) as the holder of Libyan governmental authority is inseparable from the conduct of France's international relations and therefore escapes any judicial review.

Thus, the French court denied the claim brought by Colonel Gaddafi's government representative because France had recognized the NTC, and the latter's right to act on behalf of Libya could not be challenged.

In the present case, France, together with eighteen other EU Member States, recognized Mr. Juan Guaidó as Interim President of Venezuela on 4 February 2019, by way of a joint statement:[116]

> France along with Spain, Portugal, Germany, the United Kingdom, Denmark, the Netherlands, Hungary, Austria, Finland, Belgium, Luxemburg, the Czech Republic, Latvia, Lithuania, Estonia, Poland, Sweden and Croatia takes note that Mr. Nicolas Maduro has chosen not to set in motion the electoral process. Subsequently, and in accordance with the provisions of the Venezuelan Constitution, they acknowledge and support Mr. Juan Guaidó, President of the democratically elected National Assembly, as President ad interim of Venezuela, in order for him to call for free, fair and democratic presidential elections.

The decision of France's executive to recognize Mr. Guaidó as Venezuela's Interim President as of 4 February 2019 is an Act of Government that is binding on France's administrative, civil, and criminal courts. President Guaidó's decision to appoint a Special Attorney General is similarly binding on French courts, in that it is an administrative decision issued by a properly recognized foreign authority.[117]

In these circumstances, an AF Tribunal seated in Paris, France would be justified in recognizing Mr. José Ignacio Hernández G., the Special Attorney-General of

---

[114]Cowell A, Erlanger S, France Becomes First Country to Recognize Libyan Rebels. The New York Times, 10 March 2011, www.nytimes.com/2011/03/11/world/europe/11france.html (last accessed 24 August 2020). In 2011, France's Minister for Foreign Affairs, publicly announced that Libya's National Transitional Council was the sole holder of governmental authority in France's relations with the Libyan State and its Entities.

[115]Tribunal administratif de Paris, No. 1111788, July 25, 2011.

[116]Joint Declaration on Venezuela. France Diplomatie, 4 February 2019, https://www.diplomatie.gouv.fr/IMG/pdf/2019_02_04_joint_declaration_on_venezuela_cle42db6d.pdf (last accessed 24 August 2020).

[117]Tribunal administratif de Paris, No. 1111788, 25 July 2011, holding that "it is not for the French administrative court, the ordinary court of the French administration, to rule, even by way of exception, on the legality of an administrative decision issued by a foreign authority, appointing, in this case, the Director of the Libya's Economic and Social Development Fund."

Venezuela appointed by President Guaidó, as Venezuela's representative in the proceeding as of 4 February 2019—just as any French court would do.[118]

The same is true if the seat of arbitration were located in the United States of America (or in the UK).[119] The courts of the US, which follow the Estrada Doctrine, have already decided the issue.[120] On 23 January 2019, the US President recognized Guaidó as the Interim President of Venezuela. The US courts consider that the issue of what government is to be regarded as the representative of a foreign state is a political, not a judicial question, and thus is to be determined by the Executive branch of government. Thus, the US Courts of Appeals for the D.C. Circuit ruled that, following the decision of the Executive, Guaidó's counsel could appear on behalf of Venezuela defending the State against the enforcement of an ICSID Award.[121]

This approach is consistent with international law. Indeed, Stefan Talmon—who has thoroughly studied the issue of recognition of governments under international law—is unhesitant that authorities (in exile) recognized by a state are allowed to bring action, intervene or be sued on behalf of the State:[122]

> (A)t least in national courts, authorities in exile which were formally recognized by the forum State as governments or with which the forum State government has had government-to-government dealings have as a rule, been allowed to bring an action, to intervene, or to be sued on behalf of their State. On the other hand, authorities in exile which were not recognized as governments were regarded as lacking competence to instruct counsel to act on behalf of the State.

In summary, an AF tribunal faced with the Issue must acknowledge that it lacks jurisdiction to choose which government is the representative of the State. However, it cannot overlook:

- that its award can be set aside in the competent courts of the seat of arbitration, if it has failed to give Venezuela an opportunity to present its case or if the award could be considered contrary the seat's public policy; and

[118]In fact, in the PDVSA v. Petropar case an ICC Tribunal seated in Paris decided on a request filed by the Paraguayan State entity, Petropar, to stay the proceedings and strike out the Claimant (PDVSA)'s reply on the merits on the ground that the latter represents the views of the Maduro government, which is not recognized by Paraguay. The ICC Tribunal decided in favour of the stay and reserved on the merits, after Guaidó intervened in support of the request of the Respondent. http://arbitrationblog.kluwerarbitration.com/2019/05/25/icc-tribunal-recognizes-guaidos-intervention-and-stays-proceedings-in-pdvsa-v-petropar/?doing_wp_cron=1592900903.1685969829559326171875 (last accessed 24 August 2020).

[119]Albari (2016), p. 175.

[120]Charlotin D, Hepburn J, US Courts diverge from ICSID annulment committee on Venezuela's Representation in International Disputes. IA Reporter, 23 May 2019, www.iareporter.com/Art.s/us-courts-diverge-from-icsid-annulment-committee-on-venezuelas-representation-in-international-disputes (last accessed 24 August 2020).

[121]Rusoro Mining Limited, Gold Fields Limited v. Bolivarian Republic of Venezuela (2018) USCA Case #18-7044, https://www.italaw.com/sites/default/files/case-documents/italaw10521.pdf (last accessed 24 August 2020).

[122]Talmon (1998), p. 190.

– that the award would be enforced most probably in the United States, where Venezuela holds most of its foreign assets.

Such premises necessarily imply that maintenance of the *status quo*—in other words, continuing to allow Maduro's *Procurador* to represent Venezuela and denial of participation to Guido's *Procurador*—in the cases against Venezuela may not be enough to deliver an enforceable award.[123] An award rendered under the AF rules that fails to consider the laws of the seat of arbitration and the public policy of the place where the award will most likely be enforced is dead letter.

4 Possible Practical Solutions

Having concluded that the Tribunal has no jurisdiction to decide who is the legitimate representative of a State, the tribunal or the annulment committee confronted with the Issue can still solve it in several practical ways, without exceeding its jurisdiction. The following come to mind:

First, the tribunal can let political decisions be taken by politicians. Indeed, the Tribunal could turn to the ICSID Secretariat to get information on who is recognized as the legitimate Venezuelan Government before the World Bank Group and accept the same representation as the International Organization.

The Venezuela's Procurador Especial initially requested that the decision be made by the Centre itself and not by the individual Tribunals. However, the Centre refused to take that decision and passed it to the arbitral tribunals. The reasons for such decision are unknown. However, it is reasonable to think that the fact that Venezuela is no longer part of the ICSID system and has no representative at ICSID's administrative council might have played a role.

The organizations that make up the World Bank Group are owned by the governments of member nations, which have the ultimate decision-making power within the organizations on all matters, including policy, financial or membership issues. Member countries govern the World Bank Group through the Boards of Governors and the Boards of Executive Directors; bodies that make all major decisions for the organizations.[124] In the World Bank system, voting counts as a percentage of shares, not individual membership, with the United States holding up to 16% of voting power.[125]

---

[123] Van den Berg (1999), pp. 114–145: Explaining that "(t)he ultimate purpose of the arbitration agreement is to render an enforceable award."

[124] Member Countries. The World Bank, www.worldbank.org/en/about/leadership/members (last accessed 24 August 2020).

[125] ICSID is one of the five organizations of the World Bank Group and it is in charge of providing facilities for conciliation and arbitration of international investment disputes. The Centre has a Secretariat—in charge of administering the Centre's case load—and an Administrative Council, composed of one representative of each Contracting State. Normally the person appointed by a State to the Board of Governors is also the State's representative at the Administrative Council.

ICSID is one of the five organizations of the World Bank Group,[126] and it is in charge of providing facilities for conciliation and arbitration of international investment disputes.[127] The Centre has a Secretariat—in charge of administering the Centre's case load[128]—and a governing body, the Administrative Council, composed of one representative of each Contracting State.[129] Normally, the person appointed by a State to the Board of Governors is also the State's representative at the Administrative Council. In the case of Venezuela, however, since it is not a member of ICSID it does not have a representative at the Administrative Council.

In April 2019, the International Monetary Fund ("IMF") and World Bank shareholders were still undecided on whether to recognize Guaidó as the country's leader with regard to the institutions.[130] However, a simple majority of member votes can

[126] Public Information from ICSID Webpage https://icsid.worldbank.org/en/Pages/about/ICSID%20And%20The%20World%20Bank%20Group.aspx (last accessed 24 August 2020).

[127] Public Information from ICSID Webpage https://icsid.worldbank.org/en/Pages/about/ICSID%20And%20The%20World%20Bank%20Group.aspx (last accessed 24 August 2020).

[128] Art. 3 of ICSID Convention: The Centre shall have an Administrative Council and a Secretariat and shall maintain a Panel of Conciliators and a Panel of Arbitrators.

Art. 4 of ICSID Convention: (1) The Administrative Council shall be composed of one representative of each Contracting State. An alternate may act as representative in case of his principal's absence from a meeting or inability to act. (2) In the absence of a contrary designation, each governor and alternate governor of the Bank appointed by a Contracting State shall be ex officio its representative and its alternate respectively.

[129] Art. 6 of ICSID Convention: (1) Without prejudice to the powers and functions vested in it by other provisions of this Convention, the Administrative Council shall:

(a) adopt the administrative and financial regulations of the Centre;
(b) adopt the rules of procedure for the institution of conciliation and arbitration proceedings;
(c) adopt the rules of procedure for conciliation and arbitration proceedings (hereinafter called the Conciliation Rules and the Arbitration Rules);
(d) approve arrangements with the Bank for the use of the Bank's administrative facilities and services;
(e) determine the conditions of service of the Secretary-General and of any Deputy Secretary-General;
(f) adopt the annual budget of revenues and expenditures of the Centre;
(g) approve the annual report on the operation of the Centre. The decisions referred to in sub-paragraphs (a), (b), (c) and (f) above shall be adopted by a majority of two-thirds of the members of the Administrative Council.

(2) The Administrative Council may appoint such committees as it considers necessary.

(3) The Administrative Council shall also exercise such other powers and perform such other functions as it shall determine to be necessary for the implementation of the provisions of this Convention.

[130] Campos R, Lawder D, Venezuela leadership issue still blocking IMF, World Bank aid. Reuters, 11 April 2019, www.reuters.com/Art./us-imf-worldbank-venezuela/venezuela-leadership-issue-still-blocking-imf-world-bank-aid-id (last accessed 24 August 2020).

decide who the official delegate from a country to the IMF and World Bank is, and a call for such a vote would probably have to come from the IMF's leadership.[131]

Arbitral Tribunals could recognize the Venezuelan government represented at the World Bank as the government entitled to represent the country in all disputes pending at ICSID, deferring any political decision to the World Bank as an international institution. The decision of the World Bank members on the recognition of a particular government would show a political consensus of the majority of its members.

Thus, while Guaidó's representatives remain unaccredited, the situation could change once the Bank's leadership calls for a vote, since many of the member States have recognized Guaidó as president of Venezuela.[132]

Second, a solution for cases subject to AF Rules is to allow the State to be represented by the government recognized at the seat of arbitration, for the reasons explained in the preceding section. If the same government is recognized in the country where the award would potentially be executed, then this would further reinforce the case.

Finally, taking into consideration that both procuradores purport to act in the best interest of the State, the arbitral tribunal can let both procuradores participate in the proceedings: either by allowing the State to be represented by both or by recognizing one as "legitimate" and the other as an amicus curiae. It appears that the first situation was the approach taken by the annulment committee of ConocoPhillips.[133] As regards the second situation, Arbitral Tribunals could defer the decision on the Issue to the approach taken by the World Bank or the government of the seat of arbitration, but still hear the other procurador as an amicus curiae. The tribunal would not be bound by the arguments made by the amicus curiae, but would give them the chance to be properly heard.

Both approaches will slightly increase the complexity of the case, but would shield the award from a set aside based on a manifest excess of powers and diminish any potential argument by the State of a violation of its due process rights to be represented by an agent or representative of its own choosing.

---

[131]Campos R, Lawder D, Venezuela leadership issue still blocking IMF, World Bank aid. Reuters, 11 April 2019, www.reuters.com/Art./us-imf-worldbank-venezuela/venezuela-leadership-issue-still-blocking-imf-world-bank-aid-id (last accessed 24 August 2020).

[132]Campos R, 'Large' IMF majority on Venezuela leader issue needed: Lagarde. Reuters, 13 April 2019, www.reuters.com/Art./us-imf-worldbank-venezuela/large-imf-majority-on-venezuela-leader-issue-needed-lagarde-id (last accessed 24 August 2020).

[133]Sanderson C, Jones T, ICSID committee Challenged in Venezuela Row. Global Arbitration Review, 17 April 2020, https://globalarbitrationreview.com/article/1225799/icsid-committee-challenged-in-venezuela-row (last accessed 24 August 2020).

5 Conclusion

The issue of who is the legitimate representative of the Respondent State is outside the scope of the ICSID tribunals' (or annulment committees') jurisdiction. It is a political question that ought to be left to politicians. The same is true for arbitrations under the AF Rules. This does not imply that Venezuela's representatives or agents cannot be changed in investment arbitration. It simply means that, if the award is to be protected from annulment or lack of enforceability, solutions that do not exceed the tribunal's powers must be found. This chapter suggests to allow the World Bank and its members to take the political decision of who is the legitimate government; to allow both representatives of the State to participate in the proceedings; or, in cases subject to AF Rules, to accept the representative of the government that has been recognized by the State where the seat of arbitration is located.

References

Albari LV (2016) The Estrada doctrine and the English courts: determining the legitimate government of a state in the absence of explicit recognition of governments. Hague Yearb Int Law 29:171–205

Baptista K, Riofrío Piché M (2019) Rule 18 – representation of the parties. In: Fouret J, Gerbay R, Alvarez GM (eds) The ICSID Convention, Regulations and Rules. Edward Elgar, Cheltenham, pp 1047–1057

Blackaby N, Partasides C, Redfern A, Hunter M (2015) Redfern and Hunter on international arbitration. Oxford University Press, Oxford

Born G (2015) International arbitration: cases and materials. Wolters Kluwer, Alphen aan den Rijn

Chapus R (1990) Droit administratif général, vol I. Montchrestien, Paris

Commission J, Moloo R (2018) Procedural issues in international investment arbitration. Oxford University Press, Oxford

Crawford J (2012) Brownlie's principles of public international law. Oxford University Press, Oxford

Danic O (2013) L'Évolution de la Pratique Française en Matière de Reconnaisance de Gouvernement. Annuaire Français de Droit International LIX:527–528

Schreuer C (2001) The ICSID Convention: a commentary. Cambridge University Press, Cambridge

Talmon S (1998) Recognition of governments in international law: with particular reference to governments in exile. Oxford University Press, Oxford

Talmon S (1999) Who is the legitimate government in exile? Towards normative criteria for governmental legitimacy in international law. In: Goodwin-Gill G, Talmon S (eds) The reality of international law. Oxford University Press, Oxford, pp 499–537

van den Berg AJ (1999) Improving the efficiency of arbitration agreements and awards: 40 years of application of the New York Convention. Kluwer Law International, The Hague, Boston

Webster T, Buhler M (2014) Handbook of ICC Arbitration: commentary, precedents, materials. Sweet & Maxwell, London

Krystle Baptista is an independent arbitrator based in Madrid. She intervenes as arbitrator and tribunal secretary in complex commercial and investment arbitration cases. She is also an associate professor at IE Law School and the University of Navarra. She completed her law degree at the University of Navarra with diplomas in Anglo-American Law and Global Law, and she did an LL. M. in International Legal Studies in New York University. She speaks Spanish, English, French and Portuguese. She is admitted to practice in Madrid and New York.

International Non-investment Courts and Tribunals as Transnational Actors in International Investment Law and Arbitration?

Ioannis Prezas

Contents

1 Introduction 106
2 Forms of Involvement of Non-investment Adjudicative Bodies in Investment Law and Arbitration 107
2.1 Case Law Cross-Referencing 108
2.2 Coordinating Parallel Proceedings 111
3 The Limited Jurisdiction of the ICJ Under Article 64 of the ICSID Convention 113
3.1 Interstate Disputes Over the "Application" of the ICSID Convention 114
3.2 Interstate Disputes Over the "Interpretation" of the ICSID Convention 118
4 The Impact of Interstate Proceedings Over Sovereignty Disputes on Investment Law and Arbitration 122
4.1 Sovereignty Disputes and the Legality of (the Authorization of) the Investment 123
4.2 The Territorial Applicability of the Investment Treaty 127
5 Concluding Remarks 129
References 130

Abstract While international non-investment courts and tribunals do not usually interact with investment law and arbitration, they may potentially become limited actors in this transnational legal field. First, they can contribute indirectly to the shaping of investment law though cross-references to their case law made by investment tribunals. Second, the ICJ may exceptionally become a supporting actor in international arbitration for post-award enforcement purposes under Article 64 of the ICSID Convention. This provision confers limited jurisdiction to the Court in relation to interstate disputes over the interpretation or the application of the Convention as it does not empower the Court to review arbitral awards on the merits

The author is extremely thankful to Dr Anastasios Gourgourinis for his valuable comments on an earlier draft of this study. The usual disclaimer applies.

I. Prezas (✉)
Sorbonne Law School, University Paris 1, Sorbonne Research Institute for International and European Studies, Paris, France
e-mail: ioannis.prezas@univ-paris1.fr

A. Gourgourinis (ed.), *Transnational Actors in International Investment Law*, European Yearbook of International Economic Law,
https://doi.org/10.1007/978-3-030-60679-4_5

or jurisdiction. Third, interstate proceedings over sovereignty in a disputed area may affect the legal condition of investments, as well as influence investor-state proceedings and decisions regarding the protection of the investments in the same area. The legality of the authorisation of the investment and the territorial applicability of an investment treaty are merely two of the wide variety of issues that merit attention. In any event, given the absence of a centralised and hierarchical adjudication system in international law, investor-state arbitration evolves in a fairly autonomous manner vis-à-vis all other international courts and tribunals. Specifically, the almost generalised lack of formal coordination rules between different adjudicative components of the international legal order seems to support the conclusion that non-investment courts and tribunals become actors in international investment law and arbitration, only if, and to the extent that, investment tribunals deem this necessary for the exercise of their own functions in each particular case.

1 Introduction

For more than two decades, investment arbitration between foreign investors and host states based on investment treaties has been the main and almost exclusive dispute settlement mechanism in this field of international law. In that sense, investment tribunals are undeniably the principal actors in international investment law today. Therefore, asking whether international non-investment courts and tribunals – such as, to name just a few of them, the International Court of Justice ("ICJ"), the International Tribunal for the Law of the Sea ("ITLOS"), the European Court of Human Rights ("ECtHR") or the Court of Justice of the European Union ("CJEU")—may have a role to play in investment law, seems at first sight somehow paradoxical. Indeed, due to their different ratione materiae and ratione personae jurisdiction, all these dispute settlement mechanisms are obviously of a "non-investment" nature. They do not apply investment law (as found in investment agreements), in order to settle investor-state disputes, which is the main function of investment arbitral tribunals.

Moreover, given the absence of a centralised and hierarchical adjudication system in international law, investor-state arbitration, in addition to being a widely uncoordinated legal framework as such because of its ad hoc nature, evolves in a fairly autonomous manner vis-à-vis the aforementioned international courts and tribunals. Consequently, it is difficult to see how the latter could interact with the former. As a matter of principle, they do not. Still, they are part of a wider transnational web of adjudicative mechanisms involving both states and individuals. As a result, an international non-investment adjudicative body may in some cases become a real transnational actor in investment law and arbitration, if its case law, proceedings and decisions are likely to influence or impact, one way or another, the shaping of investment law and/or the functioning of investment arbitration.

The purpose of this chapter is therefore to explore how and to what extent some[1] international non-investment courts and tribunals may be involved in, or interfere with, investment law and arbitration. To this end, Sect. 2 examines, in general, the different forms of involvement of international non-investment adjudication bodies in investment law and arbitration. Section 3 focuses on a first example of limited involvement of a non-investment court in investment arbitration by looking at the jurisdiction of the ICJ under Article 64 of the ICSID Convention over disputes concerning the interpretation and application of this Convention. Section 4 examines the potential impact of sovereignty disputes brought before non-investment adjudicative bodies on investment law and arbitration. Section 5 offers some brief concluding remarks.

2 Forms of Involvement of Non-investment Adjudicative Bodies in Investment Law and Arbitration

The potential involvement of non-investment adjudication bodies in investment law and arbitration, and, therefore, in transnational situations, may take many forms. In some cases, a decision of a non-investment court may have a *systemic* impact on investment law and especially arbitration based on international investment treaties. As it is well-known, the role of the CJEU in this field is extremely important, albeit controversial. The Court is indeed undeniably a "controlling" actor of investment dispute settlement mechanisms, whether of an intra-European Union ("EU") (between EU member states) or extra EU (between an EU member state or the EU itself and a third state) character, as shown respectively by its 2018 *Achmea* decision[2] and its 2019 Comprehensive economic and trade agreement opinion.[3] In

[1]Other international courts may exceptionally have jurisdiction over investment disputes. This is potentially the case of the Economic Community of West African States (ECOWAS) Court of Justice, see Happold and Radović (2018), pp. 105–111. An even more specific example is the ITLOS seabed disputes chamber which has jurisdiction over disputes arising out of deep seabed mining activities, and therefore investments in the Area, in accordance with the Montego Bay Convention of 1982. This regime of dispute settlement, which is yet to be tested, affords various protections to deep seabed mining contractors which may be considered as broadly equivalent to investment protection standards found in bilateral investment treaties, see Dingwall (2018). In both cases, the international adjudication bodies concerned may become specific actors in the field of investment protection in lieu of ad hoc arbitration under an investment treaty since they fulfil functions similar, albeit not identical, to those entrusted usually to arbitral tribunals.

[2]CJEU, Judgment, 6 March 2018, Case C-284/16, *Slovak Republic v. Achmea*, ECLI:EU:C:2018:158, paras 31–60 (concluding that the autonomy of the EU law precludes investor-state dispute settlement on the basis of an investment agreement, in this case the one concluded between Slovakia and the Netherlands).

[3]CJEU, Opinion 1/17, 30 April 2019, ECLI:EU:C:2019:341, paras 106–161 (concluding that the CETA Investor-State Dispute Settlement mechanism is compatible with EU primary law because it does not adversely affect the autonomy of the EU legal order).

particular, the pronouncements of the CJEU on the compatibility of investment dispute settlement mechanisms with the autonomy of the EU legal order—i.e. the exclusive jurisdiction of the CJEU to interpret EU law—or even human rights guarantees as enshrined therein, may produce far-reaching and even adverse legal consequences on the viability of investment arbitration based on existing treaties concluded by the EU and/or its members states with third states. Still, investment tribunals have a different opinion on the exact impact of such decisions on their own jurisdiction. For instance, in *Vattenfal v Germany*, the arbitral tribunal rejected the respondent's *Achmea*-based objection to its jurisdiction. It held that Article 26 of the Energy Charter Treaty ("ECT") providing for the settlement of investor-state disputes could not be interpreted so as to exclude intra-EU investor-state arbitration and that article 16 of the same instrument (governing its relation to other agreements) is a lex specialis rule prevailing over EU law.[4]

Beyond this very important, though rather specific illustration of the involvement of a non-investment court, i.e. the CJEU, in investment law and arbitration, that will not be further examined here, two other forms of possible involvement merit attention: case law cross-referencing (Sect. 2.1) and coordination of parallel proceedings by both non-investment and investment adjudicative bodies (Sect. 2.2).

2.1 Case Law Cross-Referencing

Interaction between different adjudicative components of the international legal order usually takes the form of cross-referencing of case law. Cross-referencing is a quite common phenomenon between international adjudicative bodies[5] and means that a court or tribunal expressly refers to the case law of other courts or tribunals in order, most of the time, to corroborate its own findings. While international tribunals are not bound by the rule of stare decisis, they may, nonetheless, refer to decisions and awards of other courts and tribunals as a "subsidiary means for the determination of rules of international law" according to Article 38 of the Statute of the ICJ. Substantive interaction of this kind admittedly exists between investment law as found in investment treaties and applied by investor-state tribunals and non-investment adjudication mechanisms applying in principle other, i.e. non-investment, rules of international law. Nevertheless, it is far from reciprocal.

Investment tribunals, when confronted with questions of general international law, systematically refer to the case law of the ICJ[6]—in order, for instance, to apply rules of interpretation of investment agreements or principles governing the

[4]Vattenfall AB and others v. Federal Republic of Germany, ICSID Case No. ARB/12/12, Decision on the Achmea issue, 31 August 2018, paras 208 and 229.

[5]See Boisson de Chazournes (2017), pp. 30–44.

[6]See in general Pellet (2013).

responsibility of the host state—or of human rights courts when they deem it appropriate.[7] Although the use made of these external decisions may vary considerably from one investment tribunal to another, and is, thus, likely to lead to discrepancies, external case law enjoys unquestionably some degree of intellectual authority in investment arbitration, as a means of ensuring uniformity and coherence of international law in a highly fragmented jurisdictional landscape.

From the opposite perspective, however, the place of investment (case) law in non-investment adjudication is quite limited, if any. International non-investment courts and tribunals do not usually resort to the findings of investor-state arbitral tribunals when exercising their own subject-matter jurisdiction. Interestingly, the principal judicial organ of the United Nations does not at all seem inclined to give credit to this branch of international law, even in cases where this would perhaps be appropriate, such as in the field of diplomatic protection. In the *Diallo* case, the ICJ has indeed found that the protection of shareholders by substitution, although recognized by investment agreements and case law, did not form part of customary law.[8] The evolution of investment treaty law and arbitration was not, therefore:

> sufficient to show that there has been a change in the customary rules of diplomatic protection; it could equally show the contrary.[9]

A fortiori, it does not come as a surprise that the Court, dealing with issues unrelated to economic law, is even more categorical about the limited influence of investment case law on general international law. For instance, in the Obligation to negotiate access to the Pacific Ocean case, Bolivia claimed that Chile's representations through its multiple declarations and statements over the years gave rise to the expectation of restoring Bolivia's sovereign access to the sea and that Chile's denial of its obligation to negotiate and its refusal to engage in further negotiations with Bolivia frustrated the latter's legitimate expectations. However, the Court simply noted that:

> references to legitimate expectations may be found in arbitral awards concerning disputes between a foreign investor and the host state that apply treaty clauses providing for fair and equitable treatment", before concluding that "[it] does not follow from such references that there exists in general international law a principle that would give rise to an obligation on the basis of what could be considered a legitimate expectation.[10]

The limited role of investment law in non-investment adjudication is also highlighted by the fact that human rights courts, while they may undeniably protect

---

[7]For a systematic and functional analysis of human rights references in investment arbitration see Steininger (2018). See also Dupuy and Viñuales (2015).

[8]Ahmadou Sadio Diallo (Guinea v. Democratic Republic of the Congo), Judgment, ICJ Reports 2007, p. 582, paras 89–90.

[9]Ahmadou Sadio Diallo (Guinea v. Democratic Republic of the Congo), Judgment, ICJ Reports 2007, p. 582, para 90. See also the critique by Pellet (2013), pp. 225–226.

[10]Obligation to Negotiate Access to the Pacific Ocean (Bolivia v. Chile), Judgment, ICJ Reports 2018, p. 507, para. 162.

property rights of foreign investors,[11] do not usually (need to) take into consideration investment case law. The reason is that their subject matter jurisdiction is confined to violations of human rights guarantees, and does not cover investment protection standards, even when the two may to some degree converge.

In theory, the ECtHR may apply the general principles of international law governing the expropriation of foreign nationals, which include foreign investors, through a cross-reference made to this field of law by Article 1 of the first additional protocol to the European Convention which reads as follows: "Every natural or legal person is entitled to the peaceful enjoyment of his possessions. No one shall be deprived of his possessions except in the public interest and subject to the conditions provided for by law and by *the general principles of international law*" (emphasis added). Dealing with the amount of compensation for an expropriation claim, the Court has interpreted the reference to the general principles of international law as applicable only to foreign persons and not to nationals of the defendant state.[12] In practical terms, this means that the defendant state must pay a full compensation to a foreign person, including an investor, in case of deprivation of property, i.e. expropriation, while it may pay less compensation to a national when this is justified by a special interest of the state.

While this differential treatment between foreigners and nationals is rather questionable,[13] the ECtHR has never applied these principles because it is reluctant to find an expropriation of a foreign investor (or, one might think, the Court is reluctant to find an expropriation of foreign property because it wishes to avoid applying these general principles of law). Be that as it may, it would certainly be interesting to see whether the Court will be more willing than the ICJ to take into account investment (case) law as evidence of the scope of these customary law principles governing the regime of expropriation of foreign investors, including in its indirect form, which raises the more complex issues.

Consequently, non-investment courts and tribunals are only very limited transnational legal actors because they can only contribute indirectly, and in reality, involuntarily, to the shaping of investment law, if, and to the extent that, investment tribunals decide to make cross-references to external case law. At the same time, and conversely, non-investment courts and tribunals are generally reluctant to follow investment case law. While investment tribunals see themselves as part of a wider transnational legal system, non-investment courts, and above all the ICJ, seem to treat investment law produced by ad hoc arbitral tribunals as a lex specialis, incapable of influencing the formation of rules of general international law. As a result, non-investment courts and tribunals are not willing, for the time being, to contribute directly to the expansion of the authority of investment case law.

---

[11] See e.g. El Boudouhi (2017), pp. 316–323; Fanou and Tzevelekos (2018), pp. 111–117.

[12] James and others v. United Kingdom, A/98 [1986] ECHR 2, Judgment, 21 February 1986, paras 58–66.

[13] See for instance Kriebaum (2008), pp. 664–666.

2.2 *Coordinating Parallel Proceedings*

Beyond the limited influence of the case law of non-investment adjudication bodies on investment law, their coexistence with investment tribunals raises another complex issue: what is the impact of non-investment proceedings on investment arbitration? Indeed, due to the almost generalised lack of formal rules governing the procedural coordination between a plurality of international courts and tribunals having different but sometimes overlapping jurisdictions, it may be difficult to prevent parallel proceedings before, and potentially conflicting decisions by, investment and non-investment dispute settlement mechanisms regarding similar or related factual circumstances.

Admittedly, from the perspective of some non-investment adjudication bodies, namely human rights courts, there is a mechanism capable of preventing such an outcome. To give an example, Article 35-2 (b) of the European Convention on Human Rights provides that the Court shall not deal with any application submitted under Article 34 that "is substantially the same as a matter that has already been examined by the Court or has already been submitted to another procedure of international investigation or settlement and contains no relevant new information (...)". As the ECtHR has explained, this provision

> is intended to avoid the situation where several international bodies would be simultaneously dealing with applications which are substantially the same. A situation of this type would be incompatible with the spirit and the letter of the Convention, which seeks to avoid a plurality of international proceedings relating to the same cases.[14]

Yet, this procedural effect is far from automatic, as shown by the *Yukos* case. There the ECtHR examined the Russian objection according to which the proceedings before the permanent court of arbitration initiated by the applicant company's shareholders prevented the Court from hearing the case. As a matter of principle, the Court recalled that the assessment of similarity of the cases usually involves

> the comparison of the parties in the respective proceedings, the relevant legal provisions relied on by them, the scope of their claims and the types of the redress sought.[15]

Applying this "triple identity" test, the Court found that the parties in the arbitration proceedings (the shareholders) and in the case before it (the company) were different and, therefore, concluded that the two matters were not substantially the same.[16] As a result, it went on to consider the merits of the case without examining whether the arbitral proceedings constituted "another procedure of international investigation or settlement", as required by Article 35-2 (b) of the European

[14] OAO Neftyanaya Kompaniya Yukos v. Russia, No 14902/04, Judgment, 20 September 2011, para. 520.

[15] OAO Neftyanaya Kompaniya Yukos v. Russia, No 14902/04, Judgment, 20 September 2011, para. 521.

[16] OAO Neftyanaya Kompaniya Yukos v. Russia, No 14902/04, Judgment, 20 September 2011, paras 523–526.

Convention. Such a strict assessment of the similarity of cases criterion led the ECtHR to hear, if not "substantially" in the technical legal sense, at least from an economic point of view, the same cases as the ones submitted to arbitration. Be that as it may, if the ECtHR declares an application as inadmissible, finding that it is substantially the same as a matter that has already been submitted to investment arbitration, it would at least in theory recognise the procedural priority of investor-state arbitration over the case, thereby performing a specific coordinating function designed to prevent potential conflicting decisions.

However, is the opposite also true? How should an investment tribunal deal with parallel proceedings brought before other non-investment courts and tribunals regarding a case similar to that submitted to it? Admittedly, formal coordination rules, such the one established by Article 35-2 (b) of the European Convention, are inserted in investment treaties. Still, they govern almost exclusively parallel proceedings between investment tribunals and domestic courts. For instance, the so-called fork-in-the-road clause provides for a choice between recourse to domestic courts, or, as the case may be, other agreed dispute settlement mechanisms, and ad hoc investment arbitration. Once a choice has been made, the other means of settlement of disputes cannot be resorted to.[17] Moreover, such coordination techniques may certainly be applicable, by extension, to non-investment international courts and tribunals dealing with cases initially brought before domestic courts. Yet, even in such a scenario, it does not necessarily follow that an investor-state tribunal will be willing to give priority to a non-investment adjudicative body, as shown by the *Yukos Universal Limited (Isle of Man) v Russia* case. Confronted, like the ECtHR, with the similarity of cases objection, the arbitral tribunal found that the various Russian court proceedings and applications to the ECtHR, brought by different parties, failed to trigger the "fork-in-the-road provision" of the ECT,[18] considering that the "triple identity" test was applicable to such provision.[19]

Hence, the two adjudicative bodies reached different conclusions on certain similar points, namely the protection of property and indirect expropriation, including issues of compensation.[20] Admittedly, since the applicable law and the cause of action are different before these two mechanisms, it would seem that potential conflicting decisions are not even possible. It is even arguable that such cases are not really parallel proceedings to which the principles of litis pendence (lis alibi pendens) or res judicata would be applicable.[21] Still, since investor-state tribunal and

---

[17] See Boisson de Chazournes (2017), pp. 52–57.

[18] Article 26(3) of the ECT conditions the consent of a state party to arbitration on the absence of proceedings commenced by the investor before either domestic courts or "in accordance with any applicable, previously agreed dispute settlement procedure". It is unclear whether the latter possibility covers resort to an international non-investment court such as the ECtHR, but the arbitral tribunal seems to implicitly consider it does.

[19] Yukos Universal Limited (Isle of Man) v. The Russian Federation, UNCITRAL, PCA Case No. 2005-04/AA227, Interim Award, 30 November 2009, paras 594, 598–600.

[20] See for an overview of these divergences De Brabandere (2015).

[21] See De Brabandere (2015), p. 348.

human rights courts fulfil to a certain extent similar functions (i.e. the protection of property rights), potential conflicts seem more likely to arise between them than between investment tribunals and other international non-investment courts.

Indeed, the risk of truly conflicting decisions is at first sight less visible in the latter scenario, because non-investment adjudication bodies (at least other than human rights courts) do not fulfil functions similar to those entrusted to arbitral tribunals. This is especially true for interstate courts that, needless to say, have no jurisdiction to settle disputes between a host state and a foreign investor. For that reason, applying procedural techniques such a lis alibi pendens or res judicata[22] does not even seem necessary in order to coordinate proceedings that cannot possibly overlap. These two techniques are based on the "triple identity" test, meaning that the parties, the object of the dispute and the legal grounds invoked must be the same in the two proceedings. If this is the case, the second seized tribunal will have either to stay proceedings (lis alibi pendens)—until the first seized tribunal decides its own jurisdiction and, if it finds it established, the second seized tribunal must decline its jurisdiction—or declare the application inadmissible—if the same dispute has been the object of a final decision by another adjudicative body (res judicata).

But it is obvious that this test will be impossible to meet at least when one considers the relationship between interstate non-investment adjudicative bodies and investor-state tribunals. As shown in Sect. 3, no need of procedural coordination really exists between investment tribunals and the ICJ acting under Article 64 of the ICSID Convention. Still, an investment tribunal may find itself, in some exceptional circumstances, in a position where it would have to take a decision to assert or decline jurisdiction, to stay proceedings or even to defer to the views of another non-investment tribunal on a specific issue, when the disputes brought before the two set of proceedings are to a certain extent *closely related, albeit formally plainly distinct*. This is illustrated by Sect. 4 discussing the possible impact of interstate proceedings over sovereignty disputes on investment law and arbitration.

3 The Limited Jurisdiction of the ICJ Under Article 64 of the ICSID Convention

Dealing with the role of the ICJ in the field of investment law may seem today anachronistic in view of the spectacular development of investment arbitration. It is of course true that enjoying general jurisdiction ratione materiae for interstate disputes, the Court may be directly involved in the settlement of a dispute arising out of foreign investment through a diplomatic protection claim. But this is rather exceptional, because such eventuality is limited to cases where no direct adjudicative mechanism is available to the foreign investor on the basis of an investment treaty.

[22]On these and other procedural techniques designed as tools for organizing plurality of international courts and tribunals see Boisson de Chazournes (2017), p. 45 ff.

Indeed, only a handful of cases of this type have been submitted to the Court, such as the *Diallo* case mentioned above.

Be that as it may, while creating the prominent adjudication forum regarding the settlement of investor-state disputes, the ICSID Convention reserves at the same time a role for the principal judicial organ of the United Nations in its Article 64. This provision confers, under certain conditions, such as prior negotiation, jurisdiction on the ICJ over disputes arising between contracting states "concerning the interpretation or application of the Convention". In a sense, thanks to this provision, the ICJ may become a kind of investment tribunal. Still, the scope and nature of the interstate disputes that may be submitted to the ICJ under Article 64 need some clarification. More particularly, since interstate proceedings before the Court and investor-state arbitral proceedings before the International Centre for the Settlement of Investment Disputed ("ICSID") are not expressly articulated, the question arises if and how the former could impact the latter. Although Article 64 has never been resorted to by contracting states, it is therefore interesting to examine the scope of the jurisdiction of the ICJ under this provision on interstate disputes over the application of the ICSID Convention (Sect. 3.1) as well as its interpretation (Sect. 3.2).

3.1 Interstate Disputes Over the "Application" of the ICSID Convention

As a matter of principle, the jurisdiction of the ICJ under Article 64 of the ICSID Convention on interstate disputes over the application of the same Convention cannot visibly interfere with ICSID arbitration over the *substance* of an investor-state dispute under an investment agreement. This is valid regardless of whether investor-state proceedings concerning the same set of facts have been initiated or not.

In the first scenario, i.e. when investor-state proceedings have been initiated or concluded, parallel proceedings before the ICJ concerning the same set of facts are obviously precluded. The Report of the executive directors to the ICSID Convention makes it clear that Article 64 does not:

> empower a state to institute proceedings before the Court in respect of a dispute which one of its nationals and another Contracting State have consented to submit or have submitted to arbitration, since such proceedings would contravene the provisions of Article 27 (. . .).[23]

As it is well-known, the latter provision prohibits contracting states from giving diplomatic protection, or bringing an international claim, in respect of a dispute which one of their nationals and another contracting state shall have consented to

[23]Report of the Executive Directors on the Convention on the Settlement of Investment Disputes between States and Nationals of Other States, 1 ICSID Reports, pp. 32–33, para. 45.

submit or shall have submitted to arbitration under the Convention. Therefore, it fulfils a coordinating function between interstate and investor-state proceedings. More particularly, this provision is designed to prevent the submission to a state-to-state adjudicative mechanism (including the ICJ) of the same substantive issues and factual circumstances as those already submitted to, or settled by, an investor-state tribunal. As a consequence, Article 64 does not confer upon the ICJ the power to review on appeal the decisions of ICSID arbitral tribunals. This is especially true since the ICSID Convention establishes its own exclusive procedures for the revision and annulment of awards in its Articles 51 and 52.[24] Applying Article 64, in conjunction with Article 27 as the case may be, the ICJ would, thus, have to decline jurisdiction if, for instance, the home state of the investor attempts to institute diplomatic protection proceedings against the host state of the investment, in order to challenge an ICSID award on the merits that would not be favourable to its national.

However, reference to Article 27 of the ICSID Convention is arguably even irrelevant here. Not only because this provision is meant to operate in relation to diplomatic protection disputes brought before any interstate adjudication forum (and not necessarily before the ICJ under Article 64), including state-to-state arbitration under an investment agreement. But also, and foremost, because Article 64 of the ICSID Convention appears to cover exclusively disputes between contracting parties over the application of the Convention *by the parties themselves* (such as disputes arising from the non-compliance of a contracting state with an award as we will see below). By contrast, it does not encompass disagreements between contracting parties over the application of substantive protection standards *by ICSID arbitral tribunals*. In other terms, how an arbitral tribunal concretely decides a case on the merits cannot form the object of a dispute between two contracting states over the application of the ICSID Convention before the ICJ.

As far as the second scenario is concerned, i.e. when investor-state proceedings have not yet been initiated, there is in principle nothing to preclude an interstate investment dispute concerning the same set of facts from being submitted to adjudication though a diplomatic protection claim. The reason is that the prohibition of Article 27 is not applicable to the extent that the investor had neither consented to arbitrate (e.g. in a contract, before requesting the institution of arbitral proceedings) nor submitted the dispute to investor-state arbitration by requesting proceedings before the ICSID on the basis of an investment agreement. However, this provision, while in principle allowing for state-to-state investment arbitration when no investor-state proceedings have been initiated, seems again irrelevant when it comes to the jurisdiction of the ICJ concerning interstate disputes over the application of the ICSID Convention under Article 64 of that instrument. In order to understand why, it is necessary to distinguish between the following two possibilities.

---

[24] Schreuer et al. (2009), Article 64, pp. 1261–1262, paras 12-13. See also Schreuer et al. (2009), Article 27, p. 422, para. 23.

On the one hand, the home state of the foreign investor is entitled to bring a diplomatic protection claim against the host state before a state-to-state ad hoc tribunal under an applicable investment agreement, *before* the investor initiates investor-state arbitration under the same instrument and involving the same factual circumstances. This is possible due to the fact that most investment agreements provide, in addition to investor-state arbitration, state-to-state arbitration concerning disputes over the interpretation and the application of the agreement, albeit without most of the time specifying what the articulation between the two should be. Moreover, even if the applicable BIT does not contain a principle as the one set out in Article 27 of the ICSID Convention, some tribunals did not hesitate to apply this provision by analogy. For instance, doing that, an ad hoc state-to-state investment tribunal rejected the argument put forward by Cuba that the mere availability of investor-state arbitration under the 1993 Italy-Cuba investment agreement barred Italy from bringing a diplomatic protection claim before an interstate arbitral tribunal as provided for in the same agreement. The reason was that in that case no investor-state arbitration proceedings had been initiated between any of the investors and Cuba.[25] But what if, to give just an example, the investor decided to initiate arbitration against the host state after his home state failed to win its interstate case? Obviously, parallel, successive and therefore potentially conflicting investor-state and interstate arbitral proceedings over the same set of facts and under the same investment agreement are not to be excluded and raise some quite complex issues regarding the respective scope and coordination of the two mechanisms.[26]

Be that as it may, the ICJ cannot be involved in such conflictual scenarios. As a matter of fact, investment agreement clauses providing for settlement mechanisms for interstate disputes (in addition to investor-state arbitration) do not, to the best of our knowledge, confer jurisdiction to the ICJ, but to ad hoc arbitral tribunals, as noted above. Accordingly, the ICJ does not have jurisdiction over interstate investment disputes involving facts and substantive issues over which an investor-state tribunal would also have (concurrent as the case may be) jurisdiction under an investment agreement.

On the other hand, under Article 64 of the ICSID Convention the ICJ cannot decide the merits of an interstate diplomatic protection claim involving issues that would potentially fall also under the jurisdiction of an ICSID investor-state tribunal by virtue of an investment agreement. This is true even when ICSID investor-state arbitration has not been initiated and the prohibition of Article 27 of the ICSID Convention is not applicable. The reason is simply that the jurisdiction of the Court under Article 64 covers only disputes arising out of the application (and interpretation) of the ICSID Convention as such, which is obviously not an investment treaty setting substantive standards of treatment of foreign investors. Therefore, interstate

[25] *Republic of Italy v Republic of Cuba*, Interim Award (Ad Hoc Arbitral Tribunal 15 March 2005), para 65 (noting that "[l]'absence dans l'Accord d'une disposition semblable à l'article 27 de la Convention de Washington de 1965 n'empêche pas l'application de ce principe par analogie").

[26] See in general on these issues Potestà (2013), Wong (2014), Roberts (2014), Trevino (2014).

proceedings before the ICJ under Article 64 can never have an impact whatsoever on pending, completed or, potentially, even future investor-state arbitrations within the ICSID framework in relation to the merits of a case.

It is clear from the foregoing that the term "application" of the ICSID Convention under Article 64 does not confer jurisdiction to the ICJ to review an arbitral award on its merits or to settle investment disputes between states under investment agreements. In addition, Article 27 of the ICSID Convention is arguably irrelevant in all these respects given the limited material scope of the jurisdiction of the ICJ under Article 64. Yet, it may have an important role to play in relation to the main, and seemingly only, issue pertaining to the "application" of the ICSID Convention by the parties in this field, namely compliance with awards. Indeed, nothing in Article 27 bars diplomatic protection against a contracting state that "failed to abide by and comply with the award rendered" in a dispute submitted to ICSID arbitration. More particularly, according to Article 53, paragraph 1 of the ICSID Convention "[e]ach party shall abide by and comply with the terms of the award", while Article 54, paragraph 1 of the same instrument provides that each contracting state "shall recognize an award rendered pursuant to this Convention as binding and enforce the pecuniary obligations imposed by that award within its territories as if it were a final judgment of a court in that state". Paragraph 3 of the same Article, in turn, clarifies that the execution of the award "shall be governed by the laws concerning the execution of judgments in force in the state in whose territories such execution is sought". Article 53 imposes, thus, an obligation to comply with ICSID awards on the parties, including obviously the host state. Article 54, for its part, governs recognition, enforcement and execution[27] of awards by any contracting state.

Against this background, the home state of the aggrieved investor has the right to exercise diplomatic protection, including before the ICJ in accordance with Article 64, against the host state of the investment in case of failure to comply with the award in accordance with articles 53 and 54 of the Convention. Of course, according to Article 55 of the ICSID Convention, nothing in Article 54 of the ICSID Convention mentioned above, "shall be construed as derogating from the law in force in any contracting state relating to immunity of that state or of any foreign state from execution". But the revival of the right of diplomatic protection at the post-award enforcement stage, is not affected by any procedural bar under domestic law that may affect the award's enforcement such as state immunity. Indeed, though state immunity "may be used to thwart enforcement against certain types of property of the award debtor (...) it does not affect the obligation to comply with the award".[28] In other terms, "a state that successfully relies on the laws concerning

[27]For present purposes, it is not necessary to discuss the potential distinction between enforcement and execution.

[28]Schreuer et al. (2009), Article 53, p. 1107, para 37 and in general pp. 1106–1107, paras 36–38 (with further references). See Schreuer et al. (2009), Article 64, p. 1261, para. 14; Schreuer et al. (2009), Article 55, pp. 1153–1154.

state immunity from execution will be in violation of its obligation under the Convention".[29]

Having said that, while the ICSID Convention appears to support the idea that the duty of the host state party to an arbitration to comply with an award is independent from any domestic procedural hurdles to its enforcement, such as immunity from execution, it remains unclear if and to what extent disputes over the application of Article 55 and, as consequence, over state immunity issues could be submitted to the ICJ under Article 64. It is perhaps likely, if not obvious, that the host state of the investment will not be successful in invoking an immunity defence before the ICJ in order to justify the breach of its obligation to comply with an ICSID award. But what about a contracting state which was not a party to the ICSID arbitration but failed to enforce the award in violation of Article 54? It is arguable that diplomatic protection, including resort to the ICJ, by the home state of the investor against this forum state is also possible in this scenario.[30] Still, what if the latter invokes its domestic laws on sovereign immunities? More particularly, in order to deal with the alleged violation of Article 54, would the ICJ have to assess the compatibility of such domestic laws, including case law, with the relevant rules of customary international law governing immunity from enforcement?

In any case, it is unquestionable that ICJ has jurisdiction under Article 64 of the ICSID Convention to hear all cases which pertain to the "application" *of the ICSID Convention* (and not of investment agreements) *by contracting states* (and not by investment tribunals).[31] Still, no claims of this type have yet been submitted to the Court considering that in general states comply with their obligations under ICSID awards. Be that as it may, the Court would probably become in this scenario an important supporting actor in investment law and arbitration by reinforcing the authority of arbitral awards and at the same time the autonomy and integrity of the ICSID mechanism.

3.2 Interstate Disputes Over the "Interpretation" of the ICSID Convention

Beyond its potential use as a post-award interstate enforcement mechanism, the ICJ may in theory be called upon to deliver abstract interpretations of the ICSID Convention, including on issues concerning for instance the jurisdiction of arbitral tribunals under its Article 25 or the legal effects of the denunciation of this

---

[29]Schreuer et al. (2009), Article 54, pp. 1149–1150, para. 115.

[30]Schreuer et al. (2009), Article 64, p. 1261, para. 15; Article 54, p. 1125, para. 28.

[31]See also Reisman (2012), para. 41, noting that Article 64 relate to violations by one of the state-parties of its obligations to the other state party, such as failure to comply with an award or, more generally, matters concerning the invalidity, termination and suspension of the operation of treaties, since all these matters are exclusively inter-state issues.

instrument under its Articles 71 and 72. Normally, all these issues fall under the jurisdiction of investor-state arbitral tribunals.[32] Suppose, however, that a defendant host state, disappointed by a decision on jurisdiction adopted by an investment tribunal, decides to bring the case before the ICJ against the home state of the investor arguing that the interpretation of the arbitral tribunal is incompatible with, say, Article 25 of the ICSID Convention. The Report of the executive directors to the ICSID Convention makes it again clear that while Article 64

> is couched in general terms, it must be read in the context of the Convention as a whole. Specifically, the provision does not confer jurisdiction on the Court to review the decision of a Conciliation Commission or Arbitral Tribunal as to its competence with respect to any dispute before it.[33]

This clarification is due to the fact that during the drafting of the Convention there was considerable debate about the ICJ's power to interpret the Convention in matters of jurisdiction.[34] Some proposed that the ICJ should be able to receive referrals concerning the competence of ICSID tribunals in specific cases. Eventually, however, the general consensus of the delegates was that Article 64 would in no case enable a state party to arbitral proceedings to frustrate those proceedings by a referral of the jurisdictional matters to the ICJ. Indeed, any other solution would be incompatible with Article 41 of the ICSID Convention which confers to arbitral tribunals the power to decide on their own jurisdiction.[35] For some scholars, while it is clear that the ICJ

> will not determine the competence of a tribunal in proceedings pending before ICSID, this does not affect the general jurisdiction of the ICJ concerning the interpretation or application of the Convention.[36]

Arguably, neither the host state of the investment nor the home state of the investor would succeed in initiating proceedings, against each other as the case may be, under Article 64, in order to challenge an arbitral award on jurisdiction (or on the merits as seen above). If this is true, what is the remaining scope of such a "general jurisdiction" of the ICJ under Article 64 to interpret the Convention?

Another scenario is indeed at first sight more problematic. Suppose that a contracting state, wishing to shield itself from such interpretations in the future, asks for an abstract interpretation of Article 25 on the meaning of the term "investment" or of Articles 71 and 72 of the Convention concerning the legal effects of the denunciation of the same instrument. Would the Court accept to deliver such an abstract interpretation and, in the affirmative, would this interpretation be binding on

---

[32]Regarding the effects of the denunciation of the ICSID Convention see Fábrica de Vidrios Los Andres v. Bolivarian Republic of Venezuela, ICSID Case No. ARB/12/21, Award, 13 November 2017.

[33]Report of the Executive Directors on the Convention on the Settlement of Investment Disputes between States and Nationals of Other States, 1 ICSID Reports, pp. 32–33, para. 45.

[34]Schreuer et al. (2009), Article 64, pp. 1259–1260, paras 7–11.

[35]Broches (1972), pp. 369–370.

[36]Schreuer et al. (2009), Article 41, p. 520, para. 10.

future arbitral tribunals? As interesting as this question might seem, it is rather academic. In order that the ICJ settles a dispute over the interpretation of the Convention, such a dispute must genuinely exist between two contracting parties in the first place. This is a fundamental precondition to the exercise by the ICJ, or for that matter any other judicial body, of its powers. Yet, it remains unclear how a dispute over the interpretation of the Convention could concretely come into existence.

Having said that, it is interesting to point out here that in an interstate arbitration under an investment treaty between Ecuador and the United States, the tribunal was confronted with this kind of problem. More particularly, the host state of the investment, Ecuador, considered as erroneous and overbroad the interpretation of a provision of the applicable bilateral investment agreement delivered by the investor-state tribunal constituted under this agreement. So, by diplomatic note, Ecuador informed the United States that it disagreed with certain aspects of the award and requested it to confirm by diplomatic note its agreement with Ecuador's own interpretation. After its interpretation request to the United States remained unanswered, Ecuador asked for an abstract interpretation of the same provision before a state-to-state tribunal constituted under the same investment agreement. The tribunal declined jurisdiction by majority, on the ground that there was no dispute between the parties. It held that the omission of the US to react to the interpretation request treaty could not be considered as a "positive opposition", thereby rejecting the existence of a dispute between the parties. Indeed, the mere silence of the US was not enough to infer a disagreement with Ecuador's position. Instead, the silence of the US could be explained by the fact that the US did not want to interfere with the decisions of investor-state tribunals.[37]

This finding seems to allow, a contrario, for an abstract interpretation of an investment treaty by a state-to-state arbitral tribunal, in case of positive opposition between the parties over an issue of interpretation initially submitted to an investor-state tribunal. The interpretation dispute brought before the interstate arbitral tribunal could, thus, result in a decision potentially contradicting the solution reached by the investment tribunal on the same issue.

Transposed to the issue under examination, this would mean that the host state of the investment could make an interpretation request to the home state of the investor raising the same legal problem (for instance the meaning of investment in Article 25) as the one submitted to and settled by the investment tribunal. Such a request could in theory be made in abstracto, i.e. without openly challenging the specific interpretation of the ICSID Convention given by an investment tribunal. The request, if opposed actively by the host state, would, thus, suffice to create an apparently new dispute between the parties over the interpretation of the Convention concerning a jurisdictional matter.

[37]Ecuador v. United States of America, PCA Case No. 2012-5, Award, 29 September 2012, para. 219. On this case see also Trevino (2014), pp. 202–204.

Still, such a scenario does not seem very likely as far as the jurisdiction of the ICJ under Article 64 of the ICSID Convention is concerned. Admittedly, it is not certain that the ICJ will follow the "positive opposition" methodology regarding the treatment of the silence of the interpretative request addressee. It is not necessary here to go into the details of the complex case law of the ICJ related to the existence of a dispute, which is very demanding on the part of the claimant, as shown by the Marshall Islands cases of 2016.[38] It is sufficient to observe that in the *Georgia v Russia* case of 2011 the Court found that:

> the existence of a dispute may be inferred from the failure of a state to respond to a claim in circumstances where a response is called for.[39]

Therefore, the silence of the state to which the interpretation request has been submitted would not at first sight preclude the ICJ from establishing the existence of a dispute between two contracting states over the interpretation of the ICSID Convention.

Having said that, one hardly imagines how an interstate dispute may arise over the abstract interpretation of the ICSID Convention on a jurisdictional issue. As seen above, interstate proceedings under Article 64 specifically designed to challenge an arbitral award on jurisdiction or to influence the outcome of the arbitral proceedings on the issue of jurisdiction seem to be precluded. The real reason is that by a "dispute over the interpretation of the ICSID Convention", Article 64 means obviously interpretation *by the contracting parties themselves of their own rights and obligations under the Convention* and not interpretation of the Convention by investment tribunals. Consequently, jurisdictional issues under the ICSID Convention do not (and cannot) fall under this category because they concern a contracting host state and a foreign investor (and not its home state as such). The ICJ would, thus, probably dismiss a claim under Article 64 concerning the abstract interpretation of the ICSID Convention, on the ground that there is no real dispute between the parties.

The ICJ would perhaps even consider such type of interpretative action as contrary to the object and purpose of the Convention, as it is likely to undermine greatly the investor-state dispute settlement framework which provides for specific mechanisms, albeit not entirely satisfactory, of review of awards and more specifically an annulment procedure under Article 52 of the ICSID Convention. By doing that, the ICJ would avoid, and for good reason, frustrating the interpretation of the Convention by investment tribunals. As a result, the Court would have to assert jurisdiction only to the extent that the interstate interpretative dispute concerns genuinely the legal condition of the parties in their relations *inter se* and is not likely

---

[38]Obligations concerning Negotiations relating to Cessation of the Nuclear Arms Race and to Nuclear Disarmament (Marshall Islands v United Kingdom; India; Pakistan), Judgment, ICJ Reports 2016, p. 255.

[39]Application of the International Convention on the Elimination of All Forms of Racial Discrimination (Georgia v. Russia), Preliminary objections, Judgment, ICJ Reports 2011, p. 70, para. 30.

to affect the exercise by investment tribunals, whether in pending or future cases, of their compétence de la compétence.

To sum up, Article 64 of the ICSID Convention empowers neither the host state of the investment, party to an arbitration, nor the home state of the investor to initiate proceedings before the ICJ, in order to challenge arbitral awards on the merits or on jurisdiction or seek abstract interpretations of the Convention especially in matters of jurisdiction. The ICJ can only hear diplomatic protection cases for post-award enforcement purposes, containing possibly an immunity dimension. It would appear therefore that the ICJ may only be a supporting actor in international arbitration, and not a disruptive one, unlike, potentially, state-to-state arbitral tribunals provided for by investment treaties alongside investor-state dispute settlement mechanisms. Hence, procedural coordination between investment tribunals and the ICJ is not even necessary since the proceedings and decisions of the Court cannot have any impact whatsoever on investor-state proceedings. By contrast, such coordination is perhaps desirable when investment tribunals and non-investment adjudicative bodies deal with sovereignty disputes.

4 The Impact of Interstate Proceedings Over Sovereignty Disputes on Investment Law and Arbitration

Apart from Article 64 of the ICSID Convention, the scope of which is quite limited, interstate proceedings before non-investment courts and tribunals may potentially impact investment law and arbitration, if they concern competing territorial or maritime claims in a given area, i.e. sovereignty disputes. Quite often, these disputes arise from investments or planned investments by one or even both parties to the dispute in areas that are precisely disputed because they contain natural resources, as is the case with many maritime delimitation cases.[40] In more exceptional instances, the dispute does not, at least directly, arise from a “natural resources” conflict, but from legally controversial territorial changes, as in the case of Crimea involving Russia and Ukraine. Whatever the case may be, interstate proceedings and decisions over sovereignty disputes are likely to affect the legal condition of investments in the disputed area, as well as influence investor-state proceedings and decisions regarding the protection of the investments in the same area.

Admittedly, for non-investment and investment proceedings to interact in the hypothesis of sovereignty disputes, there is a condition to be fulfilled. The interested state must be able to find a forum capable of adjudicating its sovereignty claim against another state. In some instances, this difficulty does not arise. This is especially true in cases of maritime delimitation disputes where a non-investment adjudication body, such as the ITLOS or an ad hoc arbitral tribunal, has clearly

[40]Tzeng (2018), p. 831.

jurisdiction to settle sovereignty claims. On the contrary, in other instances, the jurisdictional hurdle might be more difficult to overcome.

The Crimean case perfectly illustrates this problem. In 2016 Ukraine instituted proceedings against Russia before an arbitral tribunal constituted under Annex VII of the United Nations Convention on the Law of the Sea ("UNCLOS"). According to Ukraine, Russia is engaged in serious violations of the UNCLOS by excluding Ukraine from enjoying the abundant hydrocarbon and fisheries resources within Ukraine's own maritime areas in the Black Sea, the Sea of Azov, and the Kerch Strait. According to Russia, by contrast, the real dispute is about sovereignty over Crimea and has nothing to do with violations of the UNCLOS. Consequently, the dispute would fall outside the scope of the tribunal's jurisdiction under Article 288 (1) of the UNCLOS, which is the sole provision on which Ukraine relied to found jurisdiction. In its award of 21 February 2020, the arbitral tribunal unanimously found that it lacked jurisdiction to hear the case "to the extent that a ruling of the Arbitral Tribunal on the merits of Ukraine's claims necessarily requires it to decide, directly or implicitly, on the sovereignty of either Party over Crimea".[41]

But, if, for the sake of argument, an interstate non-investment court or tribunal establishes its jurisdiction to settle a sovereignty dispute, the potential impact of its decision on investment law and arbitration remains uncertain and raises very interesting and complex questions two of which merit further examination. These questions concern closely related but distinct issues. First, when a sovereignty dispute exists at the time of the authorization of an investment in a given area, what is the impact of interstate proceedings over such a dispute on the assessment by an investment tribunal of the legality of (the authorization of) that investment (Sect. 4.1)? Second, when the sovereignty dispute arises as a result of controversial territorial changes, what is the impact of interstate proceedings on the territorial applicability of an investment treaty in the disputed area and, therefore, on the jurisdiction of an investor-state tribunal (Sect. 4.2)?

4.1 *Sovereignty Disputes and the Legality of (the Authorization of) the Investment*

Suppose a state grants an oil concession to a foreign investor in a maritime area (in the exclusive economic zone or the continental shelf for instance), where another state has expressed sovereignty claims. It this authorization lawful under international law? And if an interstate adjudicative body settles this issue one way or another, would an investment tribunal hearing a claim by the foreign investor operating in the disputed maritime area be bound by it?

---

[41]PCA, Press release, 16 March 2020, https://pcacases.com/web/sendAttach/9342 (last accessed 1 June 2020).

To try to answer these questions, it is necessary to examine first, whether, under the law of the sea, the authorization of an investment in a disputed area is lawful. There are only few cases related to this specific problem. In the *Guyana v Suriname* case in 2007, an arbitral tribunal constituted under Annex VII of the UNCLOS found that exploratory oil drilling in disputed waters by a state (in this case Guyana) was, unlike seismic testing, a unilateral activity potentially leading to permanent physical change to the marine environment and, thus, affecting the other party's rights in a permanent manner. For that reason, such action was found to be contrary to the obligation of the acting state "not to jeopardize or hamper the reaching of a final delimitation agreement" established in Articles 74(3) and 83(3) of the UNCLOS. Interestingly, this was so, even though the activity in question had taken place in an area which the tribunal ultimately declared to be under Guyanese sovereignty.[42]

By contrast, in a more recent maritime delimitation dispute between Ghana and Côte d'Ivoire in the Atlantic Ocean, the special chamber of the ITLOS apparently reached a different conclusion. Ghana had conducted oil exploration and production in the area of the Gulf of Guinea, which was also claimed by Côte d'Ivoire. The latter maintained that it was its own right to select the oil companies to conduct exploration and exploitation operations and requested urgent provisional measures. In 2015 the special chamber decided in its order that, among others, Ghana had to take all necessary steps to ensure that no new drilling either by Ghana or under its control takes place in the disputed area.[43] Obviously, this provisional measure prevented, albeit indirectly, investors from operating their investment. More importantly, in its 2017 decision, delimiting the maritime boundary between the two states, the special chamber found that none of Ghana's authorized oil concessions had taken place in any area within Côte d'Ivoire's sovereignty. For this reason, it was impossible to state that Ghana had undertaken activities "jeopardizing or hampering the conclusion of a delimitation agreement" in accordance with Article 83, paragraph 3, of the UNCLOS.[44]

Having said that, what if the tribunal had decided in the exact opposite way? What if the oil concessions granted by Ghana were later found to be falling within Côte d'Ivoire's maritime area? In fact, Côte d'Ivoire also claimed that the activities undertaken unilaterally by Ghana constituted a violation of the exclusive sovereign rights of Côte d'Ivoire over its continental shelf. The special chamber rejected the argument on the ground that:

> maritime activities undertaken by a state in an area of the continental shelf which has been attributed to another state by an international judgment cannot be considered to be in violation of the sovereign rights of the latter if those activities were carried out before the

---

[42] Guyana v Suriname, PCA Case No. 2004-04, Award, 17 September 2007, paras 479–482.

[43] Dispute Concerning Delimitation of the Maritime Boundary Between Ghana and Côte d'Ivoire in the Atlantic Ocean, ITLOS Case No. 23, Order, 25 April 2015 (Provisional Measures).

[44] ITLOS, Dispute Concerning Delimitation of the Maritime Boundary between Ghana and Côte d'Ivoire in the Atlantic Ocean (Ghana/Côte d'Ivoire), ITLOS Case No. 23, Judgment, 23 September 2017, para. 633.

> judgment was delivered and if the area concerned was the subject of claims made in good faith by both sates.[45]

Of course, as already noted, none of these activities took place in areas attributed to Côte d'Ivoire by the judgment, but, still, this would make no difference. Indeed, the tribunal held that:

> the argument advanced by Côte d'Ivoire that the hydrocarbon activities carried out by Ghana in the disputed area constitute a violation of the sovereign rights of Côte d'Ivoire is not sustainable, even assuming that some of those activities took place in areas attributed to Côte d'Ivoire by the present Judgment.[46]

It is neither possible nor necessary here to offer a critical analysis of these findings under the law of the sea.[47] It would seem, however, that the bona fide authorization of an investment by a state before the delimitation decision is delivered does not violate the sovereign rights of another state in a disputed area, regardless of whether this area was finally attributed to that state or not through adjudication. Yet, does this mean that the same authorization is also lawful under an investment treaty? What would be the legal impact on investment arbitration of a ruling of an interstate non-investment court according to which the state authorizing a foreign investment in a disputed area did not have any title to do this, because the area belonged to another state party to the dispute?

These questions are crucial because the conformity of the authorization of the investment and, thus, of the investment itself, with other rules of international law could affect the investment protection mechanisms provided for by an investment treaty. More particularly, as it is well-known, many investment agreements require that the investment be made in accordance with the laws of the host state. Yet, would an investment authorized contrary to international law also be contrary to the domestic law of the authorizing state?

One might be inclined to think that this is possible considering that the domestic law of the host (authorizing) state may directly or indirectly incorporate rules of international law (e.g. law of the sea and especially Articles 74(3) and 83(3) of UNCLOS mentioned above) governing the legality of unilateral actions such as precisely the authorization of an investment in a disputed maritime area.[48] If one accepts this line of argument, however, the investor concerned will have no chance to claim any protection under an investment treaty since his investment would be unlawful. Admittedly, this outcome seems unfair, even if an investor engaging in operations in disputed maritime areas should be aware of that risk. Indeed, it is also

[45] ITLOS, Dispute Concerning Delimitation of the Maritime Boundary between Ghana and Côte d'Ivoire in the Atlantic Ocean (Ghana/Côte d'Ivoire), ITLOS Case No. 23, Judgment, 23 September 2017, para. 592.

[46] ITLOS, Dispute Concerning Delimitation of the Maritime Boundary between Ghana and Côte d'Ivoire in the Atlantic Ocean (Ghana/Côte d'Ivoire), ITLOS Case No. 23, Judgment, 23 September 2017, para. 594 (emphasis added).

[47] See for a full discussion van Logchem (2019).

[48] Tzeng (2018), p. 483.

possible to consider that a respondent state, which authorized the investment in violation of international law, would be estopped from asserting, before an investor-state tribunal, that the investment was not in compliance with international law and, by extension, with its domestic law.[49]

Be that as it may, according to some authors, the settlement of an interstate sovereignty dispute by a non-investment adjudicative body would potentially not only impact the investments made in the disputed area, but also in other areas of the world, as it would amount to an authoritative statement of the law concerning the issue of the lawfulness of the authorization of an investment in disputed areas.[50] Still, it is for investment tribunals to decide if, and to what extent, this statement of the law may influence the outcome of a case brought before them when establishing the lawfulness of an investment under the applicable treaty.

Moreover, even if the investment tribunal considers, following the *Ghana v Côte d'Ivoire* ruling, that the investment was made in accordance with both domestic and international law, another problem arises. A foreign investor, whose investment has been terminated as a result of the delimitation decision, would certainly not be entitled to claim reparations for breach of its rights under an investment treaty (e.g. protection against expropriation) to the former host state for having authorized an investment in an area that was not (finally) within its territory. The reason is that the authorization of the investment as such cannot breach investment protection standards (at least as far the rights of the authorized foreign investor are concerned). Yet, could the foreign investor claim reparation on the ground that the former host state lost in the interstate proceedings? This is also problematic because the respondent state could argue it had a duty under Articles 74 and 83 of UNCLOS to resort to the dispute settlement procedures established by that instrument.[51]

Finally, the fact that the former host state lost its sovereign claims as a result of interstate adjudication proceedings raises the question of the applicability ratione loci of the investment treaty relied upon by the foreign investor to bring its claim against this state. Would an investment tribunal be able to uphold the applicability of an investment treaty in a territory that no longer belongs to the respondent state as a result of an interstate adjudication? This bring us to the next and last question.

---

[49] Tzeng (2018), p. 487.

[50] Trevisanut and Giannopoulos (2018), p. 825.

[51] See Tzeng (2018), pp. 847–848, who raises also other very interesting questions: "Must the state give the investor certain participation rights in concluding the agreement or in litigating the dispute so as not to violate the non-expropriation and/or FET standards? Can the state violate the non-expropriation and/or FET standards for not having litigated the case effectively enough? As for FET in particular, is it within the legitimate expectations of the investor that the state could lose its rights in the disputed maritime area?".

4.2 The Territorial Applicability of the Investment Treaty

Almost all investment treaties grant investor-state tribunals jurisdiction over investments made in the territory of the respondent state. Thus, in order to establish its jurisdiction ratione loci, an investment tribunal will have to decide whether the investment has been made in that territory. However, what if the area in question is disputed between two states? This problem is different from the scenario examined above, since it is in principle unrelated to the legality of the authorization of an investment as such. Instead, it raises the issue of the territorial applicability of an investment treaty and therefore the identification of the state (including the one that has not authorized the investment) bound to provide protection to the investor in a given area.

This problem may arise in relation to territorial disputes which are not, at least directly, linked to the exploitation of natural resources, as in the case of Crimea. Yet, this case is more complex, because, in addition to numerous proceedings before non-investment adjudicative bodies, including an UNCLOS arbitral tribunal (as seen above), the ECtHR, the ICJ and the International Criminal Court, investor-state tribunals have already intervened in the matter.[52] Ukrainian investors have, indeed, instituted several investor-state arbitrations against Russia under the Russia-Ukraine bilateral investment treaty regarding investments in Crimea. Article 1 of this treaty protects investments made by investors of one contracting Party "on the territory" of the other contracting Party. But is Crimea a Russian territory?

Confronted with this preliminary and highly complex question, the arbitral tribunals "studiously avoided passing any judgment on the legality of Russia's annexation of Crimea", but at the same time they were also "conscious not to take, by their decisions, any action that might be interpreted as recognising Russia's annexation of Crimea".[53] So, what did they do? Reportedly, and without going into the details of their reasoning,[54] they asserted jurisdiction by considering the effectiveness of Russian annexation of Crimea, without addressing the problem of its lawfulness under international law and, thus, the sovereignty dispute as such.

At this point, it is necessary to stress that the issue of the incidental or preliminary jurisdiction of an investor-state tribunal to deal with a sovereignty dispute must be distinguished from the potential impact on investment law and arbitration of proceedings before non-investment courts having jurisdiction over the same sovereignty dispute. The former raises some concerns about the legitimacy of investor-state tribunals in deciding, including indirectly, territorial sovereignty matters, in order to establish their own jurisdiction ratione loci under an investment treaty, even in the

[52]The examination of all these proceedings exceed the limits of this chapter. See in general Rees-Evans (2019) and Tzeng (2016).

[53]Rees-Evans (2019), p. 186.

[54]These proceedings are confidential, but some information is available from other channels, see in relation to six out of nine known investors-state cases Rees-Evans (2019), pp. 178–180 and pp. 184–188.

absence of interstate proceedings on these same matters.[55] The latter must be briefly examined now. Indeed, while the jurisdictional hurdle may be difficult to overcome as seen above in relation the Ukraine-Russia arbitration before an UNCLOS tribunal, what if an interstate court such as the ICJ had already established its jurisdiction to hear the sovereignty dispute or even settled the issue?

In exercising its normal subject-matter jurisdiction, an interstate jurisdiction may, in fact, have an ancillary role to play in investment law and arbitration since determining territorial sovereignty issues is likely to affect the territorial applicability of an investment treaty. Still, what would be the reaction of an investor-state tribunal constituted before the non-investment court renders its decision? Would it have to stay proceedings pending interstate settlement of the sovereignty issue? And if the arbitral tribunal is constituted after the interstate court has rendered its decision on the sovereignty dispute, would it be bound by that decision? More particularly, if an interstate court decides for instance that Crimea is part of Ukraine, would the arbitral tribunal be free to ignore such a determination by maintaining that the bilateral investment treaty is still applicable to Russia in Crimea on account of the effective territorial authority, occupation or control argument? Such a finding would certainly ensure that the investors are given a fair chance to be protected, at the expense, nevertheless, of the one made by a competent interstate adjudicative body. Indeed, unless the applicability ratione loci of the investment treaty is totally dissociated from the lawfulness of the acquisition of territorial sovereignty,[56] how can a territory be part, at the same time, of one state according to the decision of an interstate non-investment adjudicative body and of another state for investment arbitration purposes? Conversely, if the arbitral tribunal decides to follow the interstate decision and to decline jurisdiction by dismissing the applicability of the investment agreement on the ground that the territory in dispute does not belong to the defendant state, which still controls it, the investors will very likely be left without any legal protection. This would be an unfair outcome, but apparently more in line with the need of legal certainty and coherence of case law within a highly fragmented jurisdictional landscape.

Settling these and many other conceivable problems obviously depends on the attitude of each investment tribunal with regard to the decision of an interstate non-investment adjudicative body settling a sovereignty dispute. As mentioned above, given the lack or, even, irrelevance of formal coordination rules between proceedings before non-investment dispute settlement mechanisms and investment tribunals, the latter are not under an obligation to stay proceedings. They may, nonetheless, proceed in this way out of comity[57] towards the non-investment courts or tribunals, if they deem that the outcome of the sovereignty dispute is fundamental

---

[55] Tzeng (2018), pp. 843–847.

[56] For other interesting aspects of the broader issue, than cannot be further explored here, such as the obligation of non-recognition before investment tribunals and the application of investment treaties to occupied territory, see, respectively, Wuschka (2019) and Ackermann (2019).

[57] See Boisson de Chazournes (2017), pp. 66–69.

to the exercise of their own jurisdiction. Moreover, even if an investment tribunal is constituted after the decision settling the sovereignty dispute, it is doubtful that it will be formally bound by such a decision. Still, one may reasonably expect that investment tribunals dealing with issues of an inherently interstate character defer to the views of non-investment competent adjudication bodies.

5 Concluding Remarks

International non-investment courts and tribunals may influence in a limited way investment law and arbitration through their case law to which investment tribunals make constant references. Moreover, while international non-investment adjudicative bodies cannot be directly involved in investor-state disputes, i.e. regarding the alleged breach of investment protection standards by a host state, or "micro-investment" disputes, still, they may potentially become transnational actors in investment law and arbitration when dealing with "macro-investment" disputes, i.e. concerning the (territorial) scope of application of investment agreements or the functioning and effectiveness of investment arbitration. Such issues would include genuine disputes over the application or the interpretation of the ICSID Convention under Article 64, such as the enforcement of awards, including perhaps the effects of its denunciation by a contracting party, or sovereignty disputes.

One might even be tempted to suggest a principle of mutually exclusive mandates: non-investment courts and tribunals deciding "macro-investment" disputes should not interfere with "micro-investment" disputes. Conversely, investor-state arbitral tribunals should perhaps refrain from deciding "macro-investment" disputes directly involving states, such as sovereignty disputes. However, there is perhaps no way to identify once and for all the issues that cannot be adjudicated by investor-state tribunals on the ground that they would be more suitable for adjudication by non-investment courts and tribunals. As a matter of fact, it would seem that the exact scope of the impact of non-investment courts and tribunals on investment law and arbitration ultimately depends on how investment tribunals perceive non-investment courts and tribunals and their respective functions. Indeed, the lack of formal coordination rules between different adjudicative components of the international legal order seems to support the conclusion that non-investment courts and tribunals become transnational actors in international investment law and arbitration only if, and to the extent that, investment tribunals deem this necessary for the exercise of their own functions in each particular case. In a nutshell, this is a question that revolves inescapably around the quest for a coordination between different mechanisms of adjudication in public international law.

References

Ackermann T (2019) Investments under occupation: the application of investment treaties to occupied territory. In: Fach Gómez K, Gourgourinis A, Titi C (eds) International investment law and the law of armed conflict. European yearbook of international economic law. Springer Nature Switzerland AG, pp 67–92

Boisson de Chazournes L (2017) Plurality in the fabric of international courts and tribunals: the threads of a managerial approach. Eur J Int Law 28(1):13–72

Broches A (1972) The Convention on the settlement of investment disputes between states and nationals of other States. Collected Courses Hague Acad Int Law 136:331–410

De Brabandere E (2015) Complementarity or conflict? Contrasting the Yukos case before the European Court of Human Rights and investment tribunals. ICSID Rev 30(2):345–355

Dingwall J (2018) International investment protection in deep seabed mining beyond national jurisdiction. J World Invest Trade 19(5–6):890–929

Dupuy PM, Viñuales JE (2015) Human rights and investment disciplines: integration in progress. In: Bungenberg M, Griebel J, Hobe S, Reinisch A (eds) International investment law: a handbook. Nomos, Baden-Baden, pp 1739–1767

El Boudouhi S (2017) L'investisseur devant les juridictions internationales des droits de l'homme: la question des droits fondamentaux de l'investisseur. In: Robert-Cuendet S (ed) Droit des investissements. Perspectives croisées. Larcier, Bruxelles, pp 301–329

Fanou M, Tzevelekos VP (2018) The shared territory of the ECHR and international investment law. In: Radi Y (ed) Research handbook on human rights and investment. Edward Elgar, Cheltenham and Northampton, pp 93–136

Happold M, Radović R (2018) The ECOWAS Court of Justice as an investment tribunal. J World Invest Trade 19(1):95–117

Kriebaum U (2008) Nationality and the protection of property under the European convention on human rights. In: Buffard I, Crawford J, Pellet A, Wittich S (eds) International law between universalism and fragmentation. Festschrift in Honour of Gerhard Hafner. Nijhoff, Leiden, pp 649–666

Pellet A (2013) The case law of the ICJ in investment arbitration. ICSID Rev 28(2):223–240

Potestà M (2013) State-to-state dispute settlement pursuant to bilateral investment treaties: is there potential? In: Boschiero N, Scovazzi T, Pitea C, Ragni C (eds) International courts and the development of international law. T.M.C. Asser Press, The Hague, pp 753–768

Rees-Evans L (2019) Litigating the use of force: reflections on the interaction between investor-state dispute settlement and other forms of international dispute settlement in the context of the conflict in Ukraine. In: Fach Gómez K, Gourgourinis A, Titi C (eds) International investment law and the law of armed conflict. Springer Nature Switzerland AG, pp 173–196

Reisman M (2012) Ecuador v. United States, expert opinion with respect to jurisdiction of Professor W. Michael Reisman (Perm. Ct. Arb. 4 April 2012)

Roberts A (2014) State-to-state investment treaty arbitration: hybrid theory of interdependent rights and shared interpretive authority. Harv Int Law J 55:1):1–1)70

Schreuer C, Malintoppi L, Reinisch A, Sinclair A (2009) The ICSID convention: a commentary, 2nd edn. Cambridge University Press, Cambridge

Steininger S (2018) What's human rights got to do with it? An empirical analysis of human rights references in investment arbitration. Leiden J Int Law 31:33–58

Trevino CJ (2014) State-to-state investment treaty arbitration and the interplay with investor–state arbitration under the same treaty. J Int Dispute Settlement 5:199–233

Trevisanut S, Giannopoulos N (2018) Investment protection in offshore energy production: bright sides of regime interaction. J World Invest Trade 19(5–6):789–827

Tzeng P (2016) Sovereignty over Crimea: case for state-to-state investment arbitration. Yale J Int Law 41(2):459–468

Tzeng P (2018) Investment protection in disputed maritime areas. J World Invest Trade 19 (5-6):828–859 van Logchem Y (2019) The rights and obligations of states in disputed maritime areas: what lessons can be learned from the maritime boundary dispute between Ghana and Cote d'Ivoire. Vanderbilt J Transnatl Law 52(1):121–178

Wong J (2014) The subversion of state-to-state investment treaty arbitration. Columbia J Transnatl Law 53(1):6–47

Wuschka S (2019) Procedural aspects of the obligation of non-recognition before international investment tribunals. In: Fach Gómez K, Gourgourinis A, Titi C (eds) International investment law and the law of armed conflict. Springer Nature Switzerland AG, pp 129–151

Ioannis Prezas is associate professor of international law at the Sorbonne Law School, University Paris 1 Panthéon-Sorbonne, France. He holds a PhD from the University Paris 2 Panthéon-Assas for which he was awarded, inter alia, the prestigious thesis prize of the French Society of international law. He is a member of the Sorbonne research institute for international and European Studies (IREDIES), the French branch of the international law association, the French society of international law and the Hellenic society of international law and international relations. He teaches public international law, the law of international adjudication, international environmental law and international economic law, including investment law. For four years he has been editor of the annual ICSID case law review in the *Hellenic review of international law*. His recent publications include an edited volume entitled *Substance et procédure en droit international public: dialectique et influences croisées*, Paris, Pedone, 2019.

Apropos of the External Precedent: Judicial Cross-Pollination Between Investment Tribunals and International Courts

Fulvio Maria Palombino and Gustavo Minervini

Contents

1 Introduction 134
2 Fragmentation and Coherence: A Definition 135
3 The Role of the External Precedent in the Investment Arbitration Caselaw 139
4 The Role of the Investment Arbitration Caselaw in the ICJ Jurisprudence 145
5 Conclusions 147
References 149

Abstract In the horizontal and decentralized international legal system, an effective judicial dialogue is a basic requirement to guarantee the harmonious development of international law. In this respect, since the international competent judge is not pre-established by law, there is a risk of fragmentation of international law as a result of a different interpretation of the same rule of law provided by distinct international judicial bodies. From this perspective, the use of external authorities has often been considered as a potential remedy to fragmentation. Indeed, by carefully examining the precedents related to the specific issues, each judge may contribute to the harmonious interpretation and development of international law. Nevertheless, the use of external authorities is not something good in itself. This chapter analyses the role of external authorities in investment arbitration and vice-versa, on the assumption that the use or misuse of external precedents by one court may affect how other tribunals will use its jurisprudence. Through the examination of four selected cases where judges strategically relied or ignored external

---

This chapter is the result of the joint work of the two Authors. However, in detail, Prof. Palombino wrote Sects. 1 and 4 while Mr Minervini wrote Sects. 2, 3 and 5. As far as Mr Minervini, this chapter is partly based on the Adv LLM Thesis the author submitted in fulfilment of the requirements of the Master of Laws: Advanced Studies Programme in Public International Law degree, Leiden Law School (Leiden University).

F. M. Palombino (✉) · G. Minervini
School of Law, University of Naples Federico II, Naples, Italy
e-mail: fulviomaria.palombino@unina.it; gustavo.minervini@unina.it

A. Gourgourinis (ed.), *Transnational Actors in International Investment Law*,
European Yearbook of International Economic Law,
https://doi.org/10.1007/978-3-030-60679-4_6

authorities, this chapter finally contends that a misuse of external jurisprudence produces a vicious circle in which international courts and tribunals are likely to ignore each other. Quite the opposite, a prerequisite for international courts and tribunals to effectively participate in the harmonious development of international law must be sought in the careful and justified use of the exogenous precedent.

1 Introduction

As far as the Italian legal order is concerned, Article 25, para. 1 of the Constitution states that "no case may be removed from the court seized with it as established by law".[1] This is nothing but a manifestation of the Rule of Law as it has been traditionally conceived by most liberal democracies: it is up to the (national) law (and exclusively to it) to determine the judge called upon to solve a certain dispute. Quite the opposite, international law does not exercise a function like this and the principle to be resorted to is that of "consent", i.e. the principle whereby "no state can, without its consent, be compelled to submit its disputes [. . .] to arbitration, or any other kind of pacific settlement".[2] In other words, whereas in domestic legal systems the competent judge is pre-established by law, in the international legal order jurisdiction and adjudication may take place only with the assent of the parties.

Despite some attempts to challenge it, the consensual paradigm, intended as a corollary of the principles of sovereignty and equality of states, continues to remain undisputed and, at least in part, explains the proliferation of international courts and tribunals ("ICTs") competent in the same subject-matter; since international law does not establish the competent judge with regard to a certain dispute, there is nothing impeding states from creating courts with overlapping, or even conflicting, jurisdiction. Thus, it emerges the problem of the potential inconsistency of international law as a result of a different interpretation or application of the same rule of law by distinct international judicial bodies.

In light of these premises, this paper is divided into three main parts. In the first part (Sect. 2), we will investigate in general terms the concepts of fragmentation of international law and of external precedent as a potential remedy to it. In this regard, our analysis is carried out on the premise that there is a single international legal system, although a decentralized, horizontal and pluricentric one. In this sense, the international legal system has been defined as a complex adaptive system, i.e.

[1]Article 25, para. 1 of the Constitution of the Italian Republic, https://www.senato.it/documenti/repository/istituzione/costituzione_inglese.pdf (last accessed 21 December 2019).

[2]Status of Eastern Carnelia (1923), Advisory Opinion, PCIJ (Series B) No. 5, p. 19.

> a system in which large networks of components with no central control and simple rules of operation give rise to complex collective behaviour, sophisticated information processing and adaptation via learning or evaluation.[3]

In part two (Sects. 3 and 4), the concepts of fragmentation and external precedent will be resorted to with the view of exploring the impact of external jurisprudence in investment arbitration and vice-versa (i.e. the impact of external investment jurisprudence on ICTs).

Finally (Sect. 5), we will inquire into the question of whether the use of external authorities is necessarily conducive to coherence or, rather, a kind of intellectual work to be carried out cautiously.

Against this background, this chapter aims to investigate the book's overall theme, namely transnational actors in international investment law. Indeed, investment arbitral tribunals inherently deal with transnational situations, which involve a foreign investor and a host state. Furthermore, one should not overlook that arbitral tribunals themselves—and, more generally, investment arbitration—can be deemed to be transnational to the extent that their activities transcend national frontiers. From this point of view, the same precedent may be seen as transnational: first, to the extent that it is outcome of such transnational activity; and second, because of its use as a tool to decide future (transnational) cases. Ultimately, the precedent transcends national frontiers of the involved States and influences the evolution of international investment law.

2 Fragmentation and Coherence: A Definition

Before analysing whether there has been a fruitful judicial dialogue between investment tribunals and international courts, as well as the extent to which the use of external authorities may further such dialogue, it is of the utmost importance to dwell on the terms of the problem: "fragmentation" and "coherence".

The issue of fragmentation is a relatively recent phenomenon, which emerged at the end of the 1990s giving rise to a frenetic and vigorous debate within the international law community.[4] For the purpose of this work, however, we should distinguish between two understandings of fragmentation: a normative and an

[3]Mitchell (2009), p. 13. A clarification of this definition has been provided by Pauwelyn (2014), p. 383 who pointed out the features of a complex adaptive system: "(i) dispersed interaction between many heterogeneous agents, (ii) leading to emergent, self-organized collective behavior, (iii) having no global controller and (iv) continual adaptation with out-of-equilibrium dynamics."

[4]The issue was firstly raised and discussed by ICJ Judges with regard to the role of the World Court in light of the creation of new international courts and tribunals. See Guillaume (1995), pp. 860–862; Abi-Saab (1999), pp. 926–930; Higgins (2001), p. 122. See also Koskenniemi and Leino (2002), pp. 553–556; Pauwelyn (2006), paras. 1–6.

interpretative one.[5] As for normative fragmentation, we mean the possible conflicts between different substantive bodies of international law, such as those between human rights law and investment law,[6] humanitarian law and human rights law,[7] or environmental law and trade law.[8] This issue was the subject of a seminal study by the United Nations International Law Commission ("ILC") whose final report

> adopt[ed] a technical approach to fragmentation that [...] focuses on the work that can be done by formal tools such as lex specialis, lex posterior, lex superior, and systemic integration.[9]

As for interpretative fragmentation, we use this wording to describe the situation where different international courts, adjudging the same legal or factual issue, render contradictory decisions on a single rule or body of law.[10] In light of the scope of this work, the focus of our analysis will be on this second understanding of fragmentation, which does require further elaboration.

First of all, the causes and risks of interpretative fragmentation should be pointed out. As far as the former, it was the sudden growth in the number of international courts and tribunals that raised most concerns. Indeed, as pointed out by Sir Christopher Greenwood,

> "[i]n the space of barely thirty years, the International Court of Justice has been joined by ITLOS, the International Criminal Court, ad hoc criminal courts or tribunals [...], the dispute settlement mechanism of the World Trade Organization" and hundreds of ad hoc investor-State arbitral tribunals.[11]

From this perspective, the coexistence of several courts with an overlapping or even conflicting jurisdiction was, and is still, perceived as a threat to the coherence or unity of international law. Indeed, if several courts and tribunals, without a formal hierarchy, can adjudge in the same subject-matter, they will probably come to conflicting interpretation or application of the same rule of law. Therefore, in a

---

[5]In this sense, see Dupuy (2007), p. 26; Webb (2013), pp. 5–7; Cohen HG (2016), Fragmentation, https://papers.ssrn.com/sol3/papers.cfm?abstract_id=2785719 (last accessed 1 June 2020), pp. 7–8.

[6]De Brabandere E (2018), Human Rights and international investment law, https://papers.ssrn.com/sol3/papers.cfm?abstract_id=3149387 (last accessed 1 June 2020), pp. 16–21.

[7]Droege (2008), pp. 501–502: "Traditionally, international human rights law (IHRL) and international humanitarian law (IHL) are two distinct bodies of law with different subject matters and different roots, and for a long time they evolved without much mutual influence. This has changed. [...] [T]here is today no question that human rights law comes to complement humanitarian law in situations of armed conflict. [...] In short, these regimes overlap, but as they were not necessarily meant to do so originally, one must ask how they can be reconciled and harmonized."

[8]Fragmentation of International Law: difficulties arising from the Diversification and Expansion of International Law: Report of the Study Group of the International Law Commission—Finalized by Martti Koskenniemi. ILC, 13 April 2006, UN Doc A/CN.4/L.682, p. 19, https://legal.un.org/ilc/documentation/english/a_cn4_l682.pdf (last accessed 21 December 2019); Knox (2004), pp. 4–29.

[9]Cohen (2016), p. 11.

[10]In this sense, Webb (2013), p. 6; Cohen (2016), pp. 7–8.

[11]Greenwood (2015), p. 46.

decentralized legal system, the same issue can be divergently decided. Such an outcome, however, runs against the fundamental principle that similar cases should be treated alike; a principle which safeguards legal systems minimizing the uncertainties and fostering the predictability of the law, and, thus, maintaining the credibility and legitimacy of the system itself. That is even more important in the international legal system which has neither a final court of appeal nor a centralized enforcement mechanism, and whose legitimacy "rests to a large extent on the international community's confidence in the way international law is [interpreted,] applied and developed."[12]

From this point of view—recalling a famous English maxim according to which "justice should not only be done, but also should manifestly and undoubtedly be seen to be done"[13]—coherent decisions of ICTs do enhance such confidence by, *inter alia*, "contribut[ing] to a perception that legal decision-makers decide in accordance with rules rather than arbitrary criteria."[14]

In light of the foregoing, one can easily understand why the fear of fragmentation has led to a quest for coherence in the international legal system and, more specifically, in international adjudication. However, in the authors' own view, coherence is "an inherently elusive and slippery concept"[15] which, despite being extensively used in all the different fields of human knowledge, should be carefully contextualized within the legal framework. Starting with a general proposition, the Cambridge Dictionary defines coherence as "the situation when the parts of something fit together in a natural or reasonable way."[16] Moving into the field of law, Schreuer pointed out that "[a] legal system is coherent if its elements are logically related to each other and if *it shows no contradictions*."[17] More specifically, focusing on coherence as a criterion of adjudication, Stefano Bertrea provided a definition of it as:

> the interpretive canon enabling one to establish and justify a specific standpoint by invoking the need to contribute to, and to preserve, the coherence – namely, the internal connectedness – of the system as a whole.[18]

This notion of internal connectedness represents the most useful theoretical and practical understanding of coherence for the purpose of this work. Indeed, from this

---

[12]Webb (2013), p. 6.

[13]Lord Chief Justice Gordon Hewart in *R v. Sussex Justices, Ex Parte McCarty* [1924] 1KB 256. This maxim is strictly linked to the concept of social legitimacy in relation to which see Hurd (1999), p. 381: "*[l]egitimacy*, as I use it here, refers to the normative belief by an actor that a rule or institution ought to be obeyed. It is a subjective quality, relational between actor and institution, and defined by the actor's *perception* of the institution."

[14]Ten Cate (2013), p. 455.

[15]Bertrea (2005), p. 371.

[16]Cambridge Online Dictionary, 'Coherence', https://dictionary.cambridge.org/it/dizionario/inglese/coherence (last accessed 21 December 2019).

[17]Schreuer (2013), p. 391 (italics added).

[18]Bertrea (2005), p. 373 (italics added).

perspective, a coherent decision on a certain legal issue will show that its result is the product of the internal connections of the system and was rendered with the awareness of the existing framework—in this sense, we can argue that the decision should offer an "image" of the system *making a sense as a whole*—.

A coherent decision, therefore, must not only be correctly underpinned by references to the rules of law, but also take into account the whole framework in which it is entailed. This framework includes, due to their prominence in both the clarification and development of international law, the decisions of other international courts and tribunals. According to this view, the reasoning of the judgment acquires an even more fundamental role than its outcome, by allowing the parties of the dispute and the whole international community to examine and appreciate the different steps leading to that result.[19]

This notion of coherence as internal connectedness that underpins a system *making sense as a whole*, however, should not be confused with a call for uniformity. Indeed, as pointed out by Leonor Soriano, "coherence in legal reasoning assists the judge in pursuing an ideal: to make sense of the diversity of law."[20] In this sense, coherence does not require tribunals to always decide in the same way but, recognizing the plurality of possible solutions, imposes the argumentative duty to fully justify a decision within the existing framework. And it is exactly from this perspective that the use of external precedents should be seen.

By definition, the concept of external or exogenous precedent refers to the use by courts and tribunals of judicial decisions rendered by other courts and tribunals.[21] In such hypothesis, precedent could never be binding. Quite the opposite, Michele Taruffo contends that an external authority could neither be properly considered as a precedent, since there is no horizontal or vertical relationship among courts pertaining to a different legal order or regime. Its aim would apparently be a more limited one: to inform the judge about the fact that a certain provision has been applied in a certain way in a certain case.[22] In this respect, Michele Taruffo suggests that it would be appropriate to consider external authorities as examples, which can neither bind nor constrain subsequent decisions.

Nonetheless, in the authors' own view, such a circumstance does not reduce the argumentative power of external precedents insofar as they are presumed "to refer to a shared corpus of international law";[23] a corpus whose interpretation, however, is

---

[19]In this sense, see Kurtz (2014), p. 274 who recognized that rather than consistency "it is even more important that there is greater coherence and integrity in reasoning employed by arbitral tribunals."

[20]Soriano (2003), p. 302.

[21]Palombino (2018), p. 156: who defines the issue of external precedent as the situation in which "a court relies on the decisions of tribunals operating under a different legal order or regime with a view to determining the scope of a certain rule of law."

[22]Taruffo (2007), p. 32. Contrariwise, Guillaume (2011), pp. 5, 19: who asserts that even in these cases judges and arbitrators should consider previous "decisions – either to follow or distinguish them – while justifying their choice."

[23]Charlotin (2017), p. 284.

susceptible to change depending on the context where it is resorted to. In other words, the judge taking into consideration the "example" provided by external authorities, is expected to contribute to the harmonious development of international law either confirming the correctness of that information or reshaping its content and value in the light of the particular circumstances of the case submitted to it. What should never lack, in any event, is a crystal-clear reasoning.

That being said as a matter of premise, and moving from the assumption that all international courts and tribunals rely on external precedents in their case law, two questions will be explored in the next few pages: (1) whether investment tribunals, when using external precedents, always do so on a sound basis, i.e. *not for merely opportunistic reasons*; (2) whether other international courts and tribunals are, in turn, willing to resort to investment case-law. Needless to say, these two questions are strictly intertwined: the kind of use of *external precedents* by one court will arguably affect the use of this court's *external jurisprudence* by other courts and vice versa.

This is because the relationship between international courts and tribunals—lacking any hierarchical structure—cannot but be based on mutual consideration. In this sense, one could expect ICTs to rely on each other's jurisprudence only to the extent that there is no misuse. Therefore, in order to create a virtuous circle of mutual consideration and reliability, they should carefully engage with each other's jurisprudence and, eventually, rely on it without any instrumentalization.

This finally brings us to consider how ICTs should, in practice, deal with an external authority. In this respect, once again, the reasoning plays a pivotal role: indeed, what seems of the utmost importance is to clearly articulate as to how the external authority fits within the different context and the issue at stake. One could define this process as a "reinforced" reasoning. While the relevance of an International Centre for Settlement of Investment Disputes ("ICSID") precedent in a subsequent ICSID case is apparent, the same does not (necessarily) hold true for an International Court of Justice ("ICJ") one. In the latter case, the arbitral tribunal should not merely recall the external authority, but it should provide a clear explanation as to why the ICJ precedent is suitable for the context and the issue at stake.

3 The Role of the External Precedent in the Investment Arbitration Caselaw

The question as to whether, why and how international courts and tribunals (should) resort to external precedent when adjudging their disputes has been the subject of an extensive scholarship as a result of the so-called judicialization of international law and the multiplication of international litigation fora.[24] However, the purpose of this

[24]Guillaume (2011), pp. 18–23; Cohen (2015), p. 270: "The precedents from one regional body are argued to others, precedents from human rights courts are argued to investment tribunals, and

section is not to provide a general overview of this topic but rather to shed some lights on the misuse of external authorities by investment tribunals.

From this perspective, it is contended that the misuse of external precedents is even more worrying than its non-use. Indeed, in light of the above-mentioned relationship based on mutual consideration, an unsound or unjustified recourse to external jurisprudence risks compromising the judicial dialogue among international courts and tribunals, instead of furthering a fruitful cross-pollination.

In greater detail, we will focus on two well-known cases where arbitral tribunals unconvincingly resorted to external jurisprudence: *Continental Casualty Company v. Argentina*[25] and *Philip Morris v. Uruguay*.[26] The choice of these two cases is not accidental: indeed, they are particularly illustrative of how the misuse of external authorities strengthens the sense of fragmentation and incoherence among the different international law fields.

As for the *Continental Casualty* case—one of the several cases stemming out from the unprecedented economic crisis which Argentina had to face at the beginning of the present century—the arbitral tribunal grappled with state's possibility of and requirements for invoking state of necessity as a circumstance precluding the wrongfulness of a conduct. Notably, the arbitral tribunal was called to adjudicate on the relationship between Article XI of the US-Argentina Bilateral Investment Treaty ("BIT")[27] and the defence of state of necessity, whose requirements contained in Article 25 of the International Law Commission Articles on Responsibility of States for Internationally Wrongful Acts ("ARSIWA")[28] are generally considered to be

precedents from ad hoc criminal tribunals are applied to domestic civil judgments. [...] So why does an ICTY decision carry weight in internal US Executive Branch discussions? Or in broader terms, when and why do particular decisions become precedents? This chapter begins to answer that question. Its goal is to develop a framework for a broader account of international precedent's emergence. To use this book's metaphor, in the game of international interpretation, what are the spoken and unspoken strategies of precedent? Why will certain prior interpretations be invoked in certain contexts and with certain audiences? When will those strategies be effective, forcing other actors to respond to a prior interpretation, echoing it, building upon it, or distinguishing it?"; De Brabandere (2016), pp. 42–52.

[25]Continental Casualty Company v. Argentina, ICSID Case No. ARB/03/09, Award, 5 September 2008.

[26]Philip Morris Brands Sàrl, Philip Morris Products S.A. and Abal Hermanos S.A. v. Uruguay, ICSID Case No. ARB/10/7, Award, 8 July 2016.

[27]Article XI of the US-Argentina BIT reads as follows: "This Treaty shall not preclude the application by either Party of measures necessary for the maintenance of public order, the fulfilment of its obligations with respect to the maintenance or restoration of international peace or security, or the Protection of its own essential security interests."

[28]Article 25 of ARSIWA reads as follows: "1. Necessity may not be invoked by a State as a ground for precluding the wrongfulness of an act not in conformity with an international obligation of that State unless the act: (a) is the only way for the State to safeguard an essential interest against a grave and imminent peril; and (b) does not seriously impair an essential interest of the State or States towards which the obligation exists, or of the international community as a whole. 2. In any case, necessity may not be invoked by a State as a ground for precluding wrongfulness if: (a) the international obligation in question excludes the possibility of invoking necessity; or (b) the State has contributed to the situation of necessity."

reflective of customary international law.[29] Indeed, by relying on both Article XI and the doctrine of state of necessity, Argentina maintained that the measures adopted in the wake of the economic crisis were justified by a state of necessity, which precluded wrongfulness and exempted the host State from the payment of an indemnity.[30]

This was not the first case where such an issue was at stake. In this sense, the *CMS* Tribunal regarded the two legal regimes as two sides of the same coin, therefore applying the requirements set out by Article 25 to Article XI.[31] Similarly, the *Enron* and *Sempra* Tribunals—although recognizing the existence of two separate legal regimes—concluded that an "appropriate analysis should look to [customary international law] [...] because Article XI did not provide specific requirements for invoking such a defence."[32]

In the *Continental Casualty* award, however, the Tribunal "took the controversial path of importing the [World Trade Organization's ("WTO")] approach to necessity under Article XX of the [General Agreement on Tariffs and Trade ("GATT")] into its interpretation of the US-Argentina BIT"[33] through a two-folded reasoning. First, the tribunal argued on the relationship between Article XI and the CIL necessity defence, concluding that, although there is a link between them, "the conditions of applications are not the same".[34] Second, in order to determine the content of the concept of necessity enshrined in Article XI, the Tribunal resorted to the GATT and WTO case law. This decision has been defined as the first example of "adjudicatory cross-fertilization" in the field of international economic law.[35]

Without getting into the substance of the decision, it is contended that such cross-fertilization would have required a sound cross-reasoning, *viz.* a clear and detailed explanation of the reasons why the interpretation provided in the General Agreement on Tariffs and Trade and WTO case law could better suit the needs of investment arbitration rather than other possible interpretations. Instead, the Tribunal only provided a single sentence to justify its approach stating that:

---

[29]In this sense, see Tanzi A (2013), State of Necessity, https://opil.ouplaw.com/ (last accessed 1 June 2020), para. 3.

[30]Zarra (2017a), p. 659.

[31]CMS Gas Transmission Company v. Argentina, ICSID Case No. ARB/01/08, Award, 12 May 2005.

[32]Martinez (2012), pp. 164–165; Enron Creditors Recovery Corp. v. Argentina, ICSID Case No. ARB/01/3, Award, 22 May 2007; Sempra Energy Int'l v. Argentina, ICSID Case No. ARB/02/16, Award, 28 September 2007.

[33]Alvarez and Brink (2012), p. 320.

[34]Continental Casualty Company v. Argentina, ICSID Case No. ARB/03/09, Award, 5 September 2008, para. 167.

[35]Reinisch (2010), p. 152.

> [s]ince the text of Article XI derives from the parallel model clause of the U.S. FCN treaties and these treaties in turn reflect the formulation of Article XX of GATT 1947, the Tribunal finds more appropriate to refer to the GATT and WTO case law.[36]

From this perspective, the approach of the Tribunal—which is appreciable in its attempt to 'build a bridge' between investment case-law and WTO jurisprudence—is undermined by the lack of a convincing reasoning as to why the WTO case law was to be applied in investment arbitration. In this respect, the Tribunal could have founded its interpretation on Articles 31(3)(c) of the Vienna Convention on the Law of the Treaties, which provides that "any relevant rules of international law applicable in the relations between the parties shall also be taken into account." Nevertheless, as pointed out by José Alvarez and Tegan Brink, it is surprising that "arbitrators spent no time in parsing the requisites of this rule."[37] From this perspective, one could argue that the recourse to the external jurisprudence of the GATT and WTO had scarce argumentative aim but, instead, completely superseded the required analysis and motivation. In this sense, the arbitral tribunal seemed to take the easiest path by using in a strategic perspective an exogenous precedent.

Another clarifying example in this respect may be found in the famous *Philip Morris v. Uruguay* case, where the multibillionaire tobacco company Philip Morris sued Uruguay claiming that its investment had lost value due to a new tobacco legislation and therefore it was entitled to have compensation. In greater detail, Philip Morris claimed that Uruguay's decisions banning the sale of different packaging of the same brand of cigarettes and requiring the images of health warning on cigarette package being increased from 50% to 80% violated several provisions of the Switzerland–Uruguay BIT.[38] In particular, according to the tobacco company, these measures violated Articles 5(1) and 3(2) of the BIT which respectively provide for protection against unlawful expropriation,[39] and the fair and equitable treatment ("FET") of foreign investments.[40]

In order to understand the majority award, however, it is of the utmost importance to briefly examine the context in which the decision took place. It is well known that

---

[36]Continental Casualty Company v. Argentina, ICSID Case No. ARB/03/09, Award, 5 September 2008, para. 192.

[37]Alvarez and Brink (2012), p. 335.

[38]Philip Morris Brands Sàrl, Philip Morris Products S.A. and Abal Hermanos S.A. v. Uruguay, ICSID Case No. ARB/10/7, Award, 8 July 2016, paras 9–14.

[39]Article 5(1) of the Switzerland-Uruguay BIT reads as follows: "Neither of the Contracting Parties shall take, either directly or indirectly, measures of expropriation, nationalization or any other measure having the same nature or the same effect against investments belonging to investors of the other Contracting Party, unless the measures are taken for the public benefit as established by law, on a non-discriminatory basis, and under due process of law, and provided that provisions be made for effective and adequate compensation. The amount of compensation, interest included, shall be settled in the currency of the country of origin of the investment and paid without delay to the person entitled thereto."

[40]The relevant part of Article 3(2) of the Switzerland-Uruguay BIT reads as follows: "Each Contracting Party shall ensure fair and equitable treatment within its territory of the investments of the investors of the other Contracting Party".

international investment arbitration has been strongly criticized for not being able to ensure states' power to protect their general interests and non-commercial values, while being overly protective of investors' rights. In particular, several authors and states point the finger at the so-called "regulatory chill", i.e. the use by foreign investors of international investment agreements and investor-state arbitration in order to unduly restrict legitimate domestic regulation in host states.[41]

As a reaction to these criticisms, arbitral tribunals started to increasingly pay attention to these non-commercial values by "giving due weight to States' reasons for the enactment of measures that can cause damage to foreign investors",[42] as well as applying standards of treatment in a way that recognizes states a certain margin of deference.

Following this tendency, the majority in *Philip Morris v. Uruguay* referred to the margin of appreciation doctrine as developed in the caselaw of the European Court of Human Rights (ECtHR). In greater detail, as for the alleged violation of the FET, the Tribunal underlined that all the measures were implemented in order to protect public health. In this respect, the majority stressed that regulatory authorities deserve a certain margin of appreciation while making public policy determinations.[43] That is because

> [t]he responsibility for public health measures rests with the government and investment tribunals should pay great deference to governmental judgments of national needs in matters such as the protection of public health. In such cases respect is due to the 'discretionary exercise of sovereign power, not made irrationally and not exercised in bad faith ... involving many complex factors.' As held by another investment tribunal, 'the sole inquiry for the Tribunal ... is whether or not there was a manifest lack of reasons for the legislation.'

In light of the foregoing, the majority

> did not find it necessary to decide whether the measures were actually able to reach the goals that were originally intended by the State, being sufficient that they were a good faith attempt to address a real public health concern.[44]

---

[41]As for different conceptualisations of this phenomenon, see Tienhaara (2011), p. 607: "Some authors appear to consider regulatory chill to be a broad phenomenon whereby regulatory progress is dampened across all areas that impact on foreign investors because government officials are aware of, and seriously concerned about, the risk of an investor–State dispute arising. In other words, policy-makers take into account potential disputes with foreign investors before they even begin to draft a policy and prioritise avoiding such disputes over the development of efficient regulation in the public interest. [...] A second conceptualisation of regulatory chill commonly employed by authors and commentators focuses on the chilling of specific regulatory measures that have been proposed or adopted by governments. This form of regulatory chill would emerge only when a government has been made aware of the risk of an investor–State dispute by an investor or group of investors that oppose the adoption or enforcement of a regulatory measure."

[42]Zarra (2017b), p. 96.

[43]Philip Morris Brands Sàrl, Philip Morris Products S.A. and Abal Hermanos S.A. v. Uruguay, ICSID Case No. ARB/10/7, Award, 8 July 2016, para 398.

[44]Zarra (2017b), p. 100.

In short, the majority of the tribunal relied on the margin of appreciation (allegedly) belonging to the host State so as to justify all the measures taken by Uruguay to safeguard public health. Nevertheless, as clearly highlighted by Gary Born in his dissenting opinion,[45] this doctrine seems hardly applicable with regard to the BIT at stake and, more generally, unsuitable for the investment arbitration context.

As for the Switzerland-Uruguay BIT, Gary Born pointed out that—contrariwise to the European Convention on Human Rights ("ECHR") and other international treaties—such "BIT does not contain language reserving any particular sphere of discretion or immunity for state actions."[46] Therefore, the Tribunal should have only considered the text of the BIT. In this respect the dissenting arbitrator contended that, while a certain degree of deference to sovereign measures must be recognized, such "deference does not, however, free a tribunal from its obligation ... to decide whether a particular measure is fair and equitable, or proportionate, in light of the state's articulated objectives."[47] From this perspective, the deference towards State sovereignty was to be only an element of a wider proportionality test.

Furthermore, Gary Born contended that the margin of appreciation doctrine was generally ill-suited for investment disputes. Indeed, while the ECHR is a multilateral convention which aims at ensuring the protection of human rights in 47 States, BITs are bilateral treaties for the promotion and protection of foreign investments between the Contracting Parties. Notably, in the context of the ECHR, the plurality of the contracting states may have substantial differences in the perception of the rights enshrined in the Convention as well as in the identification of the reasons why such rights could be limited.[48] This is the reason why the ECtHR, through the margin of appreciation doctrine, guarantees "an essential element of flexibility, adaptability, and pluralism among states that share a common goal but remain quite different in their approach as to how best implement it."[49]

Contrariwise, BITs are bilateral treaties through which two states accept limitations to their sovereignty for the specific purpose of attracting foreign capitals. From this perspective, these treaties neither involve rights in relation to which there could be different cultural understandings nor problems of uniformity, as is the case in the

[45]Philip Morris Brands Sàrl, Philip Morris Products S.A. and Abal Hermanos S.A. v. Uruguay, ICSID Case No. ARB/10/7, Award, 8 July 2016, Concurring and Dissenting Opinion by Gary Born, paras 87, 180–191.

[46]Philip Morris Brands Sàrl, Philip Morris Products S.A. and Abal Hermanos S.A. v. Uruguay, ICSID Case No. ARB/10/7, Award, 8 July 2016, Concurring and Dissenting Opinion by Gary Born, para. 143.

[47]Philip Morris Brands Sàrl, Philip Morris Products S.A. and Abal Hermanos S.A. v. Uruguay, ICSID Case No. ARB/10/7, Award, 8 July 2016, Concurring and Dissenting Opinion by Gary Born, para. 145.

[48]Megret (2018), p. 102: "Margin of appreciation reasoning has featured prominently in cases involving sexual minorities and the place of religion in society, to mention only some examples." In this sense, consider the jurisprudence of the ECtHR concerning the Islamic veil and its ban by several European states.

[49]Megret (2018), p. 103.

application of human rights. Furthermore, unlike the investor-state system, the coherence and success of the margin doctrine in the ECHR context is strictly related to the fact that the European system entails a standing court "charged with the adjudication of claims against a consistent set of parties to a single overarching treaty".[50] Therefore, it is not surprising that in the cases where arbitral tribunals had the chance to consider the applicability of the margin doctrine in international investment arbitration, they usually refused that possibility.[51]

In conclusion, one could argue that the recourse to the margin of appreciation doctrine as developed by the ECtHR had the—arguably commendable—purpose of ensuring states the power to protect and guarantee non-economical values. However, for the above reasons, this doctrine is unsuitable to the context of investment arbitration, which has little in common with the ECHR one. In this respect, as maintained by Julian Arato, the real issue behind the invocation of the margin doctrine was the unsolved question of the applicable standard(s) of review in investment arbitration. Such a question, nonetheless, cannot be solved by invoking the margin of appreciation which merely indicates that some deference is appropriate but not how much.[52] In this sense, once again, the arbitral tribunal seemed to take the easy way out by introducing an exogenous precedent and a doctrine which seem hardly fitting investment arbitration.[53]

4 The Role of the Investment Arbitration Caselaw in the ICJ Jurisprudence

The examples referred to above are quite symptomatic of how external precedents are susceptible to be used from a merely strategic perspective: this is a circumstance that may prove useful in order to reach a given result within a judicial proceeding, but detrimental to the development and uniform application of international law. The same circumstance, at least in part, could explain why investment tribunals so far

[50] Arato (2014), p. 550.

[51] Siemens v. Argentina, ICSID Case No. ARB/02/8, Award, 6 February 2007, para. 354; Quasar de Valors SICAV S.A., Orgor de Valores SICAV S.A., GBI 9000 SICAV S.A. v. Russia, SCC No. 24/2007, Award, 20 July 2012, para. 22; Bernhard von Pezold and Others v. Zimbabwe, ICSID Case No. ARB/10/15, Award, 28 July 2015, paras 465–466.

[52] Arato (2014), p. 565: "To be sure, different standards of review may be appropriate in different circumstances. The point is rather that the doctrine of the margin does no work in actually determining what the rights standards should be." In this sense see also Fukunaga (2019), pp. 71–77.

[53] Arato (2014), p. 565: "At least in the context of ad hoc investment arbitration, the problem is that the doctrine appears to be doing work, but in reality amounts to a mere pseudostandard — a substitute for real reasoning. In other words, the invocation of the margin of appreciation as a rubric creates a false impression of consistency across cases like Continental Casualty, Frontier Petroleum, Electrabel, Saluka, and Micula, while obscuring significant differences in the type and degree of deference afforded therein."

"failed . . .to leave a deep mark on international jurisprudence",[54] with the effect that while they cite external sources unashamedly, the opposite is not true, even where investment case-law significantly contribute to the consolidation and clarification of a rule of general international law. In other words, the unclear use of external precedents by investment tribunals sometimes generates the erroneous impression that they not participate in a common international judicial practice. Neither could one contend that it depends on the subject matter: if subject-matter was such a determining factor, one would expect the ICJ to rely on investment jurisprudence at least when dealing with issues which are at the heart of investment law practice. However, this is not the case. The ICJ judgments in *Diallo* and *Obligation to Negotiate Access to the Pacific Ocean* might shed some light in that respect.

As regards the *Diallo* saga, we refer to the judgment on preliminary objections[55] and in particular to that passage of the judgment where the ICJ rejects Guinea's argument whereby investment arbitration practice would be symptomatic of the existence of an exception allowing shareholders' states to exercise diplomatic protection. In the view of the Court, indeed, the investment jurisprudence invoked by Guinea would be:

> special cases, whether based on specific international agreements between two or more States, including the one responsible for the allegedly unlawful acts regarding the companies concerned [. . .] or based on agreements concluded directly between a company and the State allegedly responsible for the prejudice to it.[56]

By doing so, the ICJ seems to adhere to the idea whereby international investment law would be special in nature, which means, on the one hand, that rules of general international law are excluded in its administration; and, on the other hand, that investment treaties, and the practice they generate, would not contribute to the progressive development of general international law. A perspective of this kind is quite questionable and the authors' own view is exactly the opposite. Indeed, as observed by Campbell McLachlan the relationship between BITs and general international law proves symbiotic:

> the content of the treaty obligation may be informed by general international law. In turn, the promulgation of the treaty obligation, and its application by arbitral tribunals, may inform the progressive development of general international law.[57]

Still, the uncertainty, which continues to characterize the figure of diplomatic protection, and that could not even be mentioned here, may make the ICJ's argument more tolerable.

[54]Charlotin (2017), p. 294.

[55]Ahmadou Sadio Diallo (Republic of Guinea v. Democratic Republic of the Congo), Preliminary Objections Judgment, ICJ Reports 2007.

[56]Ahmadou Sadio Diallo (Republic of Guinea v. Democratic Republic of the Congo), Preliminary Objections Judgment, ICJ Reports 2007, para. 90.

[57]McLachlan (2008), p. 364.

The same is not true as far as the judgment in *Obligation to Negotiate Access to the Pacific Ocean* is concerned.[58] In this case, in particular, the Court dismissed Bolivia's claims based on legitimate expectations. In its view:

> references to legitimate expectations may be found in arbitral awards concerning disputes between a foreign investor and the host State that apply treaty clauses providing for fair and equitable treatment. It does not follow from such references that there exists in general international law a principle that would give rise to an obligation on the basis of what could be considered a legitimate expectation.[59]

This judgment's passage is very superficial and there exists more than one reason to be fairly critical. First, the Court does not give any weight to all those investment tribunals' decisions that apply the principle of legitimate expectations assuming that it belongs to general international law (such as in *Total*).[60] In doing so the Court ends up ignoring the circumstance whereby all rules of international law involve legitimate expectations and that the existence of a general principle in this matter, as observed by several prominent scholars, is difficult to contest.[61] Second, in any event, a departure from the investment case law in this regard should have required a crystal clear reasoning. And this precisely with the view to fostering the harmonious development of international law referred to above.

Third, the flawed reasoning behind the Court's judgment will, in turn, most likely bring investment tribunals to ignore it, thus producing a vicious circle. In other words, the lack of an appropriate assessment of investment case-law will prevent the judgment from exercising an external influence not only on investment tribunals but more generally on ICTs.

5 Conclusions

In light of the foregoing, it is finally possible to draw some conclusions on the use of external precedents in the judicial dialogue between investment tribunals and international courts.

This chapter first defined the notions of fragmentation and coherence in international law: we argued that these concepts are strictly related since the fears of interpretative fragmentation has led to a quest for coherence in international

[58] Obligation to Negotiate Access to the Pacific Ocean (Bolivia v. Chile), https://www.icj-cij.org/files/case-related/153/153-20181001-JUD-01-00-EN.pdf (last accessed 21 December 2019).

[59] Obligation to Negotiate Access to the Pacific Ocean (Bolivia v. Chile), https://www.icj-cij.org/files/case-related/153/153-20181001-JUD-01-00-EN.pdf (last accessed 21 December 2019), para. 162.

[60] Total S.A. v. Argentina, ICSID Case No. ARB/04/1, Award, 27 November 2013.

[61] Byers (1999), p. 107; Snodgrass (2006), p. 2; Brown (2009), p. 10: "A preliminary conclusion might be made that there is a general principle of law pursuant to which an individual's legitimate expectations are to be protected from harm caused by a public authority resiling from a previous publicly stated position."

adjudication. From this perspective, we have defined coherence as a criterion of adjudication which does not require tribunals to always decide consistently, but imposes the argumentative duty to fully justify a decision within the existing framework. By way of conclusion, therefore, a coherent decision is one which is well and reasonably grounded within the system, and gives account of the different steps leading to a certain result by, *inter alia*, carefully examining the precedents related to the specific issue and legally justifying its solution in case of inconsistency.[62]

On the basis of these concepts, we have investigated the role of external authorities in investment arbitration and vice-versa. Although the exogenous precedent has neither a binding nor a constraining value, its role in the harmonious development of international law cannot be ignored.[63] In this sense, the exogenous precedent constitutes an important link among international courts and tribunals which, through its sound use, are able to participate in a common international judicial practice.

Nevertheless, it is of the utmost importance to highlight that the mere use of external authorities does not per se bring coherence into the system. Quite the opposite! The prerequisite for international courts and tribunals to effectively participate in the harmonious development of international law must be sought in the careful and justified use of the exogenous precedent. Only through a solid and convincing legal reasoning, indeed, it can be able to further a fruitful cross-pollination among international courts and tribunals. In this regard, we have proved how external precedents are susceptible to be used or ignored in a merely strategic way. While such a (mis)use may be effective in reaching a given result within a certain proceeding, it is detrimental to the harmonious development and application of international law since it runs the risk of undermining the judicial dialogue. In this sense, a misuse of external authorities produces a vicious circle in which international courts and tribunals are likely to ignore each other and, by doing so, they enhance the sense of normative fragmentation and incoherence of international law.

As a matter of conclusion, we would like to say a few words about coherence and the external precedent. When using an external authority, "coherence can never be taken as a given, manifest or formal property of things."[64] Coherence is always a speculation which does require a clear and sound legal reasoning. In a nutshell, the use of external authorities is not something good in itself, but a kind of intellectual work to be carried out very cautiously.

---

[62] In this sense, consider the 'taking into account approach' as explained by Palombino (2018), p. 143: "The approach [which should be] followed in investor-State arbitration [. . . is] the so-called 'taking into account' approach, which means that the arbitrator is obliged to consider previous decisions, but may disregard them where reasons of substantive justice, or the mere need to foster a proper development of the law, suggest doing so."

[63] As for the role of the jurisprudence of other international courts and tribunals in international investment arbitration see Schill (2010), p. 3.

[64] Herbert (2004), p. 203.

References

Abi-Saab G (1999) Fragmentation or unification: some concluding remarks. N Y Univ J Int Law Polit 31:919–934

Alvarez JE, Brink T (2012) Revisiting the necessity defense: Continental Casualty v. Argentina. Trans Dispute Manag J 9:319–362

Arato J (2014) The margin of appreciation in international investment law. Virginia J Int Law 54:546–578

Bertrea S (2005) The arguments for coherence: analysis and evaluation. Oxf J Leg Stud 25:369–391

Brown C (2009) The protection of legitimate expectations as a 'general principle of law': some preliminary thoughts. Trans Dispute Manag J 6:1–10

Byers M (1999) Custom, power and the power of rules: international relations and customary international law. Cambridge University Press, Cambridge

Charlotin D (2017) The place of investment awards and WTO decisions in international law: a citation analysis. J Int Econ Law 20:279–299

Cohen HG (2015) Theorizing precedent in international law. In: Bianchi A, Peat D, Windsor M (eds) Interpretation in international law. Oxford University Press, Oxford, pp 268–289

De Brabandere E (2016) The use of precedent and external case law by the International Court of Justice and the International Tribunal for the Law of the Sea. Law Pract Int Courts Tribunals 15:24–55

Droege C (2008) Elective affinities? Human rights and humanitarian law. Int Rev Red Cross 90:501–548

Dupuy PM (2007) A doctrinal debate in the globalisation era: on the fragmentation of international law. Eur J Leg Stud 1:25–41

Fukunaga Y (2019) Margin of appreciation as an indicator of judicial deference: is it applicable to investment arbitration? J Int Dispute Settlement 10:69–87

Greenwood C (2015) Unity and diversity in international investment law. In: Andenas M, Bjorge E (eds) A farewell to fragmentation. Oxford University Press, Oxford, pp 37–55

Guillaume G (1995) The future of international judicial institutions. Int Comp Law Q 44:848–862

Guillaume G (2011) The use of precedent by international judges and arbitrators. J Int Dispute Settlement 2:5–23

Herbert C (2004) The conundrum of coherence. New Literary History 35:185–206

Higgins R (2001) Respecting sovereign states and running a tight courtroom. Int Comp Law Q 50:121–132

Hurd I (1999) Legitimacy and authority in international politics. Int Organ 53:379–408

Knox JH (2004) The judicial resolution of conflicts between trade and the environment. Harv Environ Law Rev 28:1–78

Koskenniemi M, Leino P (2002) Fragmentation of international law? Postmodern anxieties. Leiden J Int Law 15:553–579

Kurtz J (2014) Building legitimacy through interpretation in investor-State arbitration: on consistency, coherence, and the identification of applicable law. In: Douglas Z, Pauwelyn J, Viñuales JE (eds) The foundations of international investment law. Oxford University Press, Oxford, pp 257–296

Martinez E (2012) Understanding the debate over necessity: unanswered questions and future implications of annulments in the Argentine Gas cases. Duke J Comp Int Law 23:149–186

McLachlan QCC (2008) Investment treaties and general international law. Int Comp Law Q 57:361–400

Megret F (2018) Nature of obligations. In: Moeckli D, Shah S, Sivakumaran S (eds) International human rights law. Oxford University Press, Oxford, pp 86–109

Mitchell M (2009) Complexity: a guided tour. Oxford University Press, Oxford

Palombino FM (2018) Fair and equitable treatment and the fabric of general principles. Springer, Heidelberg

Pauwelyn J (2006) Fragmentation of international law. Max Planck encyclopedia of public international law. Online Edition. Available at http://opil.ouplaw.com
Pauwelyn J (2014) At the edge of chaos? Foreign investment law as a complex adaptive system, how it emerged and how it can be reformed. ICSID Rev 28:372–418
Reinisch A (2010) Necessity in investment arbitration. Netherlands Yearb Int Law 41:137–158
Schill SW (2010) International investment law and comparative public law – an introduction. In: Schill SW (ed) International investment law and comparative public law. Oxford University Press, Oxford, pp 3–38
Schreuer C (2013) Coherence and consistency in international investment law. In: Echandi R, Sauve P (eds) Prospects in international investment law and policy. Cambridge University Press, Cambridge, pp 391–402
Snodgrass E (2006) Protecting investors' legitimate expectations: recognizing and delimiting a general principle. ICSID Rev 21:1–58
Soriano LM (2003) A modest notion of coherence in legal reasoning. A model for the European Court of Justice. Ratio Juris 16:296–323
Taruffo M (2007) Precedente e giurisprudenza. Editoriale Scientifica, Naples
Ten Cate IM (2013) The costs of consistency: precedent in investment treaty arbitration. Columbia J Trans Law 51:418–478
Tienhaara K (2011) Regulatory chill and the threat of arbitration: a view from political science. In: Brown C, Miles K (eds) Evolution in investment treaty law and arbitration. Cambridge University Press, Cambridge, pp 606–627
Webb P (2013) International judicial integration and fragmentation. Oxford University Press, Oxford
Zarra G (2017a) Orderliness and coherence in international investment law and arbitration: an analysis through the lens of state of necessity. J Int Arbitr 34:653–678
Zarra G (2017b) Right to regulate, margin of appreciation and proportionality: current status in investment arbitration in light of Philip Morris v. Uruguay. Brazilian J Int Law 14:95–120

Fulvio Maria Palombino is Professor of International Law at the Law Department of the University of Naples Federico II and former Vice-President of the European Society of International Law. He authored several books and numerous contributions to leading Italian and international journals on issues of international litigation and arbitration, international investment law, human rights and international criminal law.

Gustavo Minervini is PhD Candidate in Law and Economics at the School of Law of the University of Naples Federico II, specializing in Public International Law. He is Teaching Assistant in Public International Law, International Human Rights Law, International Economic Law and Private International Law at the same University. He holds a combined LL.B. and LL.M (*summa cum laude*) from the University of Naples Federico II, as well as an advanced LL.M. (*cum laude*) in Public International Law from Leiden University, with a specialization in International Dispute Settlement. In July 2019, he was Visiting PhD at the University of Paris I Panthéon-Sorbonne and attended the 2019 courses of the International Academy for Arbitration Law. Currently, he is trainee lawyer with the Naples Bar in Italy.

Domestic Courts as Transnational Actors in International Investment Law: A Canadian Perspective

Ksenia Polonskaya

Contents

1 Introduction 152
2 National Legitimation: Why the Domestic Courts' Voices Matter in the Context of International Investment Law? 156
3 Courts and Investment Awards: Canadian Perspective 159
3.1 Standards of Review 160
3.2 What Does the Court Say? Looking at the Dicta of the Federal Court in Bilcon v. Clayton 164
4 Future Modes of Interaction 167
5 Concluding Remarks 168
References 169

Abstract This chapter examines the role of domestic courts as transnational actors in international investment law. In particular, this chapter examines the approaches and perspectives of the Canadian courts in the process of setting aside arbitral awards. This chapter seeks to understand how the courts themselves perceive their roles in the context of international investment law, and how the courts interact with the arbitral tribunals by legitimizing and delegitimizing certain narratives on international investment law. It suggests that the framework of "exit, voice and loyalty" developed by Albert O. Hirschman is most helpful to understand the relationships between the national courts and arbitral tribunals in the context of international investment law.

I would like to thank all participants of the Colloquium "Actors in International Investment Law: Beyond Claimants, Respondents and Arbitrators". I am also grateful to Gillian McNeil for her suggestions. Usual disclaimer applies.

K. Polonskaya (✉)
Carleton University, Department of Law and Legal Studies, Ottawa, ON, Canada
e-mail: ksenia.polonskaya@carleton.ca

A. Gourgourinis (ed.), *Transnational Actors in International Investment Law*, European Yearbook of International Economic Law,
https://doi.org/10.1007/978-3-030-60679-4_7

1 Introduction

In recent years, domestic courts have taken an active stance on matters of international investment law ("IIL"). In 2019, the Columbian Constitutional Court rendered a decision in which it evaluated the constitutionality of the 2014 Columbia-France bilateral investment treaty ("BIT").[1] The Court reasoned that the BIT is only "conditionally constitutional" because its provisions are vaguely formulated that permits multiple (and even contradictory interpretations).[2] In 2017, the Court of Justice of the European Union ("CJEU") issued now famous judgement in the *Slovak Republic v. Achmea* where it ruled that the arbitration clause of the Netherlands-Slovakia BIT was not compatible with the European Union ("EU") law.[3]

According to the CJEU, the investment tribunals can produce inconsistent interpretations of the EU law, which in turn will jeopardize its integrity.[4] As a result of this decision, the German Federal Court of Justice decided to set aside the arbitral award.[5] These examples demonstrate that domestic courts are active participants of IIL that contribute to shaping current outlook of IIL. Of course, such interactions are by no means one way. Several arbitral tribunals have already issued arbitral awards after the CJEU rendered its judgement in *Achmea*.[6] For example, in one award, the tribunal refused to decline jurisdiction over the investment dispute despite the CJEU's decision.[7]

It is well-established fact that interaction between domestic courts and IIL occurs on multiple levels.[8] As Christoph Schreuer has pointed out, the domestic courts interact with IIL as *gatekeepers* through exhaustion of local remedies provisions in the applicable IIAs; as *competitors* by means of fork in the road provisions; as

---

[1]Prieto G (2019) The Columbian Constitutional Court Judgement C-252/19: A New Frontier for Reform in International Investment Law. EJIL-Talk, https://www.ejiltalk.org/the-colombian-constitutional-court-judgment-c-252-19-a-new-frontier-for-reform-in-international-investment-law/ (last accessed 24 June 2020).

[2]Prieto G (2019), The Columbian Constitutional Court judgement C-252/19: a new frontier for reform in international investment law. EJIL-Talk, https://www.ejiltalk.org/the-colombian-constitutional-court-judgment-c-252-19-a-new-frontier-for-reform-in-international-investment-law/ (last accessed 8 April 2020).

[3]CJEU, Judgment, 6 March 2018, Case C-284/16, *Slovak Republic v. Achmea*, ECLI:EU:C:2018:158, para. 62.

[4]CJEU, Judgment, 6 March 2018, Case C-284/16, *Slovak Republic v. Achmea*, ECLI:EU:C:2018:158, paras 57–59.

[5]Pohl (2018), p. 767.

[6]For example, Eskoqsol in Liquidation v. Italian Republic, ICSID Case No. ARB/15/50, Decision on Italy's Request for Immediate Termination and Italy's Jurisdictional Objection Based on Inapplicability of the Energy Charter Treaty to Intra-EU Disputes, 7 May 2019, paras 230–231, 236.

[7]Vattenfall v. Federal Republic of Germany, ICSID Case No. ARB/12/12, Decision on the Achmea Issue, 31 August 2018, para. 232.

[8]Schreuer (2012), p. 72.

supporters by authorizing interim measures, and providing for enforcement of the arbitral awards.[9] Schreuer also acknowledges that domestic courts and investment tribunals also interact with each other as mutual *supervisors*. In this role, he emphasizes that the tribunals can examine the decisions of domestic courts for their compatibility with the investment obligations in IIAs, and domestic courts can review the awards at the stage of setting aside under Article V of the United Nations Convention on the Recognition and Enforcement of Foreign Arbitral Awards (the New York Convention).[10] It is worth noting here that the domestic courts can play this role in IIL context only when the investment disputes are adjudicated outside of the framework of the Convention on the Settlement of Investment Disputes between States and Nationals of Other States (the ICSID Convention).[11] The ICSID Convention removes the investment disputes from scrutiny of the domestic courts entirely and only permits for annulment of the awards outside of the domestic courts' purviews.

This chapter focuses on the supervisory role of the Canadian courts by reference to the paradigm of the Canadian courts as transnational actors in IIL. By looking at the national courts as transnational actors, we can capture the ways in which different judicial voices contribute to IIL's development by means of interaction.[12] Accordingly, domestic courts are no longer viewed as merely public domestic institutions that exercise limited supervision over arbitral tribunals (a traditional role accorded to them under the New York Convention and the national statutes on arbitration) but rather as active participants in IIL with (de)legitimizing authority. Here, it is important to recall that through their decisions and procedures, domestic courts and investment tribunals communicate with different epistemic communities, and thus domestic courts wield power to legitimize the system of investment protection for national audiences of legal and non-legal professionals. The term "legitimation" here is used in a sociological sense, i.e. to ensure that exercise of authority is perceived as just by the users of the system and by those impacted by the arbitral decisions i.e. public at large.[13] Given that governments have to pay the awards, the investment awards have a broad impact, not confined exclusively to the parties of the dispute as in purely private commercial arbitration.[14]

---

[9]Schreuer (2012), p. 73.

[10]United Nations Convention on the Recognition and Enforcement of Foreign Arbitral Awards, 10 June 1958, 330 UNTS 38 (entered into force 7 June 1959).

[11]Convention on the Settlement of Investment Disputes Between States and Nationals of Other States (ICSID Convention), 18 March 1965, 575 UNTS 159; 4 ILM 524 (1965) (entered into force 14 October 1966).

[12]For example, Onyema (2018), pp. 27–30 (on the roles of judges in the context of arbitration).

[13]For example, Tucker (2018), p. 150.

[14]Eberhardt P, Olivet C (2012), Profiting from Injustice: How law firms, arbitrators and financiers are fueling an investment arbitration boom, https://www.tni.org/files/download/profitingfrominjustice.pdf (last accessed 29 June 2020), p. 15.

Accordingly, this chapter examines the role of the domestic courts in IIL through the prism of judicial interaction in a pluralist sense.[15] The framework requires some unpacking, since pluralist vision can have different meanings in different settings. In the context of this chapter, pluralist vision accounts for transnational nature of authority in IIL that permits co-existence of different levels of normativity.[16] Thus, from a pluralist perspective it is of utmost importance to understand how conflicts are resolved between different levels of authority and in what way different actors contribute to the process of creating and resolving such conflicts. Paul Schiff Berman explains that from a pluralist perspective, interaction between domestic courts and investor-state tribunals represents "dialectical and iterative process" that "exist without an official hierarchical relationship based on coercive power".[17] For the purposes of this chapter, it is such process that is a subject-matter of interest, however, not from the perspective of the arbitral tribunals but from a courts' point of view.

Note that the chapter does not employ the term "dialogue" to describe the ways in which domestic courts interact transnationally with their counterparts, and/or international courts and tribunals. The reason for it is that the chapter does not seek to advance liberal cosmopolitan vision of the courts' involvement in transnational social ordering.[18] The term "dialogue" is morally charged with a vision of progress as it suggests that the courts communicate (even if spontaneously) with some sort of conscious objective to reassert common values such as rule of law, and to achieve, if not universality and integration, at least common ground on certain legal issues.[19] That is not to say that some courts in some circumstances do not aspire to achieve such objectives (they might) but merely to capture an idea that the courts' independent communications can exist outside of "dialogue" as a framework and constitute a type of normative contestation.[20] In the context of IIL, such pluralist perspective is most warranted because distinctive voices of the courts emerge despite the overarching normative framework of the New York Convention and UNCITRAL Model Law that seeks to impose uniformity of values and approaches to reasoning in the context of international arbitration.[21] For example, recall repeated attempts of some

[15]Pasquet (2017), p. 476.

[16]Bianchi (2016), p. 234.

[17]Berman (2012), p. 154. Note: This process is by no means unique for the field of investment arbitration. Berman persuasively argues that margin of appreciation doctrine constitutes a pluralist device for managing the process of interaction between the European Court of Human Rights ("ECtHR") and the national courts. Margin of appreciation gives a rise to "local variation". Also Recall Nico Krisch scholarly findings on the interaction of the European Court of Human Rights and the national courts. Krisch (2008), p. 183.

[18]Slaughter (2000), p. 1108; Kennedy (2007), p. 641.

[19]Pasquet (2017), pp. 470–473.

[20]Berman (2012), pp. 14, 11–12.

[21]Lewis (2016), p. 143; Born (2009), p. 96 ("the Convention's drafters sought to establish a single uniform set of international legal standards for the enforcement of arbitration agreements and arbitral awards").

members of the arbitration community to promote further harmonisation for the standard of review across different jurisdictions.[22]

The pluralist account encourages to ask (and answer) questions about a (possible) role of the domestic courts in IIL. What do distinctive judicial voices contribute to the narrative on IIL? Why are they important? This chapter focuses on the Canadian courts as the first step in studying the role of domestic courts as transnational actors in IIL. This chapter seeks to understand what are the approaches to the standard of review in the Canadian context, and how do the Canadian courts perceive their own role in IIL? Also, how IIL should frame interaction between domestic courts and investor-state tribunals in future? For instance, in the context of international human rights law, the European Court on Human Rights ("ECtHR") have developed certain legal doctrines and approaches to legal interpretation to manage the relationships with the domestic constitutional courts.[23] What are possible paths for future relationships between the domestic courts and investor-state tribunals?

This chapter will examine the approaches of the Canadian courts to setting aside the arbitral awards in order to identify the contribution of domestic courts to the broader narrative on the nature of IIL and the scope of the courts' supervisory function (as they themselves view it). In particular, the chapter argues that first, the Canadian courts have continued to assert their supervisory role over investment tribunals; and second, they have initially struggled to identify appropriate standard of judicial review for the investment awards. Eventually, the courts have settled on reviewing the investment awards on the standard of "correctness" as it is defined under the rules of Canadian administrative law. While the courts exercised restraint with regards to the scope and depth of judicial review, the Federal Court ("FC") in the most recent case critically assessed the reasoning of investment tribunal in the *Bilcon* case and reaffirmed the narrative of regulatory chill as a major concern against investment arbitration.[24] The court acknowledged that investment awards such as the *Bilcon* award can invoke regulatory chill for environmental regulations.[25]

This chapter shows that Canadian courts continue to exercise restraint in reviewing the awards to signal that Canada is an arbitration friendly jurisdiction. Two aspects of judicial review deserve special attention. The application of the administrative law principles and logic is problematic for a number of reasons. First, Canadian administrative law (and particularly standard of review) remains at a stage

[22]Bianchi A (2017) Epistemic communities in international arbitration, https://papers.ssrn.com/sol3/papers.cfm?abstract_id=3217633 (last accessed 24 June 2020), pp. 11, 20–21, 24–25. Also discussed in Dezalay and Garth (1996), p. 16; Lynch (2003), pp. 94–104.

[23]For example, Krisch (2012), p. 145 (discussing the margin of appreciation doctrine as a "political tool in a pluralist order"); Kerr (2015), pp. 31–39.

[24]Miles (2013), pp. 181–187 (Miles discusses a possibility of regulatory chill and explains the concept).

[25]Canada (Attorney General) v. Clayton, 2018 FC 436, paras 198–199, https://www.canlii.org/en/ca/fct/doc/2018/2018fc436/2018fc436.html?searchUrlHash=AAAAAQArQ2FuYWRhIChBdHRvcm5leSBHZW5lcmFsKSB2LiBDbGF5dG9uIEZDIDQzNgAAAAB&resultIndex=1 (last accessed 13 April 2020).

of turbulence, as the Supreme Court's perspective on the applicable standard continues to evolve.[26] Second, the federal and provincial commercial arbitration acts are based on the United Nations Commission on International Trade Law ("UNCITRAL") Model Law which does not set any autonomous standard for domestic judicial review. However, the logic of the Model Law is to set a specialized regime for dispute resolution. Arguably, such logic dictates a need to develop an autonomous standard of review, which is not tied to the principles of domestic administrative law. In addition, the most recent judicial review in *Canada (Attorney General) v. Clayton* case demonstrates that the FC adopted a critical narrative on regulatory chill in IIL. In particular, the court signalled potential problems for environmental regulations if Canada continues to engage in investment arbitration. While the dicta in *Bilcon* can have only persuasive authority, it remains an element of judicial communication that illustrates the court's voice in IIL.

Accordingly, the chapter proceeds as follows. First, the chapter examines the issue of national legitimation and why such legitimation is important in the context of IIL. Second, it reviews the decisions of the Canadian courts on the standards of review. Third, it scrutinizes the decision of the FC of Canada on the *Bilcon* case to demonstrate how the courts can question legitimacy of arbitral decisions through dicta. Forth, it examines future of the interaction between the domestic courts and arbitral tribunals through a theoretical framework of "exit, voice and loyalty". Finally, it draws concluding remarks.

2 National Legitimation: Why the Domestic Courts' Voices Matter in the Context of International Investment Law?

Any scholarly conversation on IIL begins with an (almost ritual) recital of the number of international investment agreements ("IIAs").[27] Such conversation usually continues with the examination of the roles of the investor-state tribunals, states, investors, and arbitration institutions ("AIs") in IIL. For example, Dupont and Schultz recently proposed a useful conceptual framework for thinking about IILs, under which they view states, investors, AIs and Investor State Dispute Settlement ("ISDS") tribunals as active participants of IIL that shape IIL's development through

[26]Note: and it will yet to shift again as Canadian lawyers consider the implications of the *Vavilov* case rendered by the Supreme Court of Canada in December 2019. See: Canada (Minister of Citizenship and Immigration) v. Vavilov 2019 SCC 65. Daly (2018), The supreme court of Canada's administrative law trilogy: what to expect, https://www.administrativelawmatters.com/blog/2018/11/26/the-supreme-court-of-canadas-administrative-law-trilogy-what-to-expect/, (last accessed 8 April 2020).

[27]For example, Alschner and Skougarevskiy (2016), p. 561.

the inputs, outputs, and outcomes.[28] According to Dupont and Schultz, such inputs, outputs and outcomes are context specific.[29]

They can take the form of arbitral awards, investors' claims, states' withdrawals from the treaties. Under this framework, states are viewed as respondents in the investment disputes and as the negotiators of IIAs. Investors are claimants for whose benefit IIAs are in place. Investor-state tribunals adjudicate the disputes between investors and states. Finally, AIs administer the disputes. Dupont and Schultz have masterfully captured interaction between the participants as a driving force that shapes current outlook of IIL. They, however, did not account for domestic courts as participants of IIL that can actively contributing to shaping its outlook.

Arguably, such approach materialised in light of historical context under which the system of international arbitration emerged as it is "by its essence contemplates minimal court intervention".[30] According to Florian Grisel, the International Chamber of Commerce ("ICC") spared no effort to increase autonomy of international arbitration by limiting possibility of review of foreign awards by the national courts.[31] To achieve this objective, the ICC exerted considerable influence at the New York Convention's negotiations at United Nations Economic and Social Council ("ECOSOC"), and subsequently encouraged the implementation of the UNCITRAL Model Law through their expert networks in different jurisdictions to "denationalize" international arbitration entirely.[32] Won Kidane critically notes that "the Convention requires courts of law to recognize and enforce awards rendered by institutions of justice that no one meaningfully controls".[33] Article V of the New York Convention and Article 34 of the Model Law permit national courts to set aside the arbitral awards only on a limited number of grounds.

However, the interpretation of these grounds (for example, the notion of public policy) can be a subject-matter of the court's discretion and, as such, the courts' approaches to interpreting Article V of the Convention can vary considerably. At the conference on 40 years of the New York Convention, Pieter Sanders, the author of the "Dutch Draft" and a delegate at 1958 Conference, argued in favour of further harmonization national arbitration laws, particularly with regards to recognition and enforcement.[34] The objective of such calls is to minimize value of the courts' individual voices and to foster autonomy of international arbitration from national

[28] Dupont and Schultz (2016), p. 3.

[29] Dupont and Schultz (2016), p. 5.

[30] Paulsson (2008), p. 26.

[31] Grisel (2017), p. 73.

[32] Note: not surprisingly so, the initial ICC draft included the term "international arbitration award" as opposed to "foreign arbitration award". The term reportedly invoked strong disagreement of the United Nations Economic and Social Council ("ECOSOC").

[33] Kidane (2017), p. 130.

[34] Sanders (1999), pp. 3–4.

courts' supervision to increase efficiency of dispute resolution in globalized world.[35] As Kidane points out, legal framework for international arbitration creates

> infrastructure for outsourcing the resolution of disputes to arbitral tribunals. It assumes that the chronic and inherent problems that plague courts of law around the world, such as incompetence, conflict, ethical violations, prejudice, bias, negligence, greed, fear, and even outright corruption, is less likely to afflict arbitral tribunals.[36]

Ongoing backlash against investment arbitration demonstrates that such presumption does not necessarily hold scrutiny in reality. In this context, does it mean that relationships between the national courts and arbitral tribunals should be re-examined? If so, to what extent and for what purpose? Does it mean that there is a need to resort to pre-New York Convention model in which national courts played greater role in the supervising the arbitral tribunals? Related and not least important concern whether such push back again international arbitration would not be perceived as undermining the rule of law internationally. Further discussion on the setting aside decisions by Canadian courts demonstrates that national courts can play independent role in IIL even under constraints of limited grounds for judicial review. Most importantly, it shows that the courts can play an important (1) supervising function and (2) (de)legitimizing function of the arbitral decisions even under the existing constraints in the context of IIL.

Arguably, participation of the domestic courts provides legitimation to the exercise of authority by the arbitral tribunals. The need for such legitimation arises because the outcomes of the participants' interactions result in exercise of authority that has consequences beyond the parties to the disputes (i.e. states and investors). Accordingly, "party autonomy" and "party consent" by themselves are not sufficient to legitimize the exercise of such authority. Indeed, in the context of investor-state arbitration not only individual commercial interests are involved. In this context, as Stephan Schill observes, "national legitimacy" becomes important aspect of the discourse. National legitimacy, "designates the conditions under which arbitration is seen as legitimate from the perspective of a specific country and its society. This aspect of legitimacy is generally expressed in the State's laws regarding arbitration and in the relevant practice of its supervising courts".[37]

The courts' voices, thus, are important for the purposes of national legitimation of international authority exercised by the investment tribunals. Such legitimation occurs in two ways (1) by upholding the arbitral award and/or (2) translating the value and importance of the award to national audiences that may not be familiar with the discourse of relevant epistemic communities in IIL.

[35] Sanders (1999), pp. 3–4.

[36] Kidane (2017), p. 131.

[37] Schill (2015), p. 120.

3 Courts and Investment Awards: Canadian Perspective

This section examines the standard of review for setting aside investment awards applied by the Canadian courts. The decisions on standard of review at the setting aside stage matter significantly because they illustrate a way in which the courts communicate their role (as the courts themselves perceive it) in the context of IIL. In the Canadian context, both the FC and superior Courts can have jurisdiction to set aside the arbitral awards, pursuant to relevant federal and provincial international commercial arbitration acts as applicable.[38] The application to set aside is filed to the FC if "the relief is thought against the Federal Government but the superior courts have jurisdiction if the place of arbitration is within the province".[39] From the outset, it is worth noting that the Canadian courts view investment awards as international commercial arbitration awards, and, thus, apply the same standard of review for such awards.[40]

Accordingly, the courts apply the administrative law standard of review for the arbitral awards. In past years, the Canadian courts have only considered setting aside the investment awards on the basis of two grounds, when (1) "the award deals with a dispute not contemplated by or not falling within the terms of the submission to arbitration, or contains decisions on matters beyond the scope of the submission to arbitration"[41] and (2) the award violates public policy considerations in Canada.[42] As next section will demonstrate, first, with respect to the disputes outside the scope of the submission to arbitration, the Canadian courts applied the administrative standard of review known as correctness. Second, the Canadian courts did not pronounce the scope of review standards for setting aside awards on public policy grounds. The following sections will examine the evolution of the standards for reviewing investment awards by the Canadian courts on these two grounds, and will scrutinize the dicta in the *Bilcon* case under the review of the FC to identify what

---

[38]For example, International Commercial Arbitration Act, 2017, Status of Ontario (SO) 2017, c 2, Sch 5 (for Ontario).

[39]Mestral and Morgan (2017), p. 159.

[40]Interestingly, CJEU differentiated between commercial arbitration and investment arbitration. The Canadian court in *Metaclad* did not. See: United Mexican States v Metalclad, 2001 BCSC 664, para. 55, https://www.canlii.org/en/bc/bcsc/doc/2001/2001bcsc664/2001bcsc664.html?searchUrlHash=AAAAAQAxVW5pdGVkIE1leGljYW4gU3RhdGVzIHYgTWV0YWxjbGFkLCAyMDAxIEJDU0MgNjY0IAAAAAAB&resultIndex=1 (last accessed 13 April 2020). CJEU, Judgment, 6 March 2018, Case C-284/16, *Slovak Republic v. Achmea*, ECLI:EU:C:2018:158, para. 55 ("the latter originate in the freely expressed wishes of the parties, [while] the former derive from a treaty by which Member States agree to remove from the jurisdiction of their own courts, and hence from the system of judicial remedies which the second subparagraph of Article 19(1)TEU requires them to establish in the fields covered by EU law [...], disputes which may concern the application or interpretation of EU law").

[41]Commercial Arbitration Act, Revised Statutes of Canada 1985, c.17 (2ndSupp), s. 5 and Commercial Arbitration Code in Schedule 1, Article 6.

[42]Of course, there were challenges to non-investment arbitration awards on other grounds, for example, see: Casey (2012), p. 415.

narrative of IIL the FC ultimately endorsed at the stage of setting aside the arbitral award.

3.1 *Standards of Review*

The courts have repeatedly emphasized a high level of deference to investment arbitration tribunals on the basis of principles, such as respect to the parties' choice of forum and the finality of the arbitral awards. Yet, the courts have also reiterated that they exercise a supervisory function (albeit a limited one) over the arbitral tribunals. For example, in the *United Mexican States v. Cargill*, the court noted that "if courts were to defer to the decision of the tribunal on issues of true jurisdiction, that would effectively nullify the purpose and intent of the review authority of the court".[43]

The standard of review in Canada continues to evolve. In December 2019, the Supreme Court of Canada ("SCC") rendered a decision in the case *Canada (Minister of Citizenship and Immigration) v. Vavilov*.[44] According to Shaun Fluker, "Vavilov expands the presumption of reasonableness as applicable to any substantive decision made by a statutory decision-maker [. . .] This blanket presumption applies to the determination of questions of law (including jurisdiction), fact, or mixed law and fact".[45] The SCC's decision makes room for two exceptions to the presumption of reasonableness. They include (1) "presumption will be rebutted where a legislature has indicated that a different standard should apply" (2) "the presumption of reasonableness review will be rebutted is where the rule of law requires that the standard of correctness be applied".[46] In *Vavilov*, SCC has altered the standard of review once again, a choice that may change the approach of Canadian courts to the standard applicable in reviewing arbitral awards. Yet the approaches developed by the Canadian courts prior to *Vavilov* are not obsolete as they demonstrate evolving relationships of Canadian courts with the arbitral tribunals and how the domestic courts view themselves in the context of international investment law.

---

[43]United Mexican States v. Cargill, Inc, 2011 ONCA 622 para. 48, https://www.canlii.org/en/on/onca/doc/2011/2011onca622/2011onca622.html?searchUrlHash=AAAAAQAmVW5pdGVkIE1leGljYW4gU3RhdGVzIHYuIENhcmdpbGwsIEluYy4AAAAAAQ&resultIndex=2 (last accessed 13 April 2020).

[44]Canada (Minister of Citizenship and Immigration) v. Vavilov, 2019 SCC 65, https://www.canlii.org/en/ca/scc/doc/2019/2019scc65/2019scc65.html (last accessed 13 April 2020).

[45]Shaun Fluker, Vavilov on Standard of Review in Canadian Administrative Law (6 February 2020), https://ablawg.ca/2020/02/06/vavilov-on-standard-of-review-in-canadian-administrative-law/ (last accessed 13 April 2020).

[46]Shaun Fluker, Vavilov on Standard of Review in Canadian Administrative Law (6 February 2020), https://ablawg.ca/2020/02/06/vavilov-on-standard-of-review-in-canadian-administrative-law/ (last accessed 13 April 2020), paras 17, 33.

It is important to emphasize that the position of the courts on the applicable standard of review has shifted over the years before SCC rendered its judgement in *Vavilov*. Prior to *Vavilov*, the evolution of the standard of review could be examined in the terms of pre-*Dunsmuir* and post-*Dunsmuir* dynamics.[47] *Dunsmuir v. New Brunswick* set the scope and standard for judicial review of the decisions made by the domestic administrative tribunals.[48] *Dunsmuir* sets two approaches to the administrative standard of review under which the courts can review the decisions of tribunals (1) on reasonableness or (2) correctness. The administrative law standard for judicial review in Canada has evolved considerably over the years, with the practicing bar being overly concerned as to the clarity and appropriate application of the standard.[49] Most recent study of the judicial application of the administrative law standard by Robert Danay reveals that even the SCC justices grew increasingly "polarized" and frequently "dissented" on the "the identification or the application of the standard of review".[50]

Prior to *Dunsmuir*, the Canadian courts struggled to determine whether the administrative standard of review should be used in the context of setting aside international commercial arbitration awards. In reviewing the *SD Myers* award, the FC noted that "it is an error to import into that [Commercial Arbitration Act] an approach which has been developed as a branch of statutory interpretation in respect of domestic tribunals created by statute".[51] The court particularly emphasized the "considerations of international comity and the need to account for sensitivity to the international commercial system".[52] Interestingly, in reviewing the arbitral award in the *United Mexican States v. Feldman Karpa*, the Ontario Court of Appeal

---

[47]Note: *Dunsmuir* is a leading Canadian administrative law case that sets the scope and standard for judicial review of the domestic administrative tribunals.

[48]Dunsmuir v. New Brunswick, [2008] 1 SCR para. 190, https://www.canlii.org/en/ca/scc/doc/2008/2008scc9/2008scc9.html?searchUrlHash=AAAAAQAZRHVuc211aXIgdi4gTmV3IEJydW5zd2ljawAAAAAB&resultIndex=1 (last accessed 13 April 2020). Note: in the Canadian context, administrative tribunals are specialized agencies created under provincial or federal legislation. Some administrative tribunals fulfil adjudicative functions, their decisions usually can be reviewed by the domestic courts according to the applicable administrative standard of review. There is significant difference between administrative tribunals and arbitral tribunals. Administrative tribunals in Canada are creatures of Statute whereas arbitral tribunals are established on the basis of consent between the parties. For more information, see: Ellis (2013), pp. 2–7.

[49]Danay (2019), at p. 3, 7. For historical perspective on Canadian standard of review, see Sossin and Flood (2007), p. 581.

[50]Danay (2019), p. 3.

[51]Canada (Attorney General) v. SD Myers, 2004 FC 368, paras 34, 36, 39, https://www.canlii.org/en/ca/fct/doc/2004/2004fc38/2004fc38.html?searchUrlHash=AAAAAQAxQ2FuYWRhIChBdHRvcm5leSBHZW5lcmFsKSB2IFNEIE15ZXJzLCAyMDA0IEZDIDM2OAAAAAAB&resultIndex=1 (last accessed 13 April 2020).

[52]United Mexican States v. Feldman Karpa, 2005 ONCA 249, paras 34, 36, https://www.canlii.org/en/on/onca/doc/2005/2005canlii249/2005canlii249.html?searchUrlHash=AAAAAQAmVW5pdGVkIE1leGljYW4gU3RhdGVzIHYuIEZlbGRtYW4gS2FycGEAAAAAAQ&resultIndex=1 (last accessed 13 April 2020).

("ONCA") took a different stance thereby suggesting that the administrative standard for judicial review of the arbitration awards was appropriate if the court exercises the "high level of deference".[53] Arguably, this approach can be problematic since the administrative standard of review continues to shift, its application can produce uncertainty at the stage of setting aside.

In *Karpa*, the court, accordingly, proceeded through the relevant steps of judicial analysis to establish that the tribunal did not exceed its jurisdiction.[54] In particular, the court examined that the expertise of the arbitrators, the authority of the tribunals to determine facts, and again highlighted strict limitations for review at the "set aside" stage. Thus, the court in *Karpa* took a somewhat hybrid approach to judicial review by employing the domestic administrative law standard of review with the high level of deference to the arbitral tribunals.

In the aftermath of the *Dunsmuir* decision, the Canadian courts seemed to settle on the idea that administrative law standard of review is most appropriate for the judicial review of the arbitral awards. For instance, the court in *Cargill* stated that the arbitral awards should be reviewed on the standard of correctness.[55] According to the court, the standard of correctness means "the tribunal had to be correct in its determination that it had the ability to make the decision it made".[56] It also noted that "the fact that the standard of review on jurisdictional questions is correctness does not give the courts a broad scope for intervention in the decisions of international arbitral tribunals. To the contrary, courts are expected to intervene only in rare circumstances where there is a true question of jurisdiction".[57] The court set out a three-question framework as the standard of review. These questions are:

---

[53]United Mexican States v. Feldman Karpa, 2005 ONCA 249, paras 34, 36, https://www.canlii.org/en/on/onca/doc/2005/2005canlii249/2005canlii249.html?searchUrlHash=AAAAAQAmVW5pdGVkIE1leGljYW4gU3RhdGVzIHYuIEZlbGRtYW4gS2FycGEAAAAAAQ&resultIndex=1 (last accessed 13 April 2020), paras 38–39.

[54]United Mexican States v. Feldman Karpa, 2005 ONCA 249, paras 34, 36, https://www.canlii.org/en/on/onca/doc/2005/2005canlii249/2005canlii249.html?searchUrlHash=AAAAAQAmVW5pdGVkIE1leGljYW4gU3RhdGVzIHYuIEZlbGRtYW4gS2FycGEAAAAAAQ&resultIndex=1 (last accessed 13 April 2020), paras 66–69.

[55]United Mexican States v. Cargill, Inc, 2011 ONCA 622 para. 48, https://www.canlii.org/en/on/onca/doc/2011/2011onca622/2011onca622.html?searchUrlHash=AAAAAQAmVW5pdGVkIE1leGljYW4gU3RhdGVzIHYuIENhcmdpbGwsIEluYy4AAAAAAQ&resultIndex=2 (last accessed 13 April 2020), para. 35. Gold (2011), p. 721.

[56]United Mexican States v. Cargill, Inc, 2011 ONCA 622 para. 48, https://www.canlii.org/en/on/onca/doc/2011/2011onca622/2011onca622.html?searchUrlHash=AAAAAQAmVW5pdGVkIE1leGljYW4gU3RhdGVzIHYuIENhcmdpbGwsIEluYy4AAAAAAQ&resultIndex=2 (last accessed 13 April 2020), para. 42.

[57]United Mexican States v. Cargill, Inc, 2011 ONCA 622 para. 48, https://www.canlii.org/en/on/onca/doc/2011/2011onca622/2011onca622.html?searchUrlHash=AAAAAQAmVW5pdGVkIE1leGljYW4gU3RhdGVzIHYuIENhcmdpbGwsIEluYy4AAAAAAQ&resultIndex=2 (last accessed 13 April 2020), para. 44.

> [w]hat was the issue that the tribunal decided? Was that issue within the submission to arbitration made under Chapter 11 of the NAFTA? Is there anything in the NAFTA, properly interpreted, that precluded the tribunal from making the award it made?[58]

In *Attorney General of Canada v. Mobil Investments Canada*, the court followed *Cargill's* framework of analysis but clarified that "courts are obliged to take a narrow view of what constitutes a question of jurisdiction".[59] They should resist "broadening the scope of the issue to effectively decide the merits of the case".[60] This approach is particularly "magnified in the international arbitration context".[61]

Correctness as a standard of review requires the court to identify whether the tribunal correctly established jurisdiction. Consequences of reviewing on correctness can be far reaching. However, as Marc Gold has observed, "regardless of the standard of review being applied, judges have a degree of choice as to how broadly or narrowly they define jurisdictional issues".[62] So even if the courts stop employing administrative law language in conducting the review, and develop a different autonomous standard—what will matter is still their choices in construing the issues of jurisdiction narrowly or broadly. Thus, the applicable standard of review remains a powerful tool to manage the relationships between the domestic courts and arbitral tribunals.

With regards to public policy, the Canadian courts emphasized that the standard of review to set aside the award on this ground was set very high, but did not actually pronounce explicitly the scope of the standard and the level of scrutiny. In their interpretation of public policy, the courts duly referenced the UNCITRAL Model Law.[63] The courts did not set out any hypothetical scenario in which investment arbitration award can be set aside on the grounds of public policy. Yet, they pointed out that public policy was "to guard against enforcement of an award which offends our local principles of justice and fairness in a fundamental way"[64] and that "does not refer to the political position or an international position of Canada but refers to

[58]United Mexican States v. Cargill, Inc, 2011 ONCA 622 para. 48, https://www.canlii.org/en/on/onca/doc/2011/2011onca622/2011onca622.html?searchUrlHash=AAAAAQAmVW5pdGVkIE1leGljYW4gU3RhdGVzIHYuIENhcmdpbGwsIElu Yy4AAAAAAQ&resultIndex=2 (last accessed 13 April 2020), para. 52.

[59]Attorney General of Canada v. Mobil Investments Canada Inc.et al., 2016 ONSC 790, paras 37, 129 OR (3d) 506, para. 37, https://www.italaw.com/sites/default/files/case-documents/italaw7160.pdf (last accessed 13 April 2020).

[60]Attorney General of Canada v. Mobil Investments Canada Inc.et al., 2016 ONSC 790, paras 37, 129 OR (3d) 506, para. 37, https://www.italaw.com/sites/default/files/case-documents/italaw7160.pdf (last accessed 13 April 2020), para. 37.

[61]Attorney General of Canada v. Mobil Investments Canada Inc.et al., 2016 ONSC 790, paras 37, 129 OR (3d) 506, para. 37, https://www.italaw.com/sites/default/files/case-documents/italaw7160.pdf (last accessed 13 April 2020), para. 37.

[62]Gold (2011), p. 725.

[63]Bayview Irrigation District #11 v Mexico, 2008 CanLII 22120 (Ont Sup Ct J), para. 63, https://www.italaw.com/sites/default/files/case-documents/ita0078_0.pdf (last accessed 13 April 2020).

[64]United Mexican States v. Feldman Karpa, 2005 ONCA 249, paras 34, 36, https://www.canlii.org/en/on/onca/doc/2005/2005canlii249/2005canlii249.html?

fundamental notions and principles of justice".[65] For example, in *Bayview Irrigation District #11 v. Mexico*, the court clarified that to succeed in setting aside the arbitral award on public policy grounds, the award must be "marked by corruption, bribery or fraud or contrary to the essential morality".[66] The court however did not clarify the meaning of the term "essential morality".

Accordingly, the Canadian courts demonstrate their commitment to promoting reputation of Canada as arbitration friendly jurisdiction by referencing international comity and finality of arbitral awards as relevant factors in the proceedings on setting aside the arbitral awards. This is apparent in the approach of the Canadian courts to reviewing the awards on public policy grounds. However, the adoption of administrative standard of review for the arbitral awards on jurisdictional grounds can arguably jeopardize any prima facie assertions on "friendliness" of the Canadian courts to international arbitration. The logic of the UNCITRAL Model Law and the New York Convention facilitates a creation of a specialized international arbitration regime that promotes universalization as a value across different jurisdictions.[67] By connecting the standard of review for arbitral awards to the unsettled administrative law standard, the courts risk to undermine the project on universalization. Thus, in this context, the national courts can play powerful role by fostering the objectives of universalization or undermining it.[68]

3.2 *What Does the Court Say? Looking at the Dicta of the Federal Court in Bilcon v. Clayton*

Zooming in to the judicial scrutiny of the *Bilcon* award provides useful perspective on how the domestic court can formally exercise restraint in judicially reviewing the arbitral award, yet, voice a deep concern over some aspects of IIL. First, this section considers briefly the facts and the outcome of the *Bilcon* arbitration. Second, it will turn to the analysis of the court's judgement at the stage of setting aside the award. Understanding the facts and the outcome (including the dissenting opinion) in this

searchUrlHash=AAAAAQAmVW5pdGVkIE1leGljYW4gU3RhdGVzIHYuIEZlbGRtYW4gS2FycGEAAAAAAQ&resultIndex=1 (last accessed 13 April 2020), para. 66.

[65] Canada (Attorney General) v. SD Myers, 2004 FC 368, paras 34, 36, 39, https://www.canlii.org/en/ca/fct/doc/2004/2004fc38/2004fc38.html?searchUrlHash=AAAAAQAxQ2FuYWRhIChBdHRvcm5leSBHZW5lcmFsKSB2IFNEIE15ZXJzLCAyMDA0IEZDIDM2OAAAAAAB&resultIndex=1 (last accessed 13 April 2020), para. 55.

[66] Bayview Irrigation District #11 v Mexico, 2008 CanLII 22120 (Ont Sup Ct J), para. 63, https://www.italaw.com/sites/default/files/case-documents/ita0078_0.pdf (last accessed 13 April 2020), para. 64.

[67] Van Den Berg (2014), p. 287.

[68] Note: This is perhaps not the step in the direction some provinces in Canada would like to take given that in 2018, Ontario adopted a new International Commercial Arbitration Act that gives the New York Convention direct effect.

case is essential because they form a larger part of the critical narrative in the decision of the court.

In *Bilcon*, the arbitral tribunal adjudicated a dispute over refusal to issue an environmental permit to the US–based investors. Clayton and Bilcon, the US based investors, proposed building the basalt quarry, and shipment facility in the highly sensitive area of Whites Point in Nova Scotia.[69] The approval of the project was contingent on successful environmental impact assessment conducted by the Joint Panel Review ("JPR") under the respective federal and provincial legislation.[70] The JPR rendered negative assessment, in particular, it specified that "the Project would have a significant adverse effect on a Valued Environmental Component represented by the 'core values' of the affected communities".[71] According to JRP, the "injection of an industrial project into the region would undermine and jeopardize community visions and expectations, and lead to irrevocable and undesired changes of quality of life".[72] A matter of particular concern was possible effect of the project on "the people, communities and economy of Digby Neck and Islands".[73]

The investors took a problem with the way the assessment was conducted. They submitted the claim under the NAFTA, Chapter 11 for breach of the minimum standard of treatment ("MST").[74] The arbitral tribunal ruled that Canada violated North American Free Trade Agreement ("NAFTA") provisions because the panel did not appropriately interpret and apply the concept of community core values.[75] Donald McRae, an arbitrator appointed by Canada dissented by submitting that (1) simple violation of domestic law cannot be elevated to the status of the breach of an international treaty and (2) "[c]ommunity core values" is a concept of domestic

---

[69]Bilcon v. Government of Canada, PCA Case No 2009-04, Award on Jurisdiction and Liability, 17 March 2015, para. 5.

[70]Bilcon v. Government of Canada, PCA Case No 2009-04, Award on Jurisdiction and Liability, 17 March 2015, para. 10.

[71]Bilcon v. Government of Canada, PCA Case No 2009-04, Award on Jurisdiction and Liability, 17 March 2015, para. 21.

[72]Canada (Attorney General) v. Clayton, 2018 FC 436, para. 18, https://www.canlii.org/en/ca/fct/doc/2018/2018fc436/2018fc436.html?searchUrlHash=AAAAAQAwQ2FuYWRhIChBdHRvcm5leSBHZW5lcmFsKSB2IENsYXl0b24sIDIwMTggRkMgNDM2AAAAAAE&resultIndex=1 (last accessed 13 April 2020).

[73]Canada (Attorney General) v. Clayton, 2018 FC 436, para. 18, https://www.canlii.org/en/ca/fct/doc/2018/2018fc436/2018fc436.html?searchUrlHash=AAAAAQAwQ2FuYWRhIChBdHRvcm5leSBHZW5lcmFsKSB2IENsYXl0b24sIDIwMTggRkMgNDM2AAAAAAE&resultIndex=1 (last accessed 13 April 2020), paras 19–20.

[74]Canada (Attorney General) v. Clayton, 2018 FC 436, para. 18, https://www.canlii.org/en/ca/fct/doc/2018/2018fc436/2018fc436.html?searchUrlHash=AAAAAQAwQ2FuYWRhIChBdHRvcm5leSBHZW5lcmFsKSB2IENsYXl0b24sIDIwMTggRkMgNDM2AAAAAAE&resultIndex=1 (last accessed 13 April 2020), para. 19.

[75]Canada (Attorney General) v. Clayton, 2018 FC 436, para. 18, https://www.canlii.org/en/ca/fct/doc/2018/2018fc436/2018fc436.html?searchUrlHash=AAAAAQAwQ2FuYWRhIChBdHRvcm5leSBHZW5lcmFsKSB2IENsYXl0b24sIDIwMTggRkMgNDM2AAAAAAE&resultIndex=1 (last accessed 13 April 2020), paras 34–36.

environmental law. According to McRae, "the Tribunal could not conclude that the JRP had violated Canadian law without the benefit of a determination of that question by the Court" and (3) neither the result, nor the process by which the JRP reached its decision "could ever be said to offend judicial propriety".[76]

The FC confirmed its limited authority to review the arbitral awards (i.e. only on correctness) and again emphasized the need to adhere to "the modern movement towards finality of arbitration awards".[77] Ultimately, on the basis of these principles, the court refused to set aside the arbitral award. In particular, the court pronounced that,

> while Canada takes issue with the majority's findings regarding Canada's non-compliance with the requirements of Canadian environmental law, it is not open to this Court, sitting on an application to set aside an Award under Chapter Eleven of NAFTA, to review the merits of the Tribunal's decision and to second-guess its findings, as any error that the Tribunal may have made in this regard was not jurisdictional in nature.[78]

The structure of the judgement reveals an acceptance by the court of the critical narrative on IIL particularly in its relation to the regulatory environmental protections. For example, the court in detailed reviewed the regulatory chill argument by relying on the relevant investment arbitration scholarship.[79] After acknowledging its limited ability to review arbitral awards, the court voiced its concerns with regards to the system,

> I accept that the majority's Award raises significant policy concerns. These include its effect on the ability of NAFTA Parties to regulate environmental matters within their jurisdiction, the ability of NAFTA tribunals to properly assess whether foreign investors have been

---

[76]Canada (Attorney General) v. Clayton, 2018 FC 436, para. 18, https://www.canlii.org/en/ca/fct/doc/2018/2018fc436/2018fc436.html?searchUrlHash=AAAAAQAwQ2FuYWRhIChBdHRvcm5leSBHZW5lcmFsKSB2IENsYXl0b24sIDIwMTggRkMgNDM2AAAAAAE&resultIndex=1 (last accessed 13 April 2020), paras 57, 60. See also Dissenting Opinion of Professor Donald McRae in the matter of an arbitration under chapter 11 of the NAFTA between Clayton & Bilcon and the Government of Canada, https://www.italaw.com/sites/default/files/case-documents/italaw4213.pdf (last accessed 13 April 2020).

[77]Canada (Attorney General) v. Clayton, 2018 FC 436, para. 18, https://www.canlii.org/en/ca/fct/doc/2018/2018fc436/2018fc436.html?searchUrlHash=AAAAAQAwQ2FuYWRhIChBdHRvcm5leSBHZW5lcmFsKSB2IENsYXl0b24sIDIwMTggRkMgNDM2AAAAAAE&resultIndex=1 (last accessed 13 April 2020), para. 154.

[78]Canada (Attorney General) v. Clayton, 2018 FC 436, para. 18, https://www.canlii.org/en/ca/fct/doc/2018/2018fc436/2018fc436.html?searchUrlHash=AAAAAQAwQ2FuYWRhIChBdHRvcm5leSBHZW5lcmFsKSB2IENsYXl0b24sIDIwMTggRkMgNDM2AAAAAAE&resultIndex=1 (last accessed 13 April 2020), para. 156.

[79]Canada (Attorney General) v. Clayton, 2018 FC 436, para. 18, https://www.canlii.org/en/ca/fct/doc/2018/2018fc436/2018fc436.html?searchUrlHash=AAAAAQAwQ2FuYWRhIChBdHRvcm5leSBHZW5lcmFsKSB2IENsYXl0b24sIDIwMTggRkMgNDM2AAAAAAE&resultIndex=1 (last accessed 13 April 2020), paras 139–147.

treated fairly under domestic environmental assessment processes, and the potential "chill" in the environmental assessment process that could result from the majority's decision.[80]

Accordingly, while Canadian courts signal that Canada is an international arbitration friendly jurisdiction where the courts will intervene in the arbitral decisions only "sparingly" and in "extraordinary" instances, arguably the courts can also fulfil a function of national (de)legitimation of IIL.

4 Future Modes of Interaction

In light of the ongoing reform of IIL, it is desirable to explore in what ways the relationships between the arbitral tribunals and domestic courts should evolve. The theoretical framework of "exit, voice and loyalty" is useful to conceptualize possible modes of future interactions between the domestic courts and investment tribunals.[81] Under the theory of "exit, voice, and loyalty" developed by Albert Hirschman, the members of an organization who have concerns about its functioning have three options. First, they can leave the organization and cut ties to it. Second, they can voice their concerns and demand the changes in the organization. Third, members can stay loyal to the organization and not voice any concerns. It is worth noting that the members can potentially combine two options.[82]

Accordingly, first possibility is "exit" or in other words, an open conflict. Under this mode, the domestic courts will engage in an open contestation of the arbitral tribunals' rulings by undermining the arbitral rulings through broad interpretations of grounds to set aside the awards under the New York Convention and Model Law. For example, Emilia Onyema explains that "in some African jurisdictions, national courts are more negatively interventionists with some judges [...] seeking to usurp the powers given to the arbitrator by their national law and the disputant over the dispute".[83]

The second possibility is that the domestic courts will raise their "voices" in the context of IIL. This option suggests that the domestic courts will not shy away from

[80]Canada (Attorney General) v. Clayton, 2018 FC 436, para. 18, https://www.canlii.org/en/ca/fct/doc/2018/2018fc436/2018fc436.html?searchUrlHash=AAAAAQAwQ2FuYWRhIChBdHRvcm5leSBHZW5lcmFsKSB2IENsYXl0b24sIDIwMTggRkMgNDM2AAAAAAE&resultIndex=1 (last accessed 13 April 2020), para. 198.

[81]Hirschman (1970), pp. 3–15. Note: the theory got limited prominence in ISDS context however has not yet been applied to analysing the relationships between domestic courts and arbitral tribunals. Katselas (2015), p. 216; Welsh et al. (2014), p. 130.

[82]For example, the members can stay loyal to the organization in principle, but use available means in the organization to introduce the changes. Shareholders can fully abandon a company by selling all their shares, or they can stay loyal to the company, but vote for new directors to ensure that the company changes course. The "exit" option means that the members lose a chance to "voice" their concerns in order to improve the organization.

[83]Onyema (2018), p. 200.

critically assessing international arbitration as a system of dispute resolution. It is possible that the courts will combine the two options in construing their relationships with arbitral tribunals. In this context, the decision of the FC in *Bilcon* is particularly interesting because the court effectively expressed loyalty to the system of international arbitration by emphasizing deference and comity as guiding principle of interpreting the grounds on setting aside the award even when reviewing on correctness. Yet the court simultaneously raised its voice by highlighting a possibility of regulatory chill for environmental regulations that the award of majority can invoke.

The third possibility is "loyalty" that provides for the domestic courts acting as "faithful trustees" of the international arbitration system.[84] Under this mode, the role of the domestic courts will be primarily supporting. As "faithful trustees", the domestic courts will interpret and apply the grounds for setting aside the arbitral awards in a narrow fashion, and continue to emphasize importance of international comity as a guiding principle in reviewing arbitral awards at the setting aside stage.

These three modes of interaction provide a useful framework of analysis for the approaches of national courts to defining their roles in IIL and their relationships with the arbitral tribunals. Most importantly for the purpose of this chapter is that any mode of interaction will lead to legitimation or, to the contrary, delegitimation of IIL. Given that domestic courts play an important role in "speaking" with national audiences (both legal expert communities and societies at large), the reformers of the investment arbitration should take another careful look at future of the relationships between arbitral tribunals and domestic courts if they seek to enhance legitimacy of the international system for protecting foreign investment for national audiences.

5 Concluding Remarks

This chapter has examined the role of the domestic courts as transnational actors in IIL. The chapter also conceptualized future modes of interaction between the domestic courts and arbitral tribunals by applying the "exit, voice and loyalty" framework. The experience of the Canadian courts on reviewing investment awards demonstrates that the domestic courts continue to possess considerable discretion with regards to the interpretation of the limited grounds for setting aside the arbitral awards under the New York Convention and the UNCITRAL Model Law.

It also shows that the Canadian courts have chosen to afford deference to the arbitral tribunals, thus, presenting Canada as an arbitration friendly jurisdiction. Canadian cases, however, demonstrate that the courts can raise serious concerns

[84] Lauterpacht (1949), pp. 25, 33–38. Note: the term "faithful trustee" was first applied by Hersh Lauterpacht in relation to the relationships between the domestic courts and the European Court of Human Rights. This term was later interpreted by Bjorje Eriik who explained that domestic courts should avoid any "friction" with the ECtHR. Bjorge (2015), pp. 245–246.

about IIL even under the constraints of limited grounds for judicial review and an ambition to present their jurisdiction as international arbitration friendly. This chapter concludes that the reformers of the system should focus their attention on the future of the relationships between the domestic courts and the arbitral tribunals to ensure cohesion between the courts and the tribunals. Arguably, lack of such cohesion can result in delegitimating of the system for the national audiences, an outcome that the reformers most likely do not desire.

References

Alschner W, Skougarevskiy S (2016) Mapping the universe of international investment agreements. J Int Econ Law 19(3):561–588

Berman P (2012) Global legal pluralism: a jurisprudence of law beyond borders. Cambridge University Press, Cambridge

Bianchi A (2016) International law theories: an inquiry into different ways of thinking. Oxford University Press, Oxford

Bjorge E (2015) Domestic application of the ECHR: courts as faithful trustees. Oxford University Press, Oxford

Born G (2009) International commercial arbitration. Kluwer Law International, The Hague

Casey B (2012) Arbitration law of Canada: practice and procedure. Juris Publishing, New York

Danay R (2019) A house divided: the Supreme Court of Canada's recent jurisprudence on the standard of review. Univ Tor Law J 69(1):3–17

Dezalay Y, Garth B (1996) Dealing in virtue. International commercial arbitration and the construction of transnational legal order. University of Chicago Press, Chicago

Dupont C, Schultz T (2016) Towards a new heuristic model: investment arbitration as a political system. J Int Dispute Settl 7:3–30

Ellis R (2013) Unjust by design: Canada's administrative justice system. University of British Columbia Press, Vancouver

Gold M (2011) Judicial review of international arbitrations in Canada: notes on Mexico Cargill. Can Bar Rev 90(3):717–725

Grisel F (2017) Treaty-making between public authority and private interests: the genealogy of the convention on the recognition and enforcement of foreign arbitral awards. Eur J Int Law 28 (1):73–87

Hirschman A (1970) Exit, voice, and loyalty: responses to decline in firms, organizations, and states. Harvard University Press, Cambridge

Katselas A (2015) Exit, voice, and loyalty in investment treaty arbitration. In: Lalani S, Lazo R (eds) The role of the state in investor-state arbitration. Martinus Nijhoff Publishers, The Hague, pp 211–220

Kennedy D (2007) One, two, three. Many legal orders: legal pluralism and the cosmopolitan dream. N Y Univ Rev Law Soc Change 31(3):641–659

Kerr T (2015) The relationship between the Strasbourg court and the national courts - as seen from the UK Supreme Court. In: Ziegler K, Wicks E, Hodson L (eds) The UK and European human rights: a strained relationship? Bloomsbury, London, pp 31–39

Kidane W (2017) The culture of international arbitration. Oxford University Press, Oxford

Krisch N (2008) The open architecture of European human rights law. Mod Law Rev 71 (2):183–216

Krisch N (2012) Beyond constitutionalism: the pluralist structure of postnational law. Oxford University Press, Oxford

Lauterpacht H (1949) The proposed European court of human rights. Trans Grotius Soc 35:25–47

Lewis D (2016) The interpretation and uniformity of the UNCITRAL model law on international commercial arbitration: focusing on Australia, Hong Kong and Singapore. Kluwer Law International, The Hague

Lynch K (2003) The forces of economic globalization: challenges to the regime of international commercial arbitration. Kluwer Arbitration, The Hague

Mestral A, Morgan R (2017) Does Canadian law provide remedies equivalent to NAFTA chapter 11 arbitration? In: Mestral A (ed) Second thoughts: investor state arbitration between developed democracies. McGill-Queen's Press, Montreal, pp 155–186

Miles K (2013) The origins of international investment law. Empire, environment and the safeguard of capital. Cambridge University Press, Cambridge

Onyema E (2018) The role of African courts and judges in arbitration. In: Onyema E (ed) Rethinking the role of African national courts. Kluwer Law International, The Hague, pp 1–37

Pasquet L (2017) Dialogue or interaction? A non-cosmopolitan reading of transjudicial communication. In: Müller A, Kjos H (eds) Judicial dialogue and human rights. Cambridge University Press, Cambridge, pp 467–504

Paulsson J (2008) Awards set aside at the place of arbitration in enforcing arbitration awards under the New York Convention experience and prospects. In: Enforcing arbitration awards under the New York Convention experience and prospects. United Nations, New York, pp 24–27

Pohl J (2018) Intra-EU investment arbitration after the Achmea case: legal autonomy bounded by mutual trust. Eur Const Law Rev 14(4):767–791

Sanders P (1999) The making of the convention in enforcing arbitration awards under the New York Convention. United Nations, New York

Schill S (2015) Conceptions of legitimacy of international arbitration. In: Caron D (ed) Practising virtue: inside international arbitration. Oxford University Press, Oxford, pp 106–127

Schreuer C (2012) Interaction of international tribunals and domestic courts in investment law. In: Rovine A (ed) International arbitration and mediation: the fordham papers (2011). Martinus Nijhoff Publishers, The Hague, pp 71–97

Slaughter AM (2000) Judicial globalization. Virginia J Int Law 40

Sossin L, Flood C (2007) The contextual turn: Iacobucci's legacy and the standard of review. Univ Tor Law J 57(2):581–606

Tucker T (2018) Judge knot: politics and development in international investment law. Anthem Press, New York

Van Den Berg A (2014) Should the setting aside of the arbitral award be abolished? ICSID Rev 29 (2):263–288

Welsh N, Schneider A, Rimpfel K (2014) Using the theories of exit, voice, loyalty, and procedural justice to reconceptualize Brazil's rejection of bilateral investment treaties. Wash Univ J Law Policy 45(1):105–143

Ksenia Polonskaya is Assistant Professor at Carleton University, Department of Law and Legal Studies. She holds a Ph.D. from Queen's University, an LL.M. from the University of Toronto and an LL.B. from Kuban State University (Russia). She is a contributor to Investment Claims (Oxford Press) and was previously an associate editor at the University of Toronto Faculty of Law Review. Her papers have appeared in Cambridge University Press publications, Melbourne Journal of International Law, The Law & Practice of International Courts and Tribunals, and Leiden Journal of International Law.

A Middle Path of ISDS Reform: The Principle of Comity as a Means of Strengthening the Role of National Courts in the Enforcement of Investment Arbitral Awards

Aikaterini Florou

Contents

1 A Changing Landscape of the Enforcement of Investment Arbitral Awards 172
2 The European Commission's Interventions as Amicus Curiae in Intra-EU Disputes 174
2.1 EU Law as a Jurisdictional Defence 174
2.2 EU Law as a Substantive Defence 176
3 The Decisions of National Courts in Enforcement Proceedings 177
3.1 The "Achmea avalanche" 177
3.2 The "Micula saga" 180
4 A Parallel World of "Autonomy"? The CJEU's Opinion on CETA 185
5 Old Solutions to New Problems: Comity as the Way Forward? 189
References 192

Abstract This chapter explores the changing dynamics of the relationship between domestic courts and investment-treaty tribunals at the stage of the enforcement of arbitral awards. The focus is on the increasing tension between EU law and international investment law in the context of intra-EU investor-state arbitration, as demonstrated in particular by the difficulties in enforcing the arbitral awards in the *Micula* and *Achmea* cases. The chapter reveals the divergent approaches that domestic courts, both within and outside the EU, have taken to the enforcement of intra-EU arbitral awards. It concludes with reflections on the role of comity as a means of coordination between courts and tribunals and a conflict-prevention mechanism and

I would like to warmly thank the organisers of the Colloquium on "Actors in International Investment Law: Beyond Claimants, Respondents and Arbitrators" who gave me the opportunity to discuss my paper with a distinct group of scholars. Any errors are my own.

A. Florou (✉)
University of Hamburg, Hamburg, Germany
e-mail: aikaterini.florou@sciencespo.fr

A. Gourgourinis (ed.), *Transnational Actors in International Investment Law*,
European Yearbook of International Economic Law,
https://doi.org/10.1007/978-3-030-60679-4_8

the potential institutionalization of the principle of comity in the context of the ongoing revision of the ICSID Arbitration Rules.

1 A Changing Landscape of the Enforcement of Investment Arbitral Awards

"Winter is coming", warned Gary Born in his recent Freshfields lecture on the future of international arbitration.[1] Adding to the alertness, in June 2019, Global Arbitration Review published a Guide to Challenging and Enforcing Arbitral Awards, noting that, while there is no source of reliable data available to test whether challenges to awards have been increasing during the last decade, there is anecdotal perception of increasing concerns about the enforceability of arbitral awards.[2] This perception marks a turn from the 2015 International Bar Association ("IBA") report, which had found that foreign awards were rarely refused recognition and enforcement on public policy grounds under the United Nations Convention on the Recognition and Enforcement of Foreign Arbitral Awards ("New York Convention").[3]

The current landscape of enforcement is changing, making the finality of arbitral awards less straightforward than it used to be. The stance that the European Commission ("EC") has taken towards investor-state dispute settlement and the judgment of the Court of Justice of the EU ("CJEU") in the *Achmea* case[4] are indicative of these emerging challenges to the enforcement of arbitral awards.

The European case is not unique in indicating an increasing scepticism of courts towards arbitral tribunals. In 2016, the Hague District Court set aside an United Nations Commission on International Trade ("UNCITRAL") award against Russia in the *Yukos* case, holding that the Permanent Court of Arbitration ("PCA") lacked jurisdiction to hear the dispute in the absence of a valid arbitration agreement.[5] Two years later, the Ontario Superior Court of Justice allowed new evidence in an application by Russia to set aside a similar UNCITRAL award finding that Russia had consented to arbitration under the Energy Charter Treaty ("ECT"). In the *Russian Federation v. Luxtona* case, Justice Dunphy held that under domestic law

[1]Gary Born, The Seasons of Arbitration, 33rd Annual Freshfields and Queen Mary University arbitration lecture, Freshfields London, 16 November 2018.

[2]Rowley (2019), p. xi.

[3]International Bar Association, Report on the Public Policy Exception in the New York Convention, October 2015, https://www.ibanet.org/LPD/Dispute_Resolution_Section/Arbitration/Recogntn_Enfrcemnt_Arbitl_Awrd/publicpolicy15.aspx (last accessed 18 February 2019), p. 18.

[4]CJEU, C-284/16, Slowakische Republik (Slovak Republic) v. Achmea BV, ECLI:EU:C:2018:158.

[5]Altenkirch and Frohloff (2016), The Hague District Court Sets Aside Yukos Awards, Global Arbitration News, https://globalarbitrationnews.com/the-hague-district-court-sets-aside-yukos-awards-20160426/ (last accessed 2 May 2020).

the court was "neither bound to defer to the decision of the tribunal on matters of jurisdiction nor explicitly confined to the record before such tribunal".[6]

The world of commercial arbitration has not been impervious to this trend either. In the widely discussed decision in *Henry Schein Inc v. Archer & White Sales Inc*,[7] two dental product distributors disputed on who should decide the arbitrability of a case—the court or the arbitrators—in circumstances where the court considers the demand for arbitration to be without basis.[8] Justice Sotomayor expressed her concern that sending the question of arbitrability to an arbitrator could cause inefficiencies, reasoning that the parties should not have to arbitrate the issue of arbitrability if they have not previously agreed to do so.[9]

However, the Supreme Court eventually followed its established line of jurisprudence, affirming that arbitrators should determine the question of arbitrability, even where a court believes the demand for arbitration to be "wholly groundless". In a unanimous decision of the court, Kavanaugh wrote that even in this situation, the court may not "override" a contract that delegates the question of arbitrability to an arbitrator.[10] To do so would be inconsistent with the US Federal Arbitration Act of 1925 and previous decisions of the court, adding that the Federal Arbitration Act contains no exception for a "wholly groundless" submission to arbitration, and courts cannot graft their own exceptions onto statutory text.[11]

Against this background of controversial courts' and judges' views on arbitration, this chapter focuses on the developments in the field in the EU. The antagonistic stance that the EC has taken towards investor-state dispute settlement together with the latest case law of the CJEU present a unique "natural experiment" for examining the interactions between domestic courts and arbitral tribunals. Moreover, the divergent positions that both the EC and the CJEU have taken towards arbitration within and outside the EU and the reasoning for this differentiation merit further scrutiny.

To explore this laboratory of new interactions between EU courts and arbitral tribunals, the following sections focus on three issues bound to affect the enforcement of arbitral awards in national courts in the EU and beyond: the interventions of

---

[6]The Russian Federation v. Luxtona Limited, 2018 ONSC 2419, para. 36, https://www.italaw.com/sites/default/files/case-documents/italaw9726_0.pdf (last accessed 25 June 2020).

[7]Henry Schein, Inc. v. Archer & White Sales, Inc., 586 U. S. ____ (2019), https://www.supremecourt.gov/opinions/18pdf/17-1272_7148.pdf (last accessed 2 May 2020).

[8]Henry Schein, Inc. v. Archer & White Sales, Inc., 586 U. S. ____ (2019), https://www.supremecourt.gov/opinions/18pdf/17-1272_7148.pdf (last accessed 2 May 2020), p. 8.

[9]US Supreme Court Hears Arguments on Arbitrability, Global Arbitration Review, https://globalarbitrationreview.com/article/1176144/us-supreme-court-hears-arguments-on-arbitrability (last accessed 2 May 2020).

[10]Jones T (2019) Arbitrators decide arbitrability: Kavanaugh gives first Supreme Court ruling, https://globalarbitrationreview.com/article/1178873/arbitrators-decide-arbitrability-kavanaugh-gives-first-supreme-court-ruling (last accessed 2 May 2020).

[11]Henry Schein, Inc. v. Archer & White Sales, Inc., 586 U. S. ____ (2019), https://www.supremecourt.gov/opinions/18pdf/17-1272_7148.pdf (last accessed 2 May 2020), p. 7.

the EC as amicus curiae in several courts where the enforcement of intra-EU arbitral awards is sought (Sect. 2); the decisions of national courts on requests to enforce intra-EU arbitral awards following the CJEU's *Achmea* judgment (Sect. 3); the CJEU's Opinion on the compatibility with EU law of the system for the resolution of investor-state disputes provided for in the Comprehensive Economic and Trade Agreement between Canada and the EU ("CETA") and its potential implications for the enforcement of awards issued under CETA (Sect. 4).

The chapter concludes with proposals for the way forward in addressing tensions between courts and arbitral tribunals and the risk of conflicting decisions (Sect. 5). The emphasis will be on comity as a solution to potential conflicts and the institutionalisation of comity at the international level, for example, in the context of the ongoing revision of the ICSID Arbitration Rules.

2 The European Commission's Interventions as Amicus Curiae in Intra-EU Disputes

2.1 EU Law as a Jurisdictional Defence

The EC has been active in intervening before arbitral tribunals deciding "intra-EU" arbitral cases both under intra-EU Bilateral Investment Treaties ("BITs") and the ECT. There are, to date, numerous amicus curiae briefs that the EC has submitted both to arbitral tribunals and national courts in the wake of the *Achmea* judgment. The arguments invoked are largely similar in cases under the BITs and the ECT and refer mostly to the lack of jurisdiction of arbitral tribunals to hear intra-EU disputes.

To elaborate on the EC's line of reasoning, it is worth examining the latest briefs that the European Union, has submitted to US courts. In *Masdar v. Spain*,[12] an intra-EU award issued under the ECT, the EC has intervened in the enforcement proceedings before the US District Court for the District of Columbia, invoking the nature and special characteristics of the EU legal order, the integrity of which is safeguarded by the EU judicial system, consisting of member state courts and the CJEU.

The EC's arguments rest on three (alternative) grounds. The first one calls for a harmonious interpretation of Article 16 of the ECT with EU law, in the sense that the ECT's dispute resolution clause was not intended to apply between EU member states. On the second alternative ground, the EC argued that Article 16 should be interpreted to apply intra-EU, but the ensuing conflict between the ECT and EU law

[12]United States District Court for the District of Columbia, Case 1:18-cv-02254-JEB, Document 18-1, Filed 05/03/19, Proposed Brief of the European Commission on behalf of the European Union as amicus curiae in support of the Kingdom of Spain, https://ec.europa.eu/competition/court/masdar_solar_wind_en.pdf (last accessed 2 May 2020).

should be resolved in favour of the latter.[13] This meant that Article 16 of the ECT would not apply as between the EU member states, with the result being that Spain had not made any valid offer for arbitration to investors from other member states and consequently there was no valid arbitration agreement between Spain and the Dutch investor.[14]

Last, the EC resorted to the principle of "international comity", asking the US court to dismiss the case before it. Invoking its role as the guardian of the EU Treaties, it contrasted the United States' lack of connection to the dispute with the EU's "overwhelming interest" in addressing the "fundamental questions of EU law" that the dispute raises. In particular, the EC noted that it had issued a decision binding on Spain, providing that the ECT does not apply in intra-EU relations and, in any case, any payment of the arbitration award would be subject to the Commission's approval.[15]

At the heart of the EC's argumentation lie the principles of autonomy and full effectiveness of EU law, combined with the principle of mutual trust between the member states.[16] Recalling the CJEU's reasoning in *Achmea*, the EC has stressed that these cornerstone principles of EU law are safeguarded by the system of judicial remedies provided for in the Treaties, with the CJEU having the exclusive jurisdiction to issue final and binding interpretations of EU law and guarantee its correct and uniform interpretation.[17] In this autonomous system of judicial protection national courts have the option (or obligation) to submit preliminary references on questions of EU law to the CJEU, while member states should refrain from submitting issues concerning the interpretation or application of the Treaties to any method of settlement other than those provided for in the Treaties.[18]

[13]United States District Court for the District of Columbia, Case 1:18-cv-02254-JEB, Document 18-1, Filed 05/03/19, Proposed Brief of the European Commission on behalf of the European Union as amicus curiae in support of the Kingdom of Spain, https://ec.europa.eu/competition/court/masdar_solar_wind_en.pdf (last accessed 2 May 2020), p. 11.

[14]United States District Court for the District of Columbia, Case 1:18-cv-02254-JEB, Document 18-1, Filed 05/03/19, Proposed Brief of the European Commission on behalf of the European Union as amicus curiae in support of the Kingdom of Spain, https://ec.europa.eu/competition/court/masdar_solar_wind_en.pdf (last accessed 2 May 2020), p. 14.

[15]United States District Court for the District of Columbia, Case 1:18-cv-02254-JEB, Document 18-1, Filed 05/03/19, Proposed Brief of the European Commission on behalf of the European Union as amicus curiae in support of the Kingdom of Spain, https://ec.europa.eu/competition/court/masdar_solar_wind_en.pdf (last accessed 2 May 2020), p. 3.

[16]United States District Court for the District of Columbia, Case 1:18-cv-02254-JEB, Document 18-1, Filed 05/03/19, Proposed Brief of the European Commission on behalf of the European Union as amicus curiae in support of the Kingdom of Spain, https://ec.europa.eu/competition/court/masdar_solar_wind_en.pdf (last accessed 2 May 2020), p. 2.

[17]United States District Court for the District of Columbia, Case 1:18-cv-02254-JEB, Document 18-1, Filed 05/03/19, Proposed Brief of the European Commission on behalf of the European Union as amicus curiae in support of the Kingdom of Spain, https://ec.europa.eu/competition/court/masdar_solar_wind_en.pdf (last accessed 2 May 2020), p. 5.

[18]Articles 267 and 344 TFEU respectively.

2.2 EU Law as a Substantive Defence

The EC has invoked EU law not only as a jurisdictional but also as a substantive defence in intra-EU disputes. Two cases serve as salient examples of the possible tension between EU law, on the one hand, and the ECT or intra-EU BITs, on the other.[19] In the *Electrabel* case, the tribunal addressed (obiter dictum) the potential conflict between the two legal orders, reasoning that EU law required Hungary (the respondent state) to terminate the contested investment agreement and, consequently, "it would be absurd if Hungary could be liable under the ECT for doing precisely that which it was ordered to do by a supranational authority whose decisions the ECT itself recognizes as legally binding on Hungary".[20]

In a similar vein, the tribunal also noted that the ECT recognized the status of the EU (a key negotiating party) as a regional economic integration organization ("REIO"), which issues binding decisions upon its member states. Consequently, "it would have made no sense for the European Union to promote and subscribe to the ECT if that had meant entering into obligations inconsistent with EU law".[21]

The tribunal, thus, considered EU law to be on the same level as international law, finding that the two legal orders should be interpreted in a "harmonious" manner. Should such a harmonious interpretation not be possible, the tribunal concluded that EU law would take precedence over the ECT, on the basis of the conflict rule of Article 351 Treaty on the Functioning of the EU, which was interpreted as precluding any treaties (both pre- and post- accession) between the member states, to the extent that their provisions are incompatible with their obligations under EU law.[22]

Another dispute revealing the tension between EU law and international law is the famous *Micula v. Romania* case.[23] In this dispute between Swedish investors and Romania, the claimants argued that the state's revocation of certain investment incentives was in breach of the Sweden-Romania BIT. More specifically, they claimed that Romania frustrated their legitimate expectations that the incentives would remain in place for a period of ten years, thus, breaching its obligation to accord fair and equitable treatment under the BIT. Romania invoked EU law as a defence, counterarguing that the revocation of the contested incentives was necessary for its compliance with EU law, as a prerequisite for acceding to the EU. In its

[19] Bermann (2017), p. 53.

[20] Electrabel S.A. v. Republic of Hungary, ICSID Case No. ARB/07/19, Award, 25 November 2015, para. 6.72.

[21] Electrabel v. Hungary, ICSID Case No. ARB/07/19, Award, 25 November 2015, para. 4.133.

[22] Electrabel v. Hungary, ICSID Case No. ARB/07/19, Award, 25 November 2015, paras 4.182–4.190.

[23] Ioan Micula, Viorel Micula, S.C European Food S.A., S.C. Starmill S.R.L. and S.C. Multipack S. R.L., ICSID Case No. ARB/05/20, Award, 11 December 2013.

amicus curiae intervention, the EC emphasized that the payment of any damages that the tribunal would award to the claimants would itself constitute illegal state aid.[24]

It ensues from the above that EU law has been establishing itself in the world of international investment arbitration as a considerable factor to take into account when rendering or enforcing an award. The following section examines how and to what extent EU law has played a role also at the stage of the enforcement of arbitral awards, in particular when enforcement is sought in jurisdictions within the EU.

3 The Decisions of National Courts in Enforcement Proceedings

Two cases have recently marked the dynamics between arbitral tribunals and national courts, particularly in the EU context; the CJEU's judgment regarding the arbitral award in the dispute between Slovakia and *Achmea*, and the ongoing proceedings before different national courts for the enforcement of the arbitral award that Micula has secured against Romania. This section examines, first, the *Achmea* case, which has reached the highest level of maturity at the EU level following the relevant CJEU decision and, second, the *Micula* dispute, where enforcement battles have been unfolding on different fronts not only before EU courts but also in jurisdictions outside the EU.

3.1 The "Achmea avalanche"

The dispute between Achmea and the Slovak Republic resulted from legislative measures adopted in the health system. In 2004, Slovakia opened its market to national operators and those of other Member States offering private sickness insurance services. Achmea, a company belonging to a Dutch insurance group, set up a subsidiary in Slovakia through which it offered private sickness insurance services on the Slovak market. In 2006, Slovakia partly reversed the liberalisation of the private sickness insurance market by enacting a law prohibiting the distribution of profits generated by private sickness insurance activities. As a consequence of its damage, Achmea brought, in 2008, arbitration proceedings against Slovakia pursuant to the arbitration provision of the 1991 BIT between the Netherlands and the Czech and Slovak Federative Republic and the UNCITRAL Arbitration Rules.

As Frankfurt was the place of arbitration, German law was applicable to the proceedings. Slovakia objected to the arbitration arguing that, as a result of its

[24]United States Court of Appeals, Case 15-3109-cv, Brief for Amicus Curiae the Commission of the European Union in support of Defendant-Appellant, https://www.italaw.com/sites/default/files/case-documents/italaw7096.pdf (last accessed 2 May 2020), p. 2.

succession to the EU, the arbitration clause included in its BIT with the Netherlands was incompatible with EU law. The arbitral tribunal dismissed the jurisdictional objection and in its award on the merits ordered the defendant to pay damages.[25]

Slovakia brought an action to set aside the award in Frankfurt's Higher Regional Court. Following the dismissal of its action, Slovakia appealed the decision of the Frankfurt Higher Regional Court to the Federal Supreme Court of Justice (Bundesgerichtshof, "BGH"), expressing doubts about the compatibility of the BIT's arbitration clause with Articles 18, 267, and 344 TFEU.[26]

The BGH did not share those doubts, noting, in particular, that Article 344 TFEU does not concern disputes between an individual and a member state and, in any case, the dispute did not refer to the interpretation and application of the Treaties but was based on the contested BIT. As regards Article 267 TFEU, the BGH considered that the review of the arbitral award by a state court prior to enforcement, with the possibility of making a preliminary reference to the CJEU at that stage, sufficed to ensure the uniform interpretation of EU law. Last, the BGH did not share Slovakia's argument that the BIT violates Article 18 TFEU, which prohibits any discrimination on grounds of nationality, observing that the reciprocal application of rights and obligations only to the nationals of the contracting member states is a consequence inherent in the BIT that the states have concluded between them.[27]

In light of the above, the BGH decided to stay the proceedings before it and referred the following questions to the CJEU for a preliminary ruling: does Article 344 TFEU preclude the application of an arbitration provision in an intra-EU BIT that had entered into force before the contracting member state acceded to the EU but the BIT claim was brought after accession? If this question is answered in the negative, do Articles 267 and 18 TFEU preclude such an intra-EU arbitration provision?[28]

The CJEU's preliminary ruling on *Achmea* is well-known and widely discussed. The Court held that Articles 267 and 344 of the TFEU must be interpreted as precluding a provision in an international agreement concluded between member states, such as the contested investor-state arbitration clause.[29] This CJEU judgment, combined with the EC's numerous amicus curiae interventions both in arbitral and court proceedings, has produced significant effects on the enforcement of arbitral awards, at least in the EU.

---

[25]Achmea B.V. and the Slovakia, PCA Case No. 2008-13, Final Award, 7 December 2012, para. 295.

[26]CJEU, case C-284/16, Slowakische Republik (Slovak Republic) v. Achmea BV, ECLI:EU:C:2018:158, para. 12.

[27]CJEU, case C-284/16, Slowakische Republik (Slovak Republic) v. Achmea BV, ECLI:EU:C:2018:158, paras 14–22.

[28]CJEU, case C-284/16, Slowakische Republik (Slovak Republic) v. Achmea BV, ECLI:EU:C:2018:158, para. 23.

[29]CJEU, case C-284/16, Slowakische Republik (Slovak Republic) v. Achmea BV, ECLI:EU:C:2018:158, para. 60.

The first court reaction to the *Achmea* judgment was the decision of the BGH, which showed full obedience to the CJEU's findings.[30] Showing obedience to the CJEU, the German Federal Supreme Court held that Slovakia's unilateral offer to arbitrate investor-State disputes under the Netherlands-Slovakia BIT was rendered inapplicable when Slovakia became a member of the European Union on May 1, 2004. As a consequence, no arbitration agreement could form between the parties when Achmea initiated arbitration proceedings in 2008.[31]

More specifically, the BGH found that, according to the German Code of the Civil Procedure, an arbitral award may be set aside if the arbitration agreement is invalid or non-existent. It also noted that, pursuant to Article 8(6) of the BIT, the law of the respondent State was part of the law applicable to the dispute. Consequently, since Achmea initiated the arbitration proceedings after Slovakia had become a member of the European Union, EU law was applicable to the dispute—including the question whether an arbitration agreement had been formed between the parties—as part of Slovakia's law.[32]

Recalling the CJEU's conclusion that the BIT's arbitration clause could endanger the autonomy of the EU legal order, and was incompatible with the principles of mutual trust and sincere cooperation of EU law, the BGH noted that, in case of conflict, EU law prevailed over any other international agreement concluded between member States of the European Union. Thus, the arbitration clause included in the BIT, since it was incompatible with EU law, became inapplicable between the parties upon Slovakia's accession to the EU in 2004. As a result, Slovakia's unilateral offer to arbitrate ceased to exist as of the accession date and could, thus, no longer be accepted by the investor.[33] Since there was no valid arbitration agreement concluded between the defendant state and the investor, the BGH decided to reverse the decision of the Frankfurt Higher Regional Court and set aside the arbitral award.[34]

As aforementioned, the *Achmea* case was an arbitral dispute brought under the UNCITRAL arbitration rules, with German law, as the law of the seat of the arbitration, thus applying in the set-aside proceedings. Notably, Article 1059 of

---

[30]BGH, 31.10.2018 - I ZB 2/15, http://juris.bundesgerichtshof.de/cgi-bin/rechtsprechung/document.py?Gericht=bgh&Art=en&nr=89393&pos=0&anz=1 (last accessed 2 May 2020).

[31]BGH, 31.10.2018 - I ZB 2/15, http://juris.bundesgerichtshof.de/cgi-bin/rechtsprechung/document.py?Gericht=bgh&Art=en&nr=89393&pos=0&anz=1 (last accessed 2 May 2020), para. 45.

[32]Bohmer L (2018) In now-public decision, reasoning of German Federal Supreme Court on set aside of BIT award is clarified, https://www.iareporter.com/articles/analysis-german-federal-supreme-court-puts-an-end-to-achmea-saga-finding-that-in-light-of-ecj-ruling-no-arbitration-agreement-existed-between-the-parties/ (last accessed 29 April 2020), p. 1.

[33]Bohmer L (2018) In now-public decision, reasoning of German Federal Supreme Court on set aside of BIT award is clarified, https://www.iareporter.com/articles/analysis-german-federal-supreme-court-puts-an-end-to-achmea-saga-finding-that-in-light-of-ecj-ruling-no-arbitration-agreement-existed-between-the-parties/ (last accessed 29 April 2020), p. 3.

[34]See supra note 30, para. 27.

the German Code of Civil Procedure, which the BGH applied, largely mirrors Article 5(1)(a) of the New York Convention on the Recognition and Enforcement of Foreign Arbitral Awards, stipulating that recognition and enforcement may be refused if the arbitration agreement is not valid under the law to which the parties have subjected it. One can thus expect the reasoning of the German Federal Supreme Court to apply also in other intra-EU arbitral awards issued under arbitration rules other than those of the Convention on the Settlement of Investment Disputes Between States and Nationals of Other States ("ICSID Convention").[35]

In contrast, the BGH's reasoning would not be transposed to cases concerning the recognition and enforcement of awards issued under the ICSID Convention. Article 53 of the said Convention reads that "the award shall be binding on the parties and shall not be subject to any appeal or to any other remedy except those provided for in this Convention." Indeed, the arbitral tribunal in *UP and C.D. v. Hungary* observed that the CJEU's ruling in *Achmea* did not make any reference to the ICSID Convention and held that, unlike the *Achmea* dispute, which was a Germany-seated arbitration where German law thus applied and the German courts had competence over the matter of the arbitration agreement, the ICSID dispute before it was delocalized, falling outside the competence of any national court, and subject only to review within the ICSID annulment system.[36]

Despite the expectation that ICSID awards would fall outside the scope of the conflict between EU law and intra-EU investment arbitration, the *Micula* case, examined below, paints a different picture of the interaction between EU law and investor-state arbitration.

3.2 The "Micula saga"

As aforementioned, the *Achmea* dispute was not the only case where diverging reasonings between different courts and arbitral tribunals have emerged. Another case—this one brought under the ICSID Convention—has presented similar challenges for the interaction between domestic courts and arbitral tribunals as well as the relationship between domestic, EU, and international laws. This section will examine the trajectory of the dispute between Swedish investors, the Micula brothers, and Romania focusing particularly on the interaction between the arbitral award, a judgment of the General Court of European Union, a decision of the United States District Court for the District of Columbia and two decisions of the UK Supreme Court.

Like the *Achmea* case, *Micula* was also an intra-EU dispute. To recall the background of the dispute, The Micula brothers were the majority shareholders of

[35] See supra note 30, para. 25.

[36] UP and C.D Holding Internationale v. Hungary, ICSID Case No. ARB/13/35, Award, 9 October 2018, paras 222, 227, 255.

the European Food and Drinks Group ("EFDG"), a company owning other companies including the three corporate claimants in the arbitral dispute. Taking advantage of incentives that Romania offered in the late 1990s, the Micula brothers expanded their operations by developing a highly integrated food and drinks production business in a disadvantaged area of Romania.

They successfully claimed that Romania had acted in breach of their legitimate expectations when it prematurely revoked many of the key incentives in 2005. The tribunal also found that Romania had acted in an intransparent manner by failing to inform the claimants in a timely manner that the favorable investment regime would be ended prior to its stated date of expiry.[37]

Seconding the Respondent's position, the EC participated as an *amicus curiae* in the arbitral proceedings pointing to the CJEU's recommendation to interpret intra-EU BITs in the light of EU law and urging the tribunal to "take into account" the EU's state aid rules when interpreting specific BIT provisions. The EC also invoked Article 30(3) of the Vienna Convention on the Law of Treaties on the application of successive treaties relating to the same subject matter, directing the Tribunal to apply the EU's state aid law rather than provisions of the BIT that would prove incompatible with the EC Treaty.[38]

Notably, the EC also warned about the risk of non-enforceability of the arbitral award within the EU in case it would contradict the EU state aid rules, which, according to the CJEU, formed part of the "public order" of member states' legal systems.[39] In a similar line, addressing the relationship between Article 54 of the ICSID Convention, providing for the automatic recognition and enforcement of ICSID awards, and EU law, the EC contended that member states' courts would be bound to stay enforcement proceedings before them and refer to the CJEU the question of the "applicability of Article 54 of the ICSID Convention, as transposed into the national law of the referring judge." The tribunal rejected the EC's arguments both in substance and on enforceability, holding that EU law was part of the "factual matrix" of the case and issues regarding enforcement of an award are irrelevant to the Tribunal's decision on the substance of the Claimants' claims.[40]

Against this background of divergent (if not conflicting) positions on the relationship between EU law and investment treaty arbitration, it is useful to examine how different courts have reacted to the *Micula* award and placed themselves in the debate on the interaction between EU law and international investment law.

---

[37]Ioan Micula, Viorel Micula, S.C European Food S.A., S.C. Starmill S.R.L. and S.C. Multipack S.R.L. v. Romania, ICSID Case No. ARB/05/20, Award, 11 December 2013, para. 872.

[38]Ioan Micula, Viorel Micula, S.C European Food S.A., S.C. Starmill S.R.L. and S.C. Multipack S.R.L. v. Romania, ICSID Case No. ARB/05/20, Award, 11 December 2013, para. 317.

[39]Ioan Micula, Viorel Micula, S.C European Food S.A., S.C. Starmill S.R.L. and S.C. Multipack S.R.L. v. Romania, ICSID Case No. ARB/05/20, Award, 11 December 2013, para. 335.

[40]Ioan Micula, Viorel Micula, S.C European Food S.A., S.C. Starmill S.R.L. and S.C. Multipack S.R.L. v. Romania, ICSID Case No. ARB/05/20, Award, 11 December 2013, paras 328, 337.

An enforcement proceeding showing the courts' efforts to reconcile the two legal orders was the one before the English Court of Appeal.[41] Confronted with the potential conflict between the United Kingdom's international obligations under the ICSID Convention, given effect by the 1966 Arbitration (International Investment Disputes) Act, and the court's duties under EU law, particularly the duty of sincere cooperation, the court tried to strike a balance.[42] It thus decided to stay the enforcement of the award until the General Court of the European Union ("GCEU") would issue its judgment on the EC's Decision finding that the payment by Romania of the aforementioned ICSID award would constitute illegal state aid.[43]

Engaging in an effort to reconcile the United Kingdom's obligations under EU law with its obligations under international investment law, the Justices Arden, Hamblen and Leggatt raised several interesting points of international law. Among the arguments emphasizing the importance of international law was the point of Justice Arden, that EU law recognizes that it is for the national court, not the CJEU, to determine the extent of obligations under international law imposed on the United Kingdom by the ICSID Convention.[44] Despite finding little overlap between the CJEU proceedings and the enforcement proceedings before them, Arden LJ agreed to stay enforcement pursuant to Article 54 of the ICSID Convention and section 2 (1) of the 1966 Act, and in line with the duty of sincere cooperation.[45]

Justice Arden also held that the Act should be interpreted consistently with the ICSID Convention and not in a way that would allow the United Kingdom to adopt new rules, for example by allowing a public policy defence when there is none allowed in the Convention, or accepting Romania's argument that ICSID awards are "equivalent" to final domestic-court judgments.[46] The Justice highlighted that the procedural rules for the enforcement of ICSID awards could not be interpreted solely as a domestic statute but their purpose was to implement, no more and no less, the obligations of the ICSID Convention. The UK's international treaty obligations would have to prevail. In a similar vein, Justice Leggatt held that a stay on the

[41][2018] EWCA Civ 1801, Case No: A3/2017/1853, 1855, 1856 & 1903, https://www.bailii.org/ew/cases/EWCA/Civ/2018/1801.html (last accessed 2 May 2020).

[42][2018] EWCA Civ 1801, Case No: A3/2017/1853, 1855, 1856 & 1903, https://www.bailii.org/ew/cases/EWCA/Civ/2018/1801.html (last accessed 2 May 2020), paras 214, 221.

[43]OJ 2015 L232: Commission Decision (EU) 2015/1470 of 30 March 2015 on State aid SA.38517 (2014/C) (ex 2014/NN) implemented by Romania – Arbitral award Micula v Romania of 11 December 2013 (notified under document C(2015) 2112).

[44][2018] EWCA Civ 1801, Case No: A3/2017/1853, 1855, 1856 & 1903, https://www.bailii.org/ew/cases/EWCA/Civ/2018/1801.html (last accessed 2 May 2020), para. 106.

[45][2018] EWCA Civ 1801, Case No: A3/2017/1853, 1855, 1856 & 1903, https://www.bailii.org/ew/cases/EWCA/Civ/2018/1801.html (last accessed 2 May 2020), para. 26.

[46]In a few words, Romania argued that, far from providing immediate enforcement, section 2(1) of the Arbitration Act required the UK Court to decline to enforce a judgment which would be contrary to EU law. See [2018] EWCA Civ 1801, Case No: A3/2017/1853, 1855, 1856 & 1903, https://www.bailii.org/ew/cases/EWCA/Civ/2018/1801.html (last accessed 2 May 2020), para. 112.

execution of an ICSID award can only be granted if it is consistent with the purposes of the ICSID Convention.[47]

On the contrary, Hamblen LJ argued that the question was not one of reviewing the arbitral award on grounds of public policy—a non-enforcement ground that was not included in the ICSID Convention—but of legality of enforcement. He held in this context that ICSID awards are equated with final judgments of the courts of the state where enforcement is sought and are thus in no better (or worse) than a final domestic judgment. Consequently, Justice Hamblen argued that the court must refrain from taking a decision which conflicts with a decision of the Commission in the same way that it would act unlawfully if it enforced a domestic judgment incompatible with EU law.[48]

In light of the above, Hamblen and Leggatt held that, if there is a conflict between the international obligations of the UK contained in the 1966 Act and the Court's EU law duties, the judge was right to conclude that there should be a stay on the grounds that the issue of whether Article 351—providing that the rights and obligations arising from agreements concluded before states' accession to the EU, between one or more Member States on the one hand, and one or more third countries on the other, shall not be affected by the provisions of the Treaties—applies in this case is a matter before the GCEU and there is a clear risk of conflicting decisions.[49]

The approach of a Swedish national court was different. In contrast to the English Court of Appeal, the Nacka District outside of Stockholm did not engage in a balancing exercise, holding instead that ICSID awards shall be treated like legally enforceable domestic rulings.[50] Echoing the arguments presented in the EC amicus curiae submission before it, the Stockholm court concluded that, although under the ICSID Convention it was required to enforce ICSID awards in the same way as a legally enforceable Swedish judgment, such a ruling could not be executed if its enforcement was contrary to EU law, and more specifically, the EC state aid decision. The court thus concluded that, by enforcing the award, it would side-step the EC's 2015 state aid decision thus putting Sweden in a position to violate its duty of sincere cooperation under EU law.[51]

---

[47] [2018] EWCA Civ 1801, Case No: A3/2017/1853, 1855, 1856 & 1903, https://www.bailii.org/ew/cases/EWCA/Civ/2018/1801.html (last accessed 2 May 2020), paras 113–114, 123.

[48] [2018] EWCA Civ 1801, Case No: A3/2017/1853, 1855, 1856 & 1903, https://www.bailii.org/ew/cases/EWCA/Civ/2018/1801.html (last accessed 2 May 2020), paras 139–145.

[49] [2018] EWCA Civ 1801, Case No: A3/2017/1853, 1855, 1856 & 1903, https://www.bailii.org/ew/cases/EWCA/Civ/2018/1801.html (last accessed 2 May 2020), paras 153 et seq.

[50] *Case no. Ä 2550-17,*https://www.italaw.com/sites/default/files/case-documents/italaw10319.pdf (last accessed on 2 May 2020).

[51] Dahlquist J (2018) ANALYSIS: Swedish Court declines to enforce an ICSID award, but on EU law grounds – without addressing question of Post-Achmea validity of intra-EU BITs, https://www.iareporter.com/articles/analysis-swedish-court-declines-to-enforce-an-icsid-award-but-on-eu-law-grounds-without-addressing-question-of-post-achmea-validity-of-intra-eu-bits/ (last accessed 2 May 2020), p. 2.

Another European front where the enforcement of the *Micula* award has been frozen is the Belgian courts. Adopting a middle ground between the positions of the English and Swedish courts, the Brussels Court of Appeal decided to stay its judgment until a determination by the GCEU of the validity of the contested EC decision.[52] The court observed that the EC's decision created a conflict for Romania, which is obliged to enforce the award under the ICSID Convention but also prohibited from doing so by the Commission's decision. The court also noted that the EU courts are still reviewing the Commission's findings.[53]

Particularly relevant in this context is the decision that the GCEU rendered on 18 June 2019. The GCEU held that the EC had acted unlawfully in finding that the payment of the award would constitute illegal state aid. In particular, the Court found that the EC lacked competence to issue the relevant state-aid decision and EU law was inapplicable to all the events relating to the repealed incentives, which pre-dated Romania's accession to the EU.[54]

Another proceeding for the enforcement of the *Micula* award was the one before the US District Court for the District of Columbia. Intervening as amicus curiae, the EC commented that the GCEU's judgment is not final, but subject to appeal before the CJEU, which may overturn it. Moreover, the EC argued that the annulment of its decision only means the reopening of the state aid investigation and not the enforceability of the award.[55] In any case—the EC added—even the annulment of the disputed state aid decision does not obviate the petitioners' obligation to comply with other acts of EU law, including all preparatory acts leading to the opening of the state investigation, which the petitioners had not challenged before the EU courts. Consequently, an order confirming the award would still "require Romania to take actions contrary to EU law" and "interfere with ongoing proceedings in the Commission and the EU courts."[56]

By means of commentary, two conflicting perspectives seem to arise from the above: from the perspective of international investment law, the EC's request to the US courts to deny enforcement for as long as the matter is pending in the EU

---

[52]Brussels Court of Appeal, 17 Civil Affairs Chamber, 2016/AR/393 and 2016/AR/394, 12 March 2019, https://www.italaw.com/sites/default/files/case-documents/italaw10446.pdf (last accessed 2 May 2020).

[53]Brussels Court of Appeal, 17 Civil Affairs Chamber, 2016/AR/393 and 2016/AR/394, 12 March 2019, https://www.italaw.com/sites/default/files/case-documents/italaw10446.pdf (last accessed 2 May 2020).

[54]GCEU, Cases T-624/15, T-694/15 and T-704/15, Micula et al. v. European Commission, ECLI: EU:T:2019:423.

[55]United States District Court for the District of Columbia, Case 1:17-cv-02332-APM, Response of amicus curiae: the European Commission to petitioners' notice of supplemental authority, https://www.transnational-dispute-management.com/legal-and-regulatory-detail.asp?key=22092 (last accessed 2 May 2020), p. 4.

[56]United States District Court for the District of Columbia, Case 1:17-cv-02332-APM, Response of amicus curiae: the European Commission to petitioners' notice of supplemental authority, https://www.transnational-dispute-management.com/legal-and-regulatory-detail.asp?key=22092 (last accessed 2 May 2020), p. 6.

institutions seems to turn the principle of comity into a requirement for exhaustion of local remedies, which is missing from the 2002 Romania-Sweden BIT. On the contrary, from the perspective of EU law, the request is simply a reflection of the primacy of EU law in intra-EU relations, the hierarchy of institutions within the EU, as well as the EC's role to act as the guardian of the Treaties.

The US District Court for the District of Columbia rejected the EC's and Romania's arguments. In its Opinion rendered on 9 September 2019, the court held that the *Achmea* ruling did not foreclose its subject-matter jurisdiction to enforce the award under the arbitration exception to sovereign immunity in US law.[57] Contrasting the case before it with *Achmea*, in which the contested action took place *after* Slovakia's accession to the EU, the District Court observed that the *Micula* dispute did not "relate to the interpretation or application of EU law", which was "not part of the applicable law", but only part of the "factual matrix" of the case. It also pointed in this regard to the GCEU's ruling which overturned the EC state aid decision and found that the Commission lacked "competence" to review Romania's pre-accession actions and the award's compatibility with EU law.[58]

The Opinion of the US District Court in *Micula* is also interesting from a policy perspective as the result of the US court's approach seems to reach the reverse result from what the EC's amicus curiae intervention had aimed at achieving. While the EC had asked the US courts to refrain from exercising any jurisdiction upon the case on the basis of "international comity" precluding "unnecessary interference with the enforcement and efficacy of the EU legal order",[59] the US court not only confirmed its jurisdiction, but also passed substantive judgment on the EU's competences and the conditions for exercising such competences according to the CJEU's case law. By the same token, the US District Court's approach is indicative of the value of court-to-court dialogue, as the court engaged with the reasoning of the GCEU and based its Opinion also on the GCEU's findings.

4 A Parallel World of "Autonomy"? The CJEU's Opinion on CETA

The US court's opinion on *Micula*, while rejecting the EC's arguments in its *amicus curiae* submission, paradoxically echoes the EU's approach in CETA, which establishes an investment court system ("ICS") replacing traditional investor-state dispute

[57]United States District Court for the District of Columbia, Case No. 1:17-cv-02332-APM, Document 86, Filed 09/11/19, https://www.courtlistener.com/recap/gov.uscourts.dcd.190875/gov.uscourts.dcd.190875.86.0.pdf (last accessed 2 May 2020).

[58]United States District Court for the District of Columbia, Case No. 1:17-cv-02332-APM, Document 86, Filed 09/11/19, https://www.courtlistener.com/recap/gov.uscourts.dcd.190875/gov.uscourts.dcd.190875.86.0.pdf (last accessed 2 May 2020), pp. 21–22.

[59]Micula v. Romania (I), United States District Court for the District of Columbia, Memorandum Opinion, Case 1:17-cv-02332-APM Document 86 Filed 09/11/19, p. 30.

settlement. The two cases share the same rationale of treating EU law as a matter of "fact" and not as part of the "law applicable" in an investor-state dispute.

Following the reasoning in *Achmea*, the US District Court linked the risk to the "autonomy and full effectiveness of EU law" with the possibility that an arbitral tribunal is called upon "to interpret or apply EU law" in a manner that is not subject to review by a court or tribunal within the EU's judicial system.[60] As the arbitral tribunal in *Micula* had not applied or interpreted EU law—which was not directly applicable to Romania at the time the contested measures were taken—there was no calling into question of the principle of mutual trust nor of the preservation of EU law's particular nature.[61]

The CJEU's Opinion 1/17 seems to lie on a similar premise.[62] Alternative investor-state dispute resolution mechanisms operating outside the system of judicial protection laid down in the EU Treaties are compatible with the EU's legal order, as long as the autonomy of EU law is safeguarded.[63] The way proposed to achieve this is to treat EU law "as a matter of fact" instead of part of the law applicable to the dispute.

Indeed, Article 8.31 of the CETA provides that:

> The Tribunal shall not have jurisdiction to determine the legality of a measure, alleged to constitute a breach of this Agreement, under the domestic law of a Party. For greater certainty, in determining the consistency of a measure with this Agreement, the Tribunal may consider, as appropriate, the domestic law of a Party as a matter of fact. In doing so, the Tribunal shall follow the prevailing interpretation given to the domestic law by the courts or authorities of that Party and any meaning given to domestic law by the Tribunal shall not be binding upon the courts or the authorities of that Party.

Addressing Belgium's question whether the ISDS mechanism envisaged in CETA is compatible with the autonomy of the EU legal order, the CJEU recalled its *jurisprudence constante* according to which the EU may enter into international agreements establishing a new court or tribunal.[64] However, the exercise of this competence is contingent upon safeguarding the constitutional characteristics and the autonomy of the EU legal order, in which the CJEU has the exclusive jurisdiction to give definitive interpretations of EU law.[65]

The CJEU observed that the applicable law in the case of the CETA was the agreement itself and not the domestic laws of the contracting parties. This did not mean, though, that the tribunal would not be called to "take into account" EU law "as a matter of fact" in assessing the effects of the contested measure. The Court

[60] Micula v. Romania (I), United States District Court for the District of Columbia, Memorandum Opinion, Case 1:17-cv-02332-APM Document 86 Filed 09/11/19, pp. 18–21.

[61] Micula v. Romania (I), United States District Court for the District of Columbia, Memorandum Opinion, Case 1:17-cv-02332-APM Document 86 Filed 09/11/19, p. 21.

[62] CJEU, Opinion 1/17, 30 April 2019, ECLI:EU:C:2019:341.

[63] CJEU, Opinion 1/17, 30 April 2019, ECLI:EU:C:2019:341, para. 107.

[64] CJEU, Opinion 1/17, 30 April 2019, ECLI:EU:C:2019:341, paras 107–108.

[65] CJEU, Opinion 1/17, 30 April 2019, ECLI:EU:C:2019:341, para. 106.

considered such "taking into account" to be distinct from "interpreting" EU law, with the additional safeguard that the tribunal would have to follow the prevailing interpretation given to the domestic law by the courts or authorities of the Party concerned.[66]

Considering these elements, the Court concluded that the ISDS mechanism established in CETA does not impinge on the autonomy of EU law and the Court's jurisdiction to safeguard such autonomy.[67] In the same vein, the Court held that the jurisdiction of CETA tribunals to declare infringements of the agreement did not prevent the Union from adopting measures necessary to protect the public interest.[68]

In this regard, the CJEU pointed to the Joint Interpretative Statement providing that "investors must continue to respect domestic requirements, including rules and regulations" and that the CETA "preserves the ability of the European Union and its Member States and Canada to adopt and apply their own laws and regulations that regulate economic activity in the public interest".[69] The Court, thus, concluded that the discretionary powers of the CETA tribunals do not call into question the level of protection of public interest determined by the Union following a democratic process.[70]

The Court's divergent approaches to the "autonomy" of EU law raises several interesting questions, primarily of conflicts of treaties and dispute settlement mechanisms. First, what will happen if a CETA tribunal does not follow an interpretation of domestic law given by a domestic court or the CJEU or a matter is not squarely covered by EU law?

As EU law is treated as mere fact and not part of the applicable law under CETA, courts would have to enforce an award under the CETA, even if the CETA tribunal has not followed the CJEU's interpretation of the contested matter. Relevant in this context is the absence of a "comity" rule in CETA, which would provide that the tribunal shall stay an arbitral proceeding if a similar case is pending in EU courts.[71] This is especially true, given the time limitation of 24 months for the tribunal to render its award.[72] The possibility of parallel proceedings and conflicting decisions is thus not precluded.

Another issue that seems to beg further clarification is that of the "interpretation or application of EU law". Like CETA tribunals, arbitral tribunals established under a BIT are not necessarily called to determine the legality of a measure under EU law.

---

[66]CJEU, Opinion 1/17, 30 April 2019, ECLI:EU:C:2019:341, paras 120–132.

[67]CJEU, Opinion 1/17, 30 April 2019, ECLI:EU:C:2019:341, para. 167.

[68]CJEU, Opinion 1/17, 30 April 2019, ECLI:EU:C:2019:341, paras 43–44.

[69]Point 1(d) and Point 2 of the Joint Interpretative Instrument on the Comprehensive Economic and Trade Agreement ("CETA") between Canada and the European Union and its Member States, OJ 2017 L11.

[70]CJEU, Opinion 1/17, 30 April 2019, ECLI:EU:C:2019:341, paras 152–156.

[71]Given the fact that EU law is treated in CETA as domestic law "to be taken into account as a matter of fact", the TFEU presumably does not qualify as "another international agreement" for the purposes of Article 8.24 CETA.

[72]Article 8.23 of the CETA.

They most commonly determine only the legality of a measure under the applicable treaty. This is the perspective that the US District Court took in the aforementioned *Micula* case. Indeed, the US court observed that "a close inspection of the Final Decision"[73] shows that the dispute before the ICSID arbitral tribunal did not "relate to the interpretation or application of EU law".[74]

On the contrary—the US court continued—before the ICSID tribunal, Petitioners and Romania had agreed that the claims put forward were based on the Sweden-Romania BIT and that the BIT's "substantive rules" supplied the "applicable law." Insofar as EU law was concerned, the tribunal held, Romania had not yet acceded to the EU at the time it repealed the economic incentives and so "EU law was not directly applicable to Romania".[75] The tribunal did determine, however, that "EU law forms part of the 'factual matrix' of the case".[76]

This is precisely the approach also taken in CETA, which treats EU law as a matter of fact and not part of the law applicable to the arbitral disputes under CETA. Does this mean that on every occasion an arbitral tribunal is not called to pass judgment on whether the contested measure is compatible with EU law but only determines its effects under the applicable international agreement, the autonomy and full effectiveness of EU law are safeguarded?

Considering the above, if the quest for the "autonomy and full effectiveness" of EU law is more of a legal fiction than a functional concept, and if it is ultimately the principle of mutual trust between the member states and not the autonomy of EU law that the CETA is premised on, how far can mutual trust go in enforcing awards that offer *ad hoc* justice? Wouldn't a situation whereby an award finds a measure illegal under the CETA, thus awarding an investor damages, possibly conflict with a subsequent CJEU judgment finding the measure to be legal? Wouldn't such conflicting decisions create discrepancies, risk promoting inequality, and undermine legal predictability?

Another question arising from the new paths of interaction between EU law and international investment law, refers to the relationship between the legality requirement stipulated in Points 1(d) and 2 of the Joint Interpretative Statement and the fact that EU law is only to be "taken into account as a matter of fact". The Statement provides that investors must continue to respect domestic requirements, including rules and regulations.

It is not clear, though, who will judge if investors have actually respected those requirements, in cases where a measure is contested both before a CETA tribunal and the CJEU (or EC proceedings), as happened in the *Micula* case. As there is no

[73]By "Final Decision" the court meant the final arbitral award.

[74]United States District Court for the District of Columbia, Case No. 1:17-cv-02332-APM, Document 86, Filed 09/11/19, https://www.courtlistener.com/recap/gov.uscourts.dcd.190875/gov.uscourts.dcd.190875.86.0.pdf (last accessed 2 May 2020), p. 20.

[75]Micula v. Romania (I), United States District Court for the District of Columbia, Memorandum Opinion, Case 1:17-cv-02332-APM Document 86 Filed 09/11/19, para. 319.

[76]Micula v. Romania (I), United States District Court for the District of Columbia, Memorandum Opinion, Case 1:17-cv-02332-APM Document 86 Filed 09/11/19, p. 20.

provision for staying the arbitral proceeding in favour of proceedings before the CJEU, the risk for conflicting decisions is still present.

What would happen, for example, if an investor is granted state aid cleared by the EC and then the CJEU finds such state aid to be illegal, as happened in the *Tempus* case?[77] If the investor argues that it had complied with domestic-law requirements (including the EC state aid decision) but ultimately suffered damage because it was asked to return the aid subsequently, won't a CETA award ordering the EU to pay damages possibly conflict with the CJEU decision finding the state aid to be illegal?

5 Old Solutions to New Problems: Comity as the Way Forward?

Placing the increasing tension between EU law and international investment law in the wider context of the proliferation of international law and dispute-resolution bodies, a wider question arises: Is the reassertion of state sovereignty a defence against interference with "domestic" affairs and a reaction to the over-reaching extra-territoriality of international investment law?

Can comity in this context offer a way out of the impasse that the conflict of EU law with international investment law has been creating? In particular, can it help overcome the lack of jurisdictional rules and principles governing the relationship of the competences of the CJEU, international arbitral tribunals, and national courts called to recognize arbitral awards involving EU Member States? How can comity operate in self-contained legal systems like the EU? Can it discipline the effects of doctrines such as sovereign compulsion and acts of state doctrine, which the EC has invoked before the US courts in its request to them to decline jurisdiction in recognizing intra-EU arbitral awards?

Before addressing these questions, it is useful to attempt a definition of comity. This chapter adopts Anne Marie Slaughter's view that comity is one of the building blocks of judicial dialogue in the "global community" of national and international courts offering "the framework and the ground rules for a global dialogue among judges in the context of specific cases".[78]

As Schultz and Ridi observe, Slaughter's approach has the merit of emphasizing the role of judges and arbitrators—national and international—as "facilitators of the coordination of legal regimes".[79] By the same token, comity also denotes a set of judicial tools and techniques developed to achieve such judicial dialogue and to facilitate the reconciliation of different legal regimes.

---

[77] GCEU, T-793/14 - Tempus Energy and Tempus Energy Technology v. Commission, 15 November 2018, ECLI:EU:T:2018:790.

[78] Slaughter (2003), pp. 206, 211.

[79] Schultz and Ridi (2017), pp. 192–193.

Given the absence of a universal rule regulating the competences of different adjudicatory bodies, comity can also serve as a meta-principle assisting courts and tribunals to coordinate their, possibly conflicting, jurisdictions, as well as balance these coordinating efforts with the need to deliver justice in individual cases. Some scholars have characterized recourse to comity as part of the international courts' and tribunals' "inherent powers", which include the power to abstain from exercising jurisdiction that they have, should this serve the integrity and general function of international adjudication. Obviously, such negative jurisdictional exercise begs the wider question what the purpose of ISDS is; resolve *ad hoc* disputes through piecemeal litigation or produce wider implications as a form of global governance (inevitably) influencing states' regulatory policies?

Whereas comity has traditionally been used mostly for preventive purposes, in particular to curb forum shopping, simultaneous proceedings and the ensuing conflicting decisions, its potential for facilitating a constructive dialogue between potentially conflicting legal orders has remained underexplored.

The EC has invoked comity as a way out of the conflict between the two legal orders. For example, in its *amicus curiae* brief to the US District Court for the District of Columbia, the EC argued that international comity—which permits U.S. courts to dismiss or stay domestic action based on the interests of the United States, a foreign government, and the international community in resolving a dispute in a foreign forum—strongly favours permitting these questions to be addressed within the EU judicial system.[80]

According to the EC, the only appropriate fora for resolving questions about the enforceability of intra-EU ECT awards are the EU courts, with the CJEU having the final say on the matter. Moreover—in an argument that resembles the transformation of comity into a requirement for the prior exhaustion of local remedies[81]—the EC claimed that Masdar's failure to challenge the relevant state-aid decision before the EU courts—the forum "best placed" to address it—estopped Masdar from bringing this issue now before the US court.[82]

In light of the above, the EC contrasted the EU's immense interests in the issues at stake with the US' lack of connection to the dispute, the only link being Masdar's assertion of jurisdiction under the ICSID Convention and the Foreign Sovereign Immunities Act. The EC concluded its intervention by inviting the US court not to

[80]Masdar Solar & Wind Cooperatief U.A.v. The Kingdom of Spain, United States District Court for the District of Columbia, Proposed Brief of the European Commission on Behalf of the European Union as *Amicus Curiae* in Support of the Kingdom of Spain, Case 1:18-cv-02254-JEB Document 18-1, Filed 05/03/19, p. 23.

[81]This is a requirement that the ECT does not include. See Article 26 of the ECT.

[82]Masdar Solar & Wind Cooperatief U.A.v. The Kingdom of Spain, United States District Court for the District of Columbia, Proposed Brief of the European Commission on Behalf of the European Union as *Amicus Curiae* in Support of the Kingdom of Spain, Case 1:18-cv-02254-JEB Document 18-1, Filed 05/03/19, p. 25.

embroil itself in the EU's internal affairs, to dismiss the petition and leave the matter to be decided by the EU courts.[83]

The US court's response was sympathetic to the Commission's view. Recognizing the idiosyncrasy of the situation, the judge observed that, "in the ordinary course, courts begin by assuring themselves of their own jurisdiction. In rare cases, however, they may avoid a jurisdictional analysis and render a decision on a non-jurisdictional ground". He, thus, held that "rather than delving prematurely into EU case law, international treaties, and sovereign constitutions, this Court decides to take door number two and issue a stay in the present matter".[84]

There are different ways in which a coordinated international approach to comity could be envisioned. For example, courts called upon to enforce such contested arbitral awards could exercise comity as part of their "inherent powers",[85] which seems to be the approach that the US court in Masdar adopted. Another form of *ex ante* coordination would be to incorporate comity-based provisions in the ICSID Arbitration Rules. The ongoing revisions of ICSID Arbitration Rule 72 on the stay of enforcement of the award present such opportunity. Integrating arbitral tribunals into a dialogue with national courts would show that courts and tribunals can coexist harmoniously and allow for cross-fertilization between them.[86]

In this context of increasing conflict of the two legal orders, on the one hand, and the contracting states' obligations under the ICSID Convention, on the other, a more coordinated approach to "comity" could prevent further fragmentation and unpredictability in the enforcement of contested arbitral awards. Similarly, limiting divergent national approaches to the enforcement of arbitral awards could also prevent what Mourre has called the "nationalization" of arbitration,[87] by allowing for a more coordinated approach to comity and promoting a court-tribunal dialogue at the international level.

---

[83]Masdar Solar & Wind Cooperatief U.A.v. The Kingdom of Spain, United States District Court for the District of Columbia, Proposed Brief of the European Commission on Behalf of the European Union as *Amicus Curiae* in Support of the Kingdom of Spain, Case 1:18-cv-02254-JEB Document 18-1, Filed 05/03/19, p. 25.

[84]Masdar Solar & Wind Cooperatief U.A.v. The Kingdom of Spain, United States District Court for the District of Columbia, Proposed Brief of the European Commission on Behalf of the European Union as *Amicus Curiae* in Support of the Kingdom of Spain, Case 1:18-cv-02254-JEB Document 18-1, Filed 05/03/19, pp. 5–6.

[85]United States District Court for the District of Columbia, Case No. 1:17-cv-02332-APM, Document 86, Filed 09/11/19, https://www.courtlistener.com/recap/gov.uscourts.dcd.190875/gov.uscourts.dcd.190875.86.0.pdf (last accessed 2 May 2020), p. 597.

[86]Giorgetti (2015).

[87]Ballantyne J (2019) Mourre warns against nationalization of arbitration, Global Arbitration Review, https://globalarbitrationreview.com/article/1197622/mourre-warns-against-"nationalisation"-of-arbitration (last accessed 2 May 2020).

References

Bermann G (2017) European Union law as a jurisdictional and substantive defence. Eur Int Arbitr Rev 5(2):51–69

Giorgetti C (2015) Cross-fertilization of procedural law among international courts and tribunals: methods and meaning. In: Sarvarian A, Fontanelli F, Baker R, Tzevelekos V (eds) Procedural fairness in international courts and tribunals. British Institute of International and Comparative Law, London, pp 220–252

Rowley J (2019) The Guide to challenging and enforcing arbitration awards, Global Arbitration Review

Schultz T, Ridi N (2017) Comity and international courts and tribunals. Cornell Int Law J 50 (3):578–609

Slaughter AM (2003) A global community of courts. Harv Int Law J 44(1):191–219

Aikaterini Florou is an Alexander von Humboldt Fellow at the Institute of Law and Economics at the University of Hamburg and an Adjunct Assistant Professor at the Fletcher School of Law and Diplomacy. She is also the Associate Editor of the Journal of World Energy Law & Business and a Member of the Scientific Council of the Energy Centre of the European University Cyprus (EUC). Previously, she worked as a legal officer at the Energy Directorate of the European Commission. Aikaterini holds a PhD in International Investment Law & Economics from Sciences Po Law School and LL.M. degrees from the Fletcher School of Law & Diplomacy and Athens Law School.

The manufacturer's authorised representative in the EU is Springer Nature Customer Service Centre GmbH, Europaplatz 3, 69115 Heidelberg, Germany. If you have any concerns regarding our products, please contact ProductSafety@springernature.com

Printed and bound by CPI Group (UK) Ltd, Croydon, CR0 4YY
30/09/2026
02225661-0016